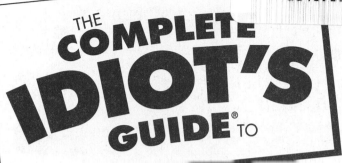

THE
COMPLETE
IDIOT'S
GUIDE® TO

Coaching for Excellence

by Jane Creswell, MCC

ALPHA
A member of Penguin Group (USA) Inc.

To my husband, Tom. What a milestone to celebrate 25 years of marriage this year and still think of you as my true love!

ALPHA BOOKS

Published by the Penguin Group

Penguin Group (USA) Inc., 375 Hudson Street, New York, New York 10014, USA

Penguin Group (Canada), 90 Eglinton Avenue East, Suite 700, Toronto, Ontario M4P 2Y3, Canada (a division of Pearson Penguin Canada Inc.)

Penguin Books Ltd., 80 Strand, London WC2R 0RL, England

Penguin Ireland, 25 St. Stephen's Green, Dublin 2, Ireland (a division of Penguin Books Ltd.)

Penguin Group (Australia), 250 Camberwell Road, Camberwell, Victoria 3124, Australia (a division of Pearson Australia Group Pty. Ltd.)

Penguin Books India Pvt. Ltd., 11 Community Centre, Panchsheel Park, New Delhi—110 017, India

Penguin Group (NZ), 67 Apollo Drive, Rosedale, North Shore, Auckland 1311, New Zealand (a division of Pearson New Zealand Ltd.)

Penguin Books (South Africa) (Pty.) Ltd., 24 Sturdee Avenue, Rosebank, Johannesburg 2196, South Africa

Penguin Books Ltd., Registered Offices: 80 Strand, London WC2R 0RL, England

Copyright © 2008 by Jane Creswell, MCC

THE COMPLETE IDIOT'S GUIDE TO and Design are registered trademarks of Penguin Group (USA) Inc.

International Standard Book Number: 978-1-59257-783-5
Library of Congress Catalog Card Number: 2008924716   3927 9822 11/08

10 09 08   8 7 6 5 4 3 2 1

Interpretation of the printing code: The rightmost number of the first series of numbers is the year of the book's printing; the rightmost number of the second series of numbers is the number of the book's printing. For example, a printing code of 08-1 shows that the first printing occurred in 2008.

Printed in the United States of America

Note: This publication contains the opinions and ideas of its author. It is intended to provide helpful and informative material on the subject matter covered. It is sold with the understanding that the author and publisher are not engaged in rendering professional services in the book. If the reader requires personal assistance or advice, a competent professional should be consulted.

The author and publisher specifically disclaim any responsibility for any liability, loss, or risk, personal or otherwise, which is incurred as a consequence, directly or indirectly, of the use and application of any of the contents of this book.

Most Alpha books are available at special quantity discounts for bulk purchases for sales promotions, premiums, fund-raising, or educational use. Special books, or book excerpts, can also be created to fit specific needs.

For details, write: Special Markets, Alpha Books, 375 Hudson Street, New York, NY 10014.

Publisher: *Marie Butler-Knight*
Editorial Director: *Mike Sanders*
Senior Managing Editor: *Billy Fields*
Senior Acquisitions Editor: *Paul Dinas*
Development Editor: *Jennifer Moore*
Senior Production Editor: *Janette Lynn*

Copy Editor: *Cate Schwenk*
Cover Designer: *Bill Thomas*
Book Designer: *Trina Wurst*
Indexer: *Angie Bess*
Layout: *Ayanna Lacey*
Proofreader: *Mary Hunt*

Contents at a Glance

Contents

Introduction

What is the biggest challenge you face in your job today?

What actions have you considered to address these challenges?

What one thing could you do this week to eliminate those barriers?

These are the kinds of questions coaches ask—of their colleagues, of their direct reports, and even of themselves. Coaching is that simple.

But coaching is more than simply asking questions. It's a way to get people to focus on the obstacles preventing them from making forward progress, to develop their own strategies for overcoming the obstacles, to put specific action plans in place, and then to evaluate the results of those actions.

This book will show you how to use a coach approach to help you and your colleagues make progress, improve productivity, and improve your working environment.

The goal of this book is not to turn you into a professional coach or even make coaching your full-time job. It's about applying coaching concepts to your current job. Throughout this book, you'll see ways to do your job better—and helps others do their job better—by using a coach approach.

This book will get you coaching in no time. It breaks down the coaching process into five easy-to-follow phases and offers a coaching model that anyone, at any level, in any organization, can use. It doesn't matter whether you're a midlevel manager in the fast food industry, a director of a non-profit foundation, a clerk in a corporate mail room, a minister at a small-town church, or an executive assistant at a Fortune 500 company.

Of course, every industry has its unique characteristics, so you'll also learn how to customize your coach approach to your particular field. Along the way you'll see lots of real-life examples of coaching in action. You'll learn how to think through any situation, what to say, and when to say it.

How This Book Is Organized

Here's a brief description of the parts that you'll find in this book.

In **Part 1, "Coaching: A New Tool at Work,"** you'll learn how coaching will help you take advantage of all the resources you already have but weren't aware of. Instead of pushing to go outside your organization for something new, you can maximize your potential with your existing resources. Coaching will help you discover those hidden resources in your company right now.

Part 2, "Coaching Basics," teaches you the fundamental coaching skills necessary for each coaching conversation. Here you'll learn what to say and when to say it to help your co-workers discover new insights and determine actions based on those insights. You'll learn how a few tweaks to your approach to conversations at work can produce positive business results. And you will be the catalyst of that positive change.

You can benefit from coaching no matter what you do for a living. Even professionals, such as lawyers and doctors (who typically do more telling than asking), find that integrating a coach approach into their practices helps them do their job better and develop stronger relationships with clients. **Part 3, "Coaching in Specific Occupations,"** walks you through the process of integrating coaching into your job.

Although coaching takes place at an individual level, a coaching culture can only be implemented at the organizational level. In **Part 4, "Coaching Challenges for Specific Organizations,"** you'll learn about the unique challenges inherent in several types of organizations. Small/Family-Owned Businesses deal with issues of growth. Large businesses deal with issues of complexity due to their size. Nonprofits, government, and faith-based organizations deal with a different set of issues regarding resource constraints, growth, and ideology. This part will dive into the differences that need to be taken into account while coaching inside these types of organizations.

In **Part 5, "Coaching as Catalyst,"** you'll learn how coaching can be used to create change in organizations. Once you understand how coaching others can help you do your job better, it will be a natural progression to start looking beyond your conversations to the processes you use to implement your job. This will reinforce the benefits that coaching can bring and produce measurable results for the organization. These chapters will inspire you to continue applying a coach approach to make a difference in your organization.

Extras

Along the way, you'll find the following extras.

Another Perspective _____

Coaching can help you see your situation from different angles. This sidebar will offer you other perspectives on coaching and other inspirational ideas.

Coaching Cautions _____

Coaching, like any form communication, can have its pitfalls. The trick is to notice the potential problems and avoid them. These cautions help you do just that.

Tips & Tools _____

It's the little things that will make your coaching more effective. Here you'll find suggestions for questions to ask and tools to use in your coaching conversations.

def•i•ni•tion _____

This sidebar offers definitions and explanations of coaching terms and expressions.

Acknowledgments

Most of what I've learned about a coach approach at work, I've learned from my clients. Thanks so much to all who have trusted me to come alongside and share your journeys with you. And thanks to those who were practicing their skills with me and coached me in the creation of this book.

In return for your trust, the confidence you have placed in me has been protected! The names, nationalities, or industries in my stories have been changed. I created composites from real experiences with multiple people and organizations that had similar experiences so that even the individuals and companies could not be identified.

This book would not have been possible without a few key people. Thanks to Judi Hayes for all your help in getting my thoughts turned into sentences and paragraphs that would convey the message I had in mind. Thanks to my husband Tom for being my sounding board and life partner in all my projects, including this one. Thanks to Judy Mikalonis and Linda Miller for seeing this opportunity, believing I could do it, and giving lots of encouragement along the way. And thanks to my colleagues who contributed ideas here and there that helped enhance this work: Ed Allen, Perry Rhue, Bev Wright, Sharon Coleman, Anita Stadler, Annie Martinez, Lily Keyes, Bill Copper, Chad Hall, Ken Kessler, Frank Skidmore, Susan Whitcomb, Jeannine Sandstrom, Jodie Wallace, Frank Aiken, Paul Higuchi, and Tracy Sullivan and the Deloitte team.

In addition, thanks go to Katharine White who joined me in the Internal Coaching Research we presented at ICF in 2003, to Ray Lamb and Pierre-Yves Driessen, who originally shared the Knowledge Model concepts with me, and Brittany F. Walls for her help with illustrations.

Big thanks go to Paul, Jennifer, Cate, and the Alpha Books team. It was a delight to work with you and benefit from your great suggestions.

Special thanks to my son, Andrew, for the hourglass illustration and my son, Bryan, for your ideas of how to get started on this book. You have both been a tremendous encouragement to me.

Trademarks

All terms mentioned in this book that are known to be or are suspected of being trademarks or service marks have been appropriately capitalized. Alpha Books and Penguin Group (USA) Inc. cannot attest to the accuracy of this information. Use of a term in this book should not be regarded as affecting the validity of any trademark or service mark.

Part 1

Coaching: A New Tool at Work

During an interview, Tony, a potential new hire, commented on the company's culture. He wasn't sure how to define it, but he liked what he observed—the way people interacted, seemed content, and focused on work. His observations helped him get the job, and he learned that what he observed was a coach approach in action.

His new boss explained that the company saw coaching as a key tool for moving the business and employees toward excellence. Since adopting the coaching culture, each employee had more input and worked more out of their strengths.

Tony learned how his new company implemented its coach approach and about the differences it continued to make in the organization. He could hardly wait to learn more.

In Part 1 you'll learn how coaching is different from other ways of interacting with employees, what a coaching culture looks like, how to get there, and how coaching benefits both the employee and company.

Coaching for Excellence

In This Chapter

- ◆ Understanding the key steps of coaching: connecting, focusing, discovering, acting, and evaluating
- ◆ Implementing action, progress, and change
- ◆ Focusing on the individual
- ◆ Comparing coaching with mentoring, consulting, and counseling

Coaching is a positive approach that looks to the future. It is an accountability process that helps the person being coached set goals, find solutions, and make forward progress. Because the entire process focuses on the person being coached, it fits the person being coached like a glove.

As a coach, you can develop skills to create positive forward progress in people, teams, and even the entire company. As a coach at work, you can help people find fulfillment, guide them to feel valuable because of their contributions, and facilitate individual and group growth. Coaching is an exciting partnership for the coach and the person being coached.

Coaching as a Tool for Work

Coaching at work is a tool for promoting discovery in others. No matter what you do for a living, others who work alongside you have untapped potential, but they may need help developing a plan for action. In fact, you can do your job better if they are working at their peak. You can use a *coach approach* to draw out their best for the benefit of your business.

def•i•ni•tion

The International Coach Federation (ICF) defines **coaching** as partnering with clients in a thought-provoking and creative process that inspires them to maximize their personal and professional potential.

A **coach approach** to your job involves looking for opportunities to help other people at work discover new insights and take new action to achieve the organization's goals. Specific attitudes, skills, and conversation models distinguish a coach approach from other ways of relating to colleagues.

Coaching is all about the other person. Whomever you interact with at work is a potential person for you to coach. They may be your team members, other colleagues in your company, your employees, boss, customers, or counterparts in other divisions.

In a business where coaching is having an impact, peers really carry their share of the load for the team, employees utilize all their potential to get the work done, and bosses focus on their job and let you do yours. When those around you are performing at their peak you will find it easier to perform your job better, too.

The Five Phases of a Coach Approach

Coaching can be broken down into five phases that are essential in every type of business. Here's a brief overview of these phases.

Connect

Coaching begins with connecting to the person being coached, or the *PBC*. Regardless of your coaching ability, you must establish trust before any real progress can be made. When people sense that you have a sincere interest in them and their progress, they will be much more open to the possibility of coaching.

def•i•ni•tion

PBC is simply shorthand for "person being coached."

Focus

Coaches and PBCs deal with one topic at a time. If the issue is complex, dealing with one segment of the situation at a time can make an overwhelming objective manageable. Sometimes a company is going through change, for example, and individuals may feel inundated with information. But in reality, only one critical transition needs focused attention. The coaching process helps the PBC concentrate on the part of the new organization that makes the most significant impact.

Or perhaps an employee has been put in charge of a new project. Although the new assignment seems overwhelming, the person in charge is capable of succeeding, leading a team to complete the project and meet all goals. Coaching skills can help the person focus on the most critical aspect of the project, address it, and then move on to the next goal.

Discover

Coaching takes advantage of just-in-time learning. This is learning what the PBC wants, needs, and can use to make an immediate difference in business situations. A coach can help a PBC focus on the current situation and resources in order to discover new insights that have been elusive up to this point.

Act

New discoveries become the basis for new actions, which will move the PBC forward. A lot of what people learn at work remains only knowledge. Coaching doesn't stop there. Coaching always has action as its goal. Coaching may involve a good bit of talking, listening, thinking, and reflecting; but the purpose is to take the right action. The goal doesn't stop with the talking; it always leads to doing. And the goal is never to do something someday if and when you have time. The goal is immediate action—taking steps right now. The action is specific. Talk leads to implementing a specific plan for what, when, how, and whom.

Evaluate

After actions are taken the PBC evaluates the results based on his or her own criteria. The question: "How will you know when you've achieved your goal?" can be useful in this stage to help the PBC set solid criteria for success. Taking the time to evaluate what he or she has learned will benefit the PBC when he or she takes on the next challenge.

Coaching means helping a person take responsibility. Whether results are positive or negative, a person who has been coached has made decisions, taken action, and knows that in large measure the results were due to his or her actions. Even if the results are not everything the PBC desired, if progress has been made, that's something to celebrate. And it's a foundation for more growth, an impetus to take the next step.

A Visual Model for Coaching

To fully grasp how the five phases of a coaching conversation work together, it helps to visualize an hourglass. The top of the hourglass at its widest point represents the discover phase—the variety of answers you could get by asking, "What would be helpful to talk about today?" In the early phase of coaching someone, you want to narrow the focus of the conversation. That focusing process is represented by the narrowing of the top of the hourglass to the center, the smallest opening that the sand goes through. That small opening represents the focus of the conversation.

Phases of a Coach Approach

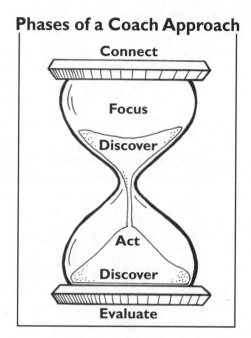

An hourglass is a great reminder of the phases of a coach approach conversation.

(Artwork courtesy of Andrew Creswell.)

Once you've focused on a single problem, you want the PBC to discover all the possibilities for how to address the issue. This discovery phase is represented by the widest part of the bottom of the hourglass where the sand falls after passing through the small center. You want to explore all the perspectives that might be helpful, options for solution, and even all the obstacles the PBC might encounter.

As the sand in an hourglass piles up in the bottom, the mound in the top lobe continually decreases in size until every grain of sand has fallen to the bottom lobe. This movement from top to bottom represents the actions that the PBC has identified and committed to accomplish.

A valuable coaching conversation is one where the actions (grains of sand at the top of the mound) line up with the focus (smallest opening in the hourglass). Not every coaching conversation fits this analogy perfectly, but it is a great mental image to help you navigate through the conversation.

Taking Responsibility

Coaching means helping people take responsibility. A person who has been coached has made decisions, taken action, and knows that in large measure the results were due to his or her actions. Even a little progress is something to celebrate. And that baby step of progress serves as a foundation for more growth, an impetus to take the next step.

Did you notice who's actually taking the steps in coaching? It is the PBC—not the coach—who does the focusing, the discovering, the acting, and the evaluating. Both of you work on connecting with each other so the coach can help the PBC take the next steps. But even in the connect phase, the primary judge of the strength of the connection is—you guessed it—the PBC.

The emphasis is on the PBC to take the steps. Consider yourself—the coach—as his or her escort. So how do you actually escort the PBC? That's what you'll find out in this book.

A Tool for Tapping into Hidden Potential

Potential is being wasted in conference rooms, cubicles, corner offices, and client lunches. If you could tap into all of that unused potential, it would be a great strategy for doing more with less. Coaching is a tool for doing just that. If you've never been coached, you may be scratching your head at this point, concluding that it sounds too good to be true.

The best way to convey the essence of coaching is for you to experience it. The next best way is to see how it has worked for others, which leads us to our first of many real-life examples:

Sharon's M.B.A. and can-do attitude put her on the fast track in the boutique clothing company she joined after completing her degree. Her enthusiasm was contagious, and people on her marketing team generally seemed willing to take on new projects. Even though her team was right in the middle of two new ad campaigns for the main product line, when management asked her team to take on a new project, Sharon agreed. She hoped her team would rise to the occasion and that success on this project would take her career to a new level.

But soon after taking on the new project, Sharon started facing challenges she'd never before encountered. Her team hit a few snags with its existing campaigns even before it began working on the new one. And then she learned that two key people on her team were leaving the company. Sharon's supervisor made it clear that Sharon's team would be expected to continue all the work until new people could be hired and brought up to speed. Progress seemed to crawl to a halt. Everything was in gridlock; Sharon didn't know what steps to take to regain momentum.

After trying to do everything herself for a few weeks, running around putting out fires and losing contact with her remaining team members, Sharon stopped, took a deep breath, and decided she needed help. Last month, she'd talked with another team leader, Rita, who had been using a coach approach with her team. Sharon decided to call Rita and ask for some coaching. Here's how their conversation went:

Sharon: Thanks for taking time to talk to me.

Rita: No problem. What's up?

Sharon: Everything's caving in all at once. We were doing pretty well on a couple of projects so we took on another one. The team was ok with it and everything. But what I didn't know was that Sam and Regina were already planning to leave. Now nothing's going right, I'm understaffed, and behind schedule. You know schedules don't change around here. What am I going to do?

Rita: I only have about 20 minutes until my next meeting. What's the most important part of all of this that you need to deal with?

Sharon: There are just not enough hours in the day to do everything. Can you fix that?

Rita: [grin] I wish! Really, where do you need to start?

Sharon: That's the thing. I don't really know.

Rita: Well, *that* sounds like a place to start. How can you figure out what's most important right now?

Sharon: OK, I do know that it is very important for my team to keep making progress even though Sam and Regina are not around anymore. I've been trying to do what I can of their jobs but it's just too difficult to do two more jobs on top of what I was already doing.

Rita: What are some other options for covering for those positions?

Sharon: Hmm. Well, I haven't really stopped to think about that. Some of the other people on my team have done those jobs before. I just didn't ask them to help out because we took on that extra assignment and everybody is already working way more hours than normal.

Rita: Ok, you can take time to think now. What about other options?

Sharon: I'm so exhausted it is hard to think. You know, I really need to ask my team. I just jumped right in and starting doing stuff before talking to them. I just assumed I could do it. This team leadership stuff is all really new to me.

Rita: When can you talk to your team?

Sharon: Right after we get off the phone.

Rita: Ok. So do you know what you're going to say?

Sharon: I'm just going to ask them what you are asking me—what are other options for dealing with our situation until I can get the empty positions filled. Is that good?

Rita: That's not for me to judge. But it brings up a thought. How will you know if the options you choose will be good?

Sharon: [grin] I'm writing that down. I'll ask them that, too.

Rita: It's not long before my meeting. Was this helpful?

Sharon: What I really wanted from you was some quick solution to my problem. So in that regard, I didn't really get what I wanted. But I did get a plan for a next step.

Rita: Well, then it was helpful. Hey, can I call you sometime when I'm in a spot, too?

Sharon: Sure thing.

From this example, you can see the key steps of coaching.

- ◆ **Connect:** Sharon and Rita had enough of a relationship that Sharon decided to call. They didn't have to be long-lost friends. They just needed enough of a connection that Sharon felt comfortable being honest about her situation.

◆ **Focus:** A key part of Rita's role as coach was to keep the conversation focused on Sharon's *agenda*. Rita began by asking questions to get Sharon to focus. She asked, "What's most important?" which didn't actually result in Sharon being focused yet, but it got her thinking in that direction. Rita kept on the path to get her focused and asked, "Where to start?". That did it. It is pretty common that it takes a few questions to get a PBC focused. Rita stayed in the role of coach and let Sharon do the actual problem solving.

◆ **Discover:** When Rita asked, twice, "What are other options?," Sharon actually took some time to think about her problem and realized she could ask the same things of her team. The *aha* was that she could draw on the brains of the whole team to help solve the problem.

def•i•ni•tion

A PBC's **agenda** is more than just his or her plan for a meeting. It conveys the fact that everything associated with coaching—the topic, the pace, the action, the evaluation—is centered around the PBC.

An **aha** is an informal way of referring to an unexpected new insight. By asking questions, coaches help PBCs experience "ahas."

◆ **Act:** Coaching is not complete until there is action. As soon as Sharon suggested that she needed to talk to her team, Rita asked her when she was going to do it. This question, followed by asking Sharon what she would say to her team, helped solidify the plan in Sharon's mind, and helped her to follow through with the planned action.

◆ **Evaluate:** At first, Sharon wanted Rita to tell her she was on the right track. But Rita, knowing it was more important for the PBC to do her own evaluation, asked Sharon how she would know if she had chosen a good option. The final step, evaluation, didn't take place during the conversation, but the discussion helped set the stage for evaluation later on.

This is only one example of how you can do your job better by coaching others. It doesn't have to take a lot of time, but it does require you to think and act very differently.

Be honest. Were you waiting to hear what brilliant solution Rita would offer? When you are in Rita's place as the coach, it is very tempting to just give the answers. Until, that is, you realize that there are greater benefits to having Sharon solve her own problem.

Where Is There More Potential?

In the preceding example, Rita helped tap into Sharon's potential. Sharon had the experience, skills, and talents necessary to come up with a plan for the next step to take, she just needed some coaching from Rita to bring it out. Similarly, Sharon recognized that she needed to tap into the potential of her team. She had not been using its ideas to help solve the problem.

The workplace is riddled with similar examples of untapped potential: in time wasted by redundancy; in the talents of people who are not using all their strengths; in all the ideas that are not being solicited and therefore, never surface; in unresolved conflicts that cause people to avoid each other; and in solutions that don't happen because the challenge doesn't arise.

Why Does Potential Remain Untapped?

Potential is hard to see. Think of coaching as mining for golden nuggets of potential that haven't yet surfaced. In order to start the mining process, though, you have to believe that "there's gold in them thar hills." In some businesses the perception exists that better answers come from outside the company. Just because those ideas have yet to surface, doesn't mean they are not there. With a coach approach at work, you are looking to those around you to come up with new solutions to existing problems.

The myth persists that it takes too much time to brainstorm, work through conflict, and find a solution. But when you use a coach approach, you are applying these idea-mining concepts to meetings and interactions that are, for the most part, already taking place. You're not setting up new meetings; instead, you're applying new techniques to already-budgeted time.

Often businesses want formulaic answers instead of individual, customized answers that result from coaching conversations. It seems that a "one size fits all" approach would be a great thing to find. You invest in one solution and use it everywhere. The problem is, often those solutions are "one size fits none." A coach approach is a formula that businesses can apply to all its challenges to produce a customized solution for each one.

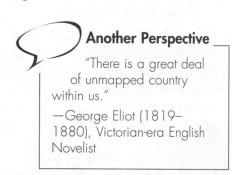

Another Perspective

"There is a great deal of unmapped country within us."

—George Eliot (1819–1880), Victorian-era English Novelist

How Does Coaching Tap Potential?

To start with, a coach assumes there is untapped potential within everyone. Each part of the coaching conversation is mining for the golden ideas businesses need to survive. Coaches employ the focus step to help PBCs look for the potential that complexity, lack of clarity, and random activity are blocking. Coaches use powerful questions to probe for bits and pieces of experience, stored knowledge, and know-how that have yet to be combined into brilliant ideas.

A coach's insistence that people actually follow through on new ideas unlocks the potential of those ideas. Action turns ideas into tangible results. When the person taking action is also responsible for evaluating that action, the coach approach transforms what's learned in the process into momentum for future actions.

A Different Kind of Coaching

If you have a whistle around your neck, a cap on your head, and a clipboard in your hands, you've bought the wrong book. In fact, if you want a playbook to help you call the shots at work, you'd better go back to the bookstore. You'll soon see that most sports analogies do not apply to coaching in the business world.

Athletic coaches are responsible for analyzing their own team's strengths and weakness and sizing members up against their opponents. Based on their analysis, coaches make executive decisions regarding practices, lineups, and particular plays. In other words, the coach gives orders and the athletes do what they are told. The goal of coaching in business is to foster personal responsibility for taking actions and moving forward. And giving orders is not the best way to engender responsibility in others.

> **Another Perspective**
>
> "The four most important words in life are: I believe in you."
>
> —Mike Krzyzewski, Duke University basketball coach

It's Not Mentoring, Consulting, or Counseling

Okay, you might be thinking, if it's not appropriate to compare business coaching to athletic coaching, then it sure sounds a lot like other business buzzwords such as mentoring, consulting, and counseling, right? Wrong. So if you were beginning to think that you didn't need to learn coaching because your company already uses mentors, consultants, or counselors, think again.

The primary difference between coaching and other types of personal help is again related to who is viewed as the expert. Just as in athletic coaching, in mentoring, consulting, and counseling, the person offering the service is clearly the expert. In business coaching the PBC is the expert. The coach is simply a guide to help the PBC keep growing, reaching goals, and achieving his or her potential.

Mentoring, counseling, and consulting are valuable personal-help processes. Many people and businesses benefit from them. But coaching is different from each of these. And coaching is something you can do!

Coaching Values People

When people are valued, they work harder. The coach approach assumes that the PBC ...

- Has lots of answers; it's just a matter of bringing them to the surface.

- Is worth investing in.

- Is intelligent and can learn more by putting together his or her knowledge in new ways.

- Is smart enough to develop his or her own action plans.

- Is responsible enough to take actions and learn from the results.

Imagine what work would be like if everyone believed these statements to be true for themselves and thought these things about all of their co-workers. That change in perspective would make a radically different working environment. Even if the people you interact with don't always demonstrate this potential, give it a try. Assume these things are true as you work with them and your interactions automatically will be different before you've even learned any coaching skills.

Bringing Out the Best in Others

A lot of businesses spend too much time assigning blame and not enough time giving credit. When a plan doesn't work as well as expected, most employees will say that they were just doing what they were told the way they were told to do it.

In a coaching climate, employees take responsibility for actions they take. *You can benefit in your job by bringing out the best in others.* That simple statement reflects the opposite of what happens in most businesses, and coaching can make it happen. It is far more common to think that the best way to get ahead is to make others look bad. So think about that statement. If this chapter hasn't convinced you, the rest of book will!

The Least You Need to Know

◆ Coaching connects people on a respectful, level ground that is not hierarchical.

◆ A coaching atmosphere is one of discovery, searching to put information together in new ways.

◆ You need others to perform at their best in order to do your job well.

◆ Coaching opportunities abound in the workplace.

◆ Coaching is not the same thing as mentoring, consulting, or leading.

◆ More good work gets done when everyone takes responsibility for their actions.

Chapter 2

What Is Different About a Coaching Culture?

In This Chapter

- ◆ Moving from busyness to making efforts count
- ◆ Creating a climate for innovation
- ◆ Leading employees to become more creative and productive
- ◆ Taking action to improve processes
- ◆ Using entrepreneurial skills in a salaried job

Even if you coach only one person in your company, that person would benefit, you would benefit, and the company would feel the impact. So imagine the benefits if everyone were to participate in coaching. When a majority of the people in a company takes part, the business has adopted a *coaching culture*.

The purpose of this chapter is to share stories that demonstrate what a coaching culture is like. Each of the scenarios took place in organizations that were working toward a coaching culture, although the names, jobs, and some details have been altered.

def·i·ni·tion

A **coaching culture** is an organizational environment in which the coaching phases of connection, focus, discovery, action, and evaluation are routinely fostered through conversations and processes.

Focus on Results

At work it's easy to get lured into busyness and wanting to get credit for the effort spent when what really matters is the results. Coaching is a bit like a "so what?" methodology: let's not just expend effort; instead, let's actually make sure the effort counts for something. Consider Chris, head of training in a large utilities company.

Chris is the kind of boss people like to see coming through their office door. He likes just about everybody, and they like him in return. Chris began to see his ability to get along well with people as one of his strengths, and he wanted to do it well—so well, in fact, that pleasing people began to shape how he made decisions. His desire to please people clouded his judgment about the projects he took on and the way he delegated work to his staff.

Part of his job was to set strategy for the whole organization. When it came time to develop his annual strategy, he would include everything anyone had asked him to do. As a result the strategy was bulky, expensive, and unorganized. The plan just kept getting bigger and bigger and less and less manageable.

Because his company embraced coaching at all levels, he approached a peer executive, Perry, for help. After a brief discussion Chris realized that he was overwhelmed.

Perry asked: How would our CEO prioritize your activities for today?

Chris: Yeah, yeah. I know how he would prioritize. But he's not aware of my latest challenges.

Perry: Well, what would be the best way to prioritize?

Chris: I need to deal with the hardest things first and get them out of the way.

For the next few minutes, Chris kept churning on how to get everything done and was right back where he started the conversation: overwhelmed.

So Perry tried a different approach with the following line of questions: Who do you need to say no to in order to make this a more reasonable work load? Who will it impact? Who do you need to talk to in order to make it right?

Chris didn't want to answer these questions. He viewed saying no to anyone as being negative and not a team player. He just didn't want to choose.

Perry said: "Not choosing is a choice. Which one do you want? Keep doing it all or get something taken off your plate?"

With this, Chris finally realized how his eagerness to please was causing him to create unrealistic plans. Chris began to make hard decisions about what he would and would not do. People continued to like him, but more important, he earned a lot more respect because he actually followed through on what he said he would do.

In a coaching culture you get really focused on what matters most, determine what makes the biggest impact, and commit to the projects you agree to do.

Tips & Tools

The One Page Business Plan at www.onepagebusinessplan.com is a great tool to use to clarify business objectives and focus on results.

Action vs. Talk

Coaching focuses on action. In fact, if there's no action, there's no coaching. Consider Teresa, an executive assistant in an accounting firm.

Teresa was an efficient worker—that's how she rose to the level of executive assistant. You could count on her to do her job well, but you could also expect to listen to her complaints and criticism the entire time. Some days her co-workers went home thinking that Teresa didn't like anything or anyone. They had good reason. They had listened to her share her opinions about what was wrong with the filing system, the supply closet, the conference room technology, and half the staff.

When Teresa met with Stephanie, the internal coach for her division, she quickly learned that coaches don't put up with whining. That's because coaching results are about action, not talk. At first Teresa was frustrated because she usually created relationship connection through her complaining: she whined, you whined back, and you become buddy whiners. Because she always got her job done, she never considered the possibility that her whining was a problem.

Stephanie insisted that Teresa stop whining during their conversations and focus on what actions she was going to take. Here's how her coach got Teresa to stop whining: whenever Teresa would complain about something, the following type of dialogue would occur:

Stephanie: That sounds like a difficult situation, what can you do about it?

Teresa: I can't do anything about it (and whined some more).

Stephanie: You know, talking about this is not going to improve the situation, but I think planning some concrete actions that you can do will help. Would you agree to that?

Tips & Tools

When the PBC resists creating any actions, you can ask: "Are you willing to take action?" This simple technique of renegotiating the agreement is often helpful to get a PBC past his or her reluctance to make progress.

When Teresa reluctantly agreed, Stephanie continued: What is under your control in this situation?

This question forced Teresa to sort out what she had control over and what was out of her control. She realized that part of her whining was due to assumptions about what she had control over. She learned that she had control over a lot more than she had first thought. Coaching conversations brought that to light.

Eventually her whining gave way to looking for actions to fix the problem. She reserved her whining for coffee breaks and at lunch and spent a lot more time in action rather than talk. She also started coaching others. She's found she doesn't much like to listen to people whine.

Coaching conversations always move in the same direction: toward an action as the end point. As more people experience coaching, the entire organization becomes more focused and action-oriented.

An Environment for Innovation

Innovation is not something you can force to happen, but it is the life-blood of companies. Coaching is a natural tool for creating an environment for innovation to thrive. Consider what happened with this high-energy group of sales reps in a pharmaceutical company.

Even before the sales manager, Rodrigo, began coaching them, the reps were doing great. But, in spite of outperforming other sales teams and their reputation for excellence, no team members were making quota. They were doing better than the other teams because each individual was a shining star. They had good processes, but they were a collection of good performers, not a team.

Rodrigo got them all together in one place so they could see and hear each other's ideas, which they thought at first was a big waste of time when they could be out making sales calls. He asked them, "What are your top challenges as a team?"

As the reps started mentioning challenges, Rodrigo listened for resonance with the other team members. When several people said "Oh yeah, I've had that problem, too," Rodrigo identified those problems for further discussion. After several problems had been identified, the team settled on five of the most pressing problems to address first and ranked them.

Rodrigo asked: "What are all the options for how this first problem can be solved?" He kept asking variations of this question until he had exhausted all the ideas from the room.

Then he asked: "Which of these ideas would be the most effective given the time and resources available?"

Everyone expressed opinions, but there was significant disagreement on several of the problems under discussion. Rodrigo employed questions like: "How much agreement do we need to be effective?" and "What would it take to get to that point?"

When they choose the top three actions to take on each problem, Rodrigo asked what specifically needed to be done, with whom, and by when for each action. One at a time the team examined those actions in greater detail to determine what obstacles might show up so they could be avoided. As the team began to coalesce they were able to divide the responsibilities fairly.

Coaching Cautions

Don't be the note taker when you coach a team! That counteracts your goal for the team to accept responsibility for their actions. Ask: "Who will take notes?" and hum the theme to *Jeopardy* until someone volunteers.

Finally Rodrigo asked: "How will you evaluate the results of your action plans?" After several more minutes of discussion they all agreed to keep each other updated weekly and to meet again for a debriefing in three weeks. And they also asked Rodrigo to join them again for another session. In their view coaching went from being a waste of time to an asset in the space of 90 minutes.

In team coaching they learned from one another what might work in different situations because the others had tried it and it had been successful. And through coaching they discovered that they needed to collaborate instead of compete. They began to see other companies as the competition rather than their teammates.

At first, when team members heard new ideas, they thought they couldn't use them because they belonged to someone else. During team coaching sessions they heard more and more new ideas, and they began to make the shift to thinking it was a good thing to use one another's ideas.

Two other things made this possible. Some long-established conventions within the company began to change. For years the unwritten norm had been to work in isolation: "This is how you call on a customer. This is how you do your job. Never call on customers in pairs or in teams." No one had ever questioned these ideas, but now they began to change. Over time the new ideas became the new norm. Team members began to visit customers together. They used one another's ideas. And the sales group that had been the best began to do even better as a team.

New ideas are a regular part of the discovery phase of the coaching conversation. An organization-wide coaching culture leads to an expectation that innovation is the norm.

Clear Communication

A by-product of coaching is clear communication. It happens for a couple reasons. For one thing, PBCs must articulate clearly to make progress, and they become more skilled in clarifying their thoughts and expressing them as they speak. In addition, specific action plans are a required part of a coaching conversation. Consider Sonja.

Sonja is an executive in the home office of a large bank. She's brilliant and detail oriented, and her goal is to reach senior VP level by the time she is 45. Then Sonja got some feedback from her current bosses that she rubbed people the wrong way. Not one to back away from bad news, Sonja set out to confirm what she had heard, and she got the same feedback from previous bosses and others with whom she worked.

Apparently she could be so focused and intense that she came off as abrupt, even terse, in her dealings with others. She had been known to brusquely dismiss any questions or objections people had during meetings. Where she thought she was providing insight and valuable, detailed information, others found her speeches tiresome and over their heads. She found that while she was admired for her intelligence and work ethic, people avoided her because of her intensity and lack of finesse in working relationships. What's more, Sonja learned that this reputation was the biggest factor in keeping her from making senior VP.

As Sonja grappled with how to handle this news she contacted a colleague, Simon, who was an exec at one of the largest branches of the company, for advice. He told her he would be glad to help with the problem and asked if she would like to be coached. She agreed and they set up several times for coaching by phone.

In her coaching sessions, Sonja would repeat statements she had made that were not well received. Simon asked questions like, "What are the possible ways this can be interpreted?" and "If you said this to a friend outside of work what would the likely reaction be?"

At times, Simon also communicated with Sonja very directly, pointing out that her lengthy explanations and terseness could be interpreted as superior and uncaring.

Coaching helped Sonja gain perspective and develop a plan to change. In coaching sessions Sonja began to practice in advance what she would say and how she would say it.

Sonja also began to realize that details she thought were important were not so important to others with whom she worked. As she added more and more detail, their eyes would glaze over, and they saw her as being arrogant instead of detail-oriented and thorough.

Her very strengths were also her biggest weaknesses. She had been assuming that she needed to dole out all the knowledge she had acquired to everyone. Instead, she needed to learn how to synthesize the information to share only what each person needed and wanted to know to do their job. She needed to accept that not sharing every detail didn't mean that she was withholding information.

Because Simon flexed to Sonja's style of communication, Sonja learned how to flex to others style of communication. By using the coaching skill of modeling behavior, her coach helped Sonja learn to assess accurately how to communicate well with different people.

> ### Another Perspective
>
> "To exist is to change, to change is to mature, to mature is to go on creating oneself endlessly."
>
> —Henri Bergson, French philosopher who was awarded the 1927 Nobel prize for literature

She began to gauge when an employee truly understood her and was not just nodding to allow a quick escape from her office. She also found that if she listened more carefully she was able to better judge how she was coming across. Her abrupt dismissals of questions were replaced by a growing willingness to listen to concerns she once considered trivial.

The result was better, more manageable communication throughout Sonja's part of the company. Her communications with others were better received, her performance reviews improved, and her bosses began to look at the possibility of a promotion in her future.

Consultants, managers, and executives frequently point to the lack of clear communication as a hindrance to progress. Working in a coaching culture promotes better communication as different perspectives are considered. Coaching can be a mirror to show how others view you.

Intra-prenuership

Entrepreneurship involves the drive to be creative and productive in order to survive. The entrepreneur has a vision and promotes it enthusiastically. You see this drive among self-employed people and small business owners, but these qualities may be lacking in salaried employees in a larger company. Instead, they may lapse into a routine that involves little creativity. This is especially true for employees far removed from the end customer.

Intra-prenuership brings the best entrepreneurial qualities into companies. Consider this story about Latoya, an executive in a medical professionals recruitment company.

Latoya is a promising young employee who just got promoted into management. Her boss, Sandra, is helping her get acclimated into the role of manager and wants to see her succeed. Sandra uses coaching as a tool with all her employees because she's found it to be effective in promoting new ideas.

def•i•ni•tion

Intra-prenuership is operating as an entrepreneur inside a large organization. It involves approaching your job with the same drive, attitude, and behaviors that you would if you owned the business.

Their early coaching sessions together typically focused on the routine problems of learning how to manage people: planning, employee conflicts, project management, and so on. It didn't take very long for the volume of decisions to pile up. She was surprised by how overwhelming this could become. She brought this problem into one of her coaching sessions with Sandra.

Sandra began the coaching session by asking what Latoya would like to focus on.

Latoya: I'm finding I have to make so many decisions every day that I'm starting to feel overwhelmed.

Sandra: How do you want to address this problem?

Latoya: I don't know where to start. I think I'm making good decisions but I'm never quite sure.

Sandra: What criteria do you use to make your decisions?

Latoya: That's just the problem. It's all so new and I worry about making the wrong decision all the time.

Sandra: What if you were the owner, how would you decide?

Latoya: This is a huge company and I'm definitely not the owner. I don't know how the owner of this corporation would think.

Sandra: No, you're not the owner. But if you changed your perspective and made decisions as if you are the owner, how would that change your behaviors?

Latoya didn't have a ready answer and ended the conversation by saying she would need to think about it. That question stayed with Latoya as she grappled with all the decisions of her new job over the next few weeks. At first, it just seemed like a ridiculous thought. She kept asking herself, *What do owner's care most about? Increasing revenue? Reducing expenses at every turn? Brand loyalty? Stakeholder value?* The more she thought about these things the more she noticed that the question of ownership was having an impact on how she behaved. She used that perspective as a starting point for all her decisions.

In a coaching culture, "thinking like the owner" is a common occurrence. As with Latoya, the shift in thinking and behavior doesn't happen overnight. But when it is a part of the culture that decisions are made this way, peers challenge you to keep this in mind, bosses expect it, difficulties with implementation are addressed as they occur, and it becomes the way the norm.

Refined Processes

Coaching is a powerful process for eliminating inefficiencies. When a person brings challenges to a coaching conversation, often the outcome is an action to refine a process that isn't working as well as it could.

Coaching insists that the PBC look at the root of what caused the challenge in the first place. What is usually at the root? Process.

A software sales team responsible for a multi-state region was floundering because its process for tracking complex sales was almost as complex as the sale itself. The software was difficult to use. The fields were confusing, and few people knew what to enter into each field, so they tended to leave fields blank.

The team met once a week to talk about what should have been put in the database fields. This wasted the time of a lot of people—the sales team, the contracts team, the sales support team, members from marketing, and people from customer service. All these people had to listen to the coordinator ask what should be typed into the database.

As a result, people put their brains on autopilot or even worked on other projects while putting the conference call on mute. When the time came to collaborate on challenges that needed all the best thinking of the various roles they represented, they were not very engaged in the conversation.

The project coordinator decided to forego the usual agenda for just one week and coach the team on how to make their weekly meetings more productive. One discovery from the coaching session was that the database needed to be streamlined. A couple of people on the call volunteered to determine which data was really crucial report back on what they learned.

Another discovery was that everyone was needed for certain topics, but only a few people needed to be involved in discussions about some of the subtopics. They decided in that meeting to have two parts of the meeting—the bigger list of attendees would come first and finish in a set amount of time. Everyone agreed not to mute or multitask for that shorter time so that the call could be efficient.

Another Perspective

"Some people have greatness thrust upon them. Very few have excellence thrust upon them .... They achieve it. They do not achieve it unwittingly by doing what comes naturally and they don't stumble into it in the course of amusing themselves. All excellence involves discipline and tenacity of purpose."

—John W. Gardner, Former Secretary of Health, Education and Welfare, and founder of Common Cause.

The final discovery was that this coaching meeting had been their most productive ever, and it was about process and not about specific sales. The project coordinator agreed to use a coach approach going forward. Someone else took on the role of database monitor and agreed to make sure the new streamlined version of the database was updated prior to each meeting.

In coaching conversations, challenges are initially addressed by looking at the symptoms. However, it is important to get the PBC to keep exploring the situation until he or she established action plans that address the source of the challenge. In a coaching culture, this happens on a regular basis.

Coaching Replicates Itself

When people experience the benefits of coaching, they pass on their experiences and what they learn to others, and they begin to experiment with coaching skills. They start to ask powerful questions, and they start to expect forward movement as the result of investing time in conversation. Often people end up coaching others without even intending to do so; but when you have a coaching culture, coaching gets multiplied throughout an organization pretty quickly. Consider Sam.

Sam, from contract management, was one of the first people in his company to see the value of coaching. Sam lacked confidence, often felt defeated before he began a new project, and was wishy-washy in his decision-making. His former boss knew him well and offered to coach him now and then after he changed jobs to a new sector. One thing Sam needed to deal with was focusing on one thing at a time. Before Sam could focus on what he would do next year, he needed to learn to focus on what he would do next week.

As Sam began to focus on results, his actions became more precise and on target. His team noticed a change and asked what had brought such clarity to Sam's work. When he told them that his former boss had been coaching him and had helped him focus more clearly on his work, they wanted to learn more about coaching. When Sam saw that others could see the changes coaching had brought about in him, he began to consider how coaching could help others on his team. He thought he could help them gain new insights about themselves and their work.

At first Sam's team members were a little skeptical. They weren't all that familiar with coaching, and they saw his questions as criticism. They thought, *If he knows so much, why doesn't he just give us the answers?* But over time each of the team members began to have new insights and to see the benefits of coaching from his or her own experiences. Sam then became the section hero because he brought coaching to their sector.

As more and more people had good experiences with coaching, they coached others; and coaching and its benefits began to spread throughout Sam's company.

Compounded Benefits

Each of the people profiled in this chapter not only benefited from coaching; others benefited as well. Multiply these benefits by the number of people and coaching opportunities in an organization, and you are on your way to creating a coaching culture.

The Least You Need to Know

- ◆ Coaching is a tool that addresses the key challenges of business.
- ◆ Organizations that are constantly exposed to coaching will experience lasting benefits.
- ◆ Coaching leads to clearer communication, refined processes, and personal responsibility.
- ◆ Coaching has a multiplying effect.

3

Creating a Coaching Culture

In This Chapter

- ◆ Starting a coaching culture in the workplace
- ◆ Understanding how work culture is shaped by coaching others
- ◆ Convincing folks at the top that coaching will help the company
- ◆ Planning for a coaching culture

Most of this book focuses on showing you that everyone can do their job better by taking advantage of coachable moments. When coaching begins to take hold in a company, an overall culture that values coaching may emerge. Other employees will see that it works and will want to coach and be coached, too.

Although it's certainly possible for a coaching culture to emerge unaided, it may not happen at all without planning and purpose. And without some orchestrated effort, a newly established coaching culture might fizzle out.

Coaching successes in a variety of companies demonstrate that there is no one right way to create a sustainable corporate coaching culture. But there are common elements that show up again and again in organizations that have successfully implemented a culture. This chapter builds on their experiences to help you learn how to create a coaching culture in your organization.

Identifying a Leader

The first thing you need to do when embarking on a coaching culture is pick someone to take the lead. The person you choose to take the lead needs to be someone who is willing to develop competency as a coach and to be a resource for the rest of the organization. That person can be in HR, training and development, organizational development, or a leader in a business unit.

Tips & Tools

Research on creating coaching cultures and the return on investment (ROI) of coaching is expanding. The International Consortium for Coaching in Organizations (ICCO) publishes *The International Journal of Coaching in Organizations* quarterly. The journal's research articles cover topics such as creating a coaching culture, the ROI of executive coaching, and case studies. The Worldwide Association of Business Coaches has also conducted research about creating a coaching culture.

Key Responsibilities

The lead person will need to take on a number of responsibilities to create a coaching culture. Good planning is essential. You will want to put plans in place that are customized to work well in the current culture. Part of your planning should include scheduling and budgeting any necessary training. You also need to establish goals for the overall coaching culture initiative.

The leader will also be responsible for connecting coaching resources with people who need them. Examples of coaching resources include coaches, coach training, assessments to use with coaching, and books and related materials.

Training

The most helpful training for creating a coaching culture teaches International Coach Federation (ICF) competencies, focuses on corporate/business coaching, and emphasizes challenges unique to internal coaching.

Creating a Coaching Culture Step-by-Step

Before you can begin the process of establishing a coaching culture in your company, you need to get executive buy-in on the project, develop plans for implementing the culture, and try a pilot project. Set goals for the scope of the project such as number of teams or departments involved. Also consider measurable goals such as impact on the company (more on this in the Chapter 20).

Getting Executive Buy-In

Always start at the top. Before you do anything else, get executive buy-in. When coaching has the blessings of the top team, a coaching culture will be that much easier to implement. The best way to get enthusiastic executive endorsement is to have the executives experience coaching personally.

Although research and experience support the fact that coaching is financially beneficial, don't begin building your case with a promise of a big jump in ROI. The increased ROI will come and will likely be impressive, but it isn't an effective sales tool. Executives rarely approve a plan for coaching based on an ROI projection alone. They need to experience coaching personally to understand the potential benefits.

Coaching Cautions

Have more than one executive sponsor the coaching culture initiative. Execs move around a lot, and you don't want your program to end just because the lone sponsoring exec moved on or got promoted.

Start by showing executives that coaching can be done informally and that an external professional isn't always needed. Then, if they choose, they can hire an external coach as a part of the initiative to create a coaching culture. Using an external coach is a common practice on the executive level because of perceived *equity of exchange* issues. Executives need to see their coach as someone who has credibility and can be objective in coaching conversations. An internal coach will typically be at a lower level than the executive and therefore, may carry less credibility with the executive. The higher the executive, the more likely that an internal coach will not be the answer.

def•i•ni•tion

Equity of exchange happens when a participant gets value from an interaction that is equal to or greater than what he/she contributes.

You know you really have your executives' support if …

- ◆ Their leadership style already involves coaching.

- ◆ They are willing to be coached and share their experience with others in the organization.

- ◆ They approve allocation of time and resources for others to participate in being coached.

- ◆ They agree that coaching is a business catalyst and has the direct ability to impact ROI.

- ◆ They can articulate a clear vision for coaching that they personally believe (not "my employees told me to say this").

- ◆ They are willing to fund the coaching initiative.

If you don't have this level of buy-in, wait until you do before you embark on a large-scale coaching culture initiative. In the meantime, employees can do their job better by seizing coachable moments with others.

Making Plans

In order to get executive buy-in, you may need to document plans for the coaching culture initiative. The larger your company, the more likely you'll need to submit a formal plan. The following planning suggestions grew out of conclusions from a coaching culture survey conducted by the ICF.

Coaching won't be sustainable unless it produces a positive ROI, so planning on how to measure it is important. (See Chapter 20 for more specifics on how to do this.) A strategy for funding and resource allocation will determine the scope of the initiative, and whether the company will have dedicated coaches or whether managers and peers will do the coaching.

Business objectives should be considered so that coaching aligns with them seamlessly. An overall plan should include information on how the plan will be renegotiated if conditions change. If your company ran a coaching pilot project, be sure to use information gained in that project when creating your plan, because what worked on a small scale in your company is likely to work in a larger initiative.

Assignments. Specify how coaches will be assigned, how teams will be coached, and how long coaches will remain with an individual, group, or team.

Assessments. Set criteria for the use of assessments. Many companies rely heavily on assessments, especially at the beginning of a coaching process, while others may not find them helpful.

Scope. Determine the scope of the project. Some companies limit the coaching initiative to career development. Others limit it to work with new employees or those moving into new positions to help them become established (onboarding). Still others only make coaching available to people who have been identified as

> **Coaching Cautions**
>
> Companies that limit coaching initiatives to working with leaders who have performance issues do not have success in creating a sustainable coaching culture. Employees figure out the selection criteria and avoid it at all costs.

executive leadership hopefuls. Your plans should include a description of any such limitations.

Training. Focus on incorporating the ICF core competencies of "facilitating learning and results" and "communicating effectively." (A full list of these is available on the ICF website: www. internationalcoachfederation.com). Plan to assess training needs for internal coaches annually. Include in your plans the need for keeping coaching skills current, encouraging coaches to work toward higher levels of ICF certification.

Communication. Implement a communication plan that includes a strong message about what coaching is and how it is relevant to business results. Be sure to celebrate the success that the business is enjoying as a result of coaching.

Process Integration. Create a process integration plan that includes connecting the coaching process to recruitment and retention, education, performance management, leadership development, reward and recognition, succession planning, and coaching as a key competency of management jobs.

Conducting a Pilot

You'll find that it's a good idea to start small; get some easy successes and then build from there. Follow these steps to conduct a successful coaching pilot:

1. Identify the participants, including PBCs and coaches. This may be easier if potential participants take a coachability assessment (see Chapter 5).

2. Identify training needs. Training for someone who is going to use coaching in his or her regular job doesn't have to be comprehensive. Even a few days of introductory training can build the groundwork for a successful pilot.

3. Set clear goals for the pilot. The goals should be concrete and reasonable, based on the expected time frame, level of participation, and scope of the project.

4. Determine in advance how long the pilot will last and how results of the pilot will be evaluated.

5. Stick to the evaluation criteria. Changing the way the project is evaluated after completion or in midstream will likely invalidate the results you are seeking to support a larger initiative.

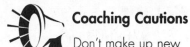

Coaching Cautions

Don't make up new metrics to monitor the success of coaching. Use the ones you already have in place: revenue, ROI, customer satisfaction, and employee satisfaction.

If your pilot is successful, begin to expand its scope. If your pilot does not produce the results you desire, consider changing the parameters of the pilot before expanding the scope.

The Phases of Coaching Culture Development

Successful coaching culture initiatives roughly follow three phases of development: the people phase, the culture phase, and the process phase. One phase does not have to be complete before you begin the next one.

People Phase

Focus on getting more people in the organization to experience the benefits of coaching.

The momentum will build. Sometimes it will build quickly enough that you are ready to move to the next phase in six months, but don't be surprised if it takes longer.

Try to expose people at all levels to coaching during this phase. People phases that are top heavy (only executives being coached) or bottom heavy (only nonmanagement being coached) tend to take longer to build momentum toward an organization-wide coaching culture.

Culture Phase

Get acquainted with your organization's culture.

Some say that you should start with the picture of what your culture is, then describe what your ideal desired culture would look like. Next lead a brainstorming session to identify the actions needed to move the organization to that ideal culture.

> **Another Perspective**
>
> In his book *Organizational Culture and Leadership* (Jossey-Bass, 1992), Edgar Schein wrote: "… culture is to a group what personality or character is to an individual. We can see the behavior that results, but often we cannot see the forces underneath that cause certain kinds of behavior."

This sounds like a good plan, but it doesn't really work. Using this plan is like saying: *Who are you now? Who would you rather be?* You might say you want to be Tom Hanks or Oprah Winfrey. Now let's brainstorm about how you can become Oprah Winfrey. What a silly exercise! There's only one Oprah—and it's not you.

Of course, you are not any more likely to be able to create a totally new culture in your organization than you can become Oprah. The missing step in this process is acknowledging who you are at the core— not your history, not your education, but at the core. You were born with a certain personality style, cognitive preferences, and strengths. When you want to make adjustments, you make them within the context of what you were born with. Some of those strengths at the core are hidden.

When it comes to an organization's culture, its core traits are here to stay. These are the culture elements you want to focus on when creating a coaching culture.

The first step of this phase is to identify the core of the organization's culture. Then focus on the strengths that make the organization successful, productive, and profitable. When creating a coaching culture, any existing elements of the culture that are congruent with a coach approach are automatically strengths. You'll want to orient any new initiatives around leveraging and developing those strengths.

Process Phase

People processes—things such as employee performance evaluations, career development, succession planning, recruiting, and retention—tend to sabotage attempts to leverage the strengths of an organization's culture. This phase is about taking the strengths identified in the culture phase and evaluating people processes to make sure each one is leveraging and developing those strengths.

One organization that went through these phases identified that "assuming untapped potential in everyone" was a strength of its culture. In the process phase they evaluated their people processes to see if "assuming untapped potential in everyone" was being strengthened or leveraged. Here's what they found about assuming untapped potential in various people processes:

Employee Performance Evaluations. Although evaluation forms listed both the strengths and weaknesses of each employee, the bulk of the annual evaluation conversation addressed action plans for the employee's weaknesses.

To leverage the untapped potential in the people process, supervisors still filled out the form in the same way, but they changed the evaluation conversation to focus on the employee's untapped potential and how it could be used. In most cases employees had strengths that weren't listed on the annual objectives and weren't being evaluated at all.

Career Development. In terms of career development, in the past supervisors simply pointed employees to career advancement information within the company.

The company tweaked the process by pointing out employee strengths and untapped potential *before* bringing up career advancement opportunities. The rest of the process stayed the same, but the conversation with the manager about possible advancement was very different due to the new way of starting the process.

Succession Planning. Before the company starting leveraging untapped potential of employees, it wasn't doing any succession planning.

The company designed a succession planning process that focused on leveraging untapped potential.

Recruiting. Under the old system, application forms, requested resumé format, and onsite interviews focused on historical performance, not on untapped potential.

They modified the application forms to add an essay question about untapped potential; requested that resumés include a list of the applicant's core strengths and a brief explanation of how potential could be tapped in new ways; and during interviews included discussion of potential and peer reviews that would be a reality check of that potential.

Retention. In the past, a process to retain employees was implemented only if an employee who had special strengths threatened to leave.

Under the new system, an annual review of untapped potential was added to the retention process as a mean of being proactive in retaining key employees.

By tweaking their people processes, the company was able to boost the momentum that was building in the people phase while more and more people were benefiting from coaching.

This is just one example of an organization addressing one of its strengths. It only takes looking at a handful of strengths for coaching to make a big difference in the life of the organization and for a coaching culture to take hold.

The Least You Need to Know

- Executive buy-in is essential if you want to create a coaching culture throughout the organization.

- Understand the strengths of your company's culture before you begin to change it through coaching.

- Plan for the success of your coaching initiative. Include desired outcomes as well as the methods you'll use to introduce coaching into your organization.

- A coaching culture will almost certainly have a positive effect on ROI, but that change is less dramatic than the positive effect it has on employees.

- Implement a pilot project in your company before beginning coaching throughout the organization.

Part 2

Coaching Basics

After Tony had been on the job for a few months, he continued to learn about coaching. He learned that most of his colleagues did a little coaching and also sought coaching when they were stuck. He was surprised to learn that he could be a coach, too. He was already beginning to learn about the basic skills of listening and asking questions. He was beginning to see his work—and his life outside of work—in new ways, even after his short time on the job. Because his peers were already coaching one another, they were happy to bring him into the mix. Then he learned that coaching was more than working with peers. Managers frequently coached employees and even teams and groups.

In Part 2 you'll learn the skills needed to help people you're coaching discover new insights and determine actions based on those insights. We'll also take a look at how coaching works within organizations at all levels—from coaching individuals to teams; from coaching someone across the hall to coaching someone on another continent.

Chapter 4

The Nuts and Bolts

In This Chapter

- ◆ Listening in a new way
- ◆ Asking powerful questions
- ◆ Protecting confidentiality
- ◆ Focusing on action
- ◆ Taking a new approach to answers

Coaching is a simple process, and the skills involved—listening carefully and asking questions—are tools that you are already familiar with. But it may not be immediately obvious how to put these skills together to make a coaching conversation. You need to know the function of each skill and then apply it in a meaningful way. That's the fun of it—putting the nuts and bolts together in unique ways that help you get your job done better.

Your first successes in this endeavor will have you anticipating the next opportunity to put the nuts and bolts together.

Timing Is Everything

You can't just walk up to a colleague whenever you feel like it and start coaching. Instead, you need to wait for an appropriate opportunity. This opportunity is called a *coachable moment*.

As a coach, you need to learn to recognize coachable moments when they present themselves to you. Then you need to know the skills you can use to bring about new learning and subsequent action. Consider these examples of coachable moments:

◆ A co-worker is stuck on a problem that is holding up everyone else on the team, including you.

◆ Your employee needs to come up with some innovative ideas for a new assignment you have given him or her.

◆ Your customer is interested in your product but not sure if he or she wants to buy it.

◆ You are in HR and responsible for helping a new employee on board.

◆ Your peer needs to have a difficult conversation with your boss, the outcome of which will impact everyone in the organization.

def•i•ni•tion

A **coachable moment** is when a person is in a position to benefit from learning something new related to a specific focus area and is ready to take action on it.

When you think you've identified a coachable moment, ask yourself these questions: *Is the person ready to look for new insights? Is this a situation the person can control, decide what to do, and take actions? Is the person searching for answers but not in deep distress or worry over the issue? Do I have a good relationship with the person so my questions won't be viewed with suspicion or as a trap?* If you can answer yes to most of these questions, it's a coachable moment.

Listen Intently

You can do your job better by listening like a coach. Coachlike listening is not just an auditory process; it's also a mental process that involves listening more intently with the purpose of facilitating learning for the PBC (person being coached). Done well, you both benefit.

It may seem obvious that if you listen more closely, you can use what you hear to come up with new ideas and help the person you are coaching take new action. That might actually happen, and would be good. But listening intently to others can also help you interact with them in such a way that *they* come up with new ideas, and *they* take action. Now that's a deal! Their action helps you do your job better, and they take personal responsibility for the consequences because they came up with the solution.

A New Way of Listening

To turn listening into a more powerful tool for you, you'll have to stop listening the old way and start listening a new way. A first step in listening a new way is to quiet the thought processes going on in your head. Listen closely to what the other person is saying without trying to determine how to fix his or her problems. Don't think about how you've solved this type of problem before. Don't start silently brainstorming new solutions for the problem; all that is just noise.

New listening means you listen for the nuances of the PBC's meaning and the importance the PBC attaches to what he or she says. Focus on what's being said rather than how you'll respond. Listen with the purpose of gathering information to guide the rest of the coaching conversation. Remember: you're not just listening to be nice. You're not waiting until the PBC finishes speaking so you can jump in with your own ideas. Rather, you are listening for information that might be pertinent to a coaching conversation.

Listen for Unspoken Messages

Pay attention to what's not said. Listen to tone of voice, word choice, importance, motivation, and level of passion. What seemed obvious to you but was not expressed in words? What tone of voice did you hear that wasn't supported by words? What seemed to be the next thing that would be said but was cut short?

For example if a PBC frequently uses "we" or "they" instead of "I" he or she may be less likely to personally take on an action. A rising intonation in the voice may signal uncertainty, even if the sentence is worded as a statement.

Unspoken messages can sometimes have as much meaning as the words that are spoken. But be careful not to assume that you know *what* was not said, just notice that it was not said. You may later have a chance to explore those unspoken messages in the course of the conversation.

Tips & Tools

While you listen, try following along in your head by silently repeating the words the person is saying as they are being said. See if it helps you focus.

You can train yourself to listen for several things at once; literal words the PBC is saying, how you both interpret those words, and how the PBC responds to your questions. Is the PBC responding in a way that says he's interested, engaged in the conversation, and wanting to learn? If not, listen to that, too.

Try this: for one day, listen for at least three minutes without saying a word to everyone you come in contact with. Notice their responses to you. Many people will come up with new ideas just by being listened to—and you haven't even said anything yet! If someone is suspicious of your new behavior, it is an indicator that you were not listening well before. Three minutes isn't really that long.

Ask Powerful Questions

You can do your job better by asking high quality, powerful questions. Powerful questions are the heart of a coaching conversation. A powerful question prompts discovery and generates new knowledge for the PBC, which now belongs to that person. Because the answer originated with the PBC, she will retain the information for much longer than if you simply told her the answer.

Impact of Powerful Questions

For your questions to have the greatest impact, they should meet the following criteria:

◆ Use questions that promote discovery for the PBC.

◆ Use questions that get the PBC to put together new ideas, using past experiences as a "database" from which to draw.

◆ Use questions to get the PBC to look at the situation from a different perspective.

◆ Use questions that are not tainted by your own premonition of an answer.

The more you use a coach approach, the more you'll find that being able to ask powerful questions is critical to unlocking new insights and facilitating *shifts* for the people you coach. It is also one of the hardest things for new coaches to figure out how to do. That's why you'll find many examples of questions throughout this book (and in Appendix C). Here are some common questions (for each phase of the coaching conversation) to get you started.

def•i•ni•tion

Shift is jargon that coaches often use to refer to the change that happens when a PBC has had such a huge new insight that his or her perspective is changed.

Focus Phase. Where are you now and where do you want to be? Where are you stuck? What is the most important thing you need to deal with today? How can you narrow your focus for greatest impact? What topic would give the biggest return for this investment of time?

Discover Phase. What have you tried already? What initial thoughts do you have about this challenge? What is another perspective on your situation? Who can you talk with to get another perspective? What is at the very root of this challenge? What are all the options for dealing with this situation? How will you determine between good and best options?

Act Phase. Of all the actions you have listed, which are the most feasible? What action do you plan to take by when? Who needs to be enlisted to help you? What resources are needed? What can you do to mitigate this risks involved with this action? How committed are you to prioritizing your day/week to take this action?

Evaluate Phase. What would be the consequences, both positive and negative, of taking that action? What would be the consequences of no action? What system do you need to put in place to hold yourself accountable? How will you evaluate the results of this action? What criteria will you use to evaluate your success?

You certainly will not use all these questions in every coaching interaction that you have. As you keep reading this book and actually start to coach, you will begin to get a sense of which questions are most appropriate for any given situation.

> **Coaching Cautions**
>
> Limit the number of questions you ask in a given conversation. If you ask too many questions to satisfy your own need for information, the PBC will feel like he or she is being interrogated rather than coached.

Powerful questions unlock new ideas in the PBC's brain. For any given coachable moment, one powerful question might be all a good coach needs to contribute to the conversation. If your question causes the PBC to think out loud, to begin talking about possibilities, you'll know you've asked a good question.

How to Ask Powerful Questions

Powerful questions should be concise and so clear and relevant that they need no explanation or elaboration.

Powerful questions are often open-ended questions. Questions that can be answered with yes or no do not generate new ideas. Most open-ended questions begin with *how* or *what*. You might think *why* questions would fit this category, but often they lead to defensiveness so *why* questions are best avoided.

Before you ask each question, ask yourself, *Who will benefit most from it?* The questions benefiting the PBC most are ones that spark new thinking and therefore, new actions that can actually move the PBC forward.

Give the PBC time to answer. He or she may need time to think before responding. A great coaching question will get a response like, "I'll have to think about that," or, "Good question. I don't know." Either of these answers is your cue to be quiet and let the PBC think things through.

Coaching Cautions

If you have an answer in mind, don't try to put it in the form of a question. That's a leading question, and it hampers the PBC's thought process. Asking leading questions is more like manipulating than coaching.

Consider these examples of average questions and powerful questions.

Average vs. Powerful Questions

Average	Powerful
What does your to-do list look like today? (no new info for the PBC)	What are the three to-do's on your list that will have the greatest impact when completed?
Can you do that? (closed question)	What will it take to do that?
Why did you do that? (creates defensiveness)	What were your underlying assumptions? Which of those assumptions need challenging?
Have you tried this idea? (your idea, not the PBC's)	What can you try next?
How might changing your mind help you move forward? (leading question, maybe their mind doesn't need to change)	How do you need to think about this to move forward?

Encourage and Challenge

Encouraging others can help you do your job better. To the extent that people lack confidence, they become a drain on the organization. At best, they slow down progress by second-guessing and waffling on decisions. At worst, they are paralyzed and can't take any action.

Encouraging is sometimes referred to as cheerleading, but that's not a word adults respond well to. Instead, think of it as infusing courage.

Consider these tips for encouraging others at work:

◆ Genuinely acknowledge the ability, intelligence, and integrity of the PBC.

◆ Express admiration for the PBC's fortitude to press forward on tough topics.

◆ Offer encouragement about the struggle you've watched in a coachable moment. For example, you might say, "The 'aha' you just had showed incredible insight in a complex situation, and that will serve you well as you take action."

Some of the best encouragement you can give a person is to believe she can succeed before she believes it. A way to communicate that belief is to challenge the PBC to go beyond the status quo in her thinking and actions.

Coaching Cautions

You can negate encouragement with the use of the word "but." If you say, "You did a nice job, but ...," the PBC won't hear anything that precedes the word "but" and will instead focus only on the negative aspect of the statement.

Challenging others in a coaching conversation is tricky because your questions need to stretch beyond what the PBC currently thinks but not so far as to be unrealistic. It really requires using the knowledge you've gained in your connection with the PBC to calibrate how much of a stretch this challenge would be.

If the timing seems to be right for challenging, you might ask:

◆ What would it take to accomplish that in half the time or with half the resources?

- What would you need to do to significantly broaden the impact?

- What would you do if you knew you could not fail?

Know When and How to Give Answers

You can do your job better by drawing out the best in others at work. Sometimes you can trigger others' thoughts by supplying some ideas of your own. When used deliberately and sparingly, giving a PBC answers can actually help him or her move forward without *hijacking* the coaching conversation or turning it into a consulting conversation.

def•i•ni•tion

Hijacking is coaching jargon for turning the focus from the PBC to you. In this case, the hijacking would focus on you as the expert. Once the conversation is hijacked, it is very hard to turn the focus back to the PBC.

When to Give Answers in Coaching

Sometimes you'll need to provide answers in the middle of a coaching conversation. Here are some situations where it might be appropriate to give answers:

- You participate in brainstorming with the PBC.

- You know the PBC knows you have some ideas or opinions on the matter and you want to preserve his or her trust.

- You feel certain that the PBC will give your information the same weight as his or her own ideas and will take action on them with the same enthusiasm.

How to Give Answers in Coaching

Once you decide to give answers, do so sparingly. Offer your ideas with humility, making sure the PBC knows your ideas are just one opinion and not the fail-proof answer.

When you are in a brainstorming conversation with a PBC, make sure that you do not offer the first suggestion. Also make sure that you don't offer most of the ideas. Hold back and let the PBC make the first—and the most—contributions.

Of course, sometimes you have to give answers because of you're role in the company—you may be the boss, for instance. Chapter 5 talks about how to switch between coaching and other roles where giving answers is more appropriate than asking questions.

Call It Like You See It

Just as you will sometimes want to answer questions in a coaching conversation, there are times when you will want to share your observations. Such comments should be like putting up a mirror for the other person to take a look. This helps the PBC see things from a different perspective and find out how he or she is viewed by others. The value of the statements you make are not in the statements themselves but in the person's ability to use the observation to consider adjustments.

This is dangerous territory in a coaching conversation. If you are not careful, your observations can sound judgmental. On the other hand, such reflections can be a great tool for creating new awareness and spurring new action.

Try these tips for effective direct communication:

◆ Share what you see and hear from the PBC, noting any inconsistencies. Leave the conclusions, summary, and/or judgment up to the PBC.

◆ Don't allow the comments of others to color your observations of whether the PBC is being consistent with her own evaluation criteria.

◆ Use direct communication sparingly so that it doesn't seem like an evaluation.

If you make too many observations, the PBC may shut down the discovery part of his or her brain and expect you to analyze the problem and prescribe action. This will undo all the good work you've done to get the PBC to take personal responsibility for his or her actions.

Tips & Tools _____

Lots of feedback can turn coaching into something more like consulting. The best path is self-evaluation. Give feedback sparingly, constructively, and only when the PBC is ready to hear it.

Keep the Conversation Confidential

Don't ever talk to others about the content of coaching conversations without permission from the PBC.

Confidentiality is key to connecting and building the trust needed for the PBC to learn. If you break that confidence and share what happened, you may embarrass the PBC. If that happens, you probably won't get another chance to coach that person or anyone else who knows that you've violated the PBC's trust.

The key to secret keeping has to do with how secure you are with yourself. If you are secure, you are OK with the knowledge that forward action is happening no matter how it came to be. If you are not, you will want to take credit for being the catalyst in the conversation.

You make the choice: keep secrets and keep the action moving forward, or divulge and give up the chance for future coaching.

Try this tip for keeping coaching secrets: think of that "aha" as belonging to the PBC. Because it is her possession, she gets to decide whom to share it with. You can't decide to share it because it doesn't belong to you.

Coaching Cautions _____

Loose lips sink shifts (with apologies to the brilliant people of the Ad Council for altering their World War II slogan).

Focus on Action

You can do your job better if you help others take action. Remember this: if the coaching conversation didn't result in the PBC taking action, it was not an effective conversation.

How do you know that the PBC is really going to do what she said she would? You don't. But how you handle the topic of action in the conversation will help you be more confident that it will happen.

Try these tips to make sure your coaching conversation leads to action:

♦ Let the PBC determine his or her own course of action.

♦ Make sure the action relates to the focus of the conversation. The more relevant the action, the more likely the PBC will follow through.

♦ Make sure that the action identified is action the PBC commits to do, not something the PBC wants someone else to do.

♦ Ask the PBC when the specific action will take place and who needs to help. For complicated actions or a series of actions, ask what the plan is for taking the action and how he will know he is making progress.

The Least You Need to Know

♦ Good coaches listen more than they talk.

♦ The most powerful questions are usually open-ended, and they prompt the PBC to generate new ideas.

♦ Never discuss your coaching conversations with others unless you have the PBC's permission to do so.

♦ Make sure the PBC leaves the coaching conversation ready to take action.

Chapter 5

You Can Be the Coach

In This Chapter

- ◆ Incorporating coaching into various roles
- ◆ Preparing to coach by understanding yourself
- ◆ Reaching a coaching agreement with the PBC (person being coached)
- ◆ Looking for opportunities to coach
- ◆ Knowing what results to expect

Coaching is a brain-altering experience. The new insights you'll help people gain through your coaching create new synapses and neural pathways in their brains. What you might be surprised to learn, however, is that it's a brain-altering experience for you, the coach, as well.

In order to coach others, you'll first have to clarify and adjust your assumptions about people. When you do that, you can interact with them better in a coach approach. That's what this chapter is about.

Adjusting Your Perspective

You'll need to make some adjustments in order to coach well. Consider this simple coaching illustration.

Lydia wasn't getting any work done one day. She was trying to decide whether or not to take vacation in order to chaperone a group of college students from her alma mater on a study trip abroad. One by one she asked her colleagues what they would do.

Her friend Amy loved to give advice and was convinced Lydia should take some much needed time for herself and not devote her vacation to being a chaperone. However, Amy had just read an introductory coaching skills book and decided to ask Lydia some questions rather than share her opinion up front. Over the course of the brief conversation, Amy asked the following questions:

◆ If you did not go on this trip, how would you choose to use your vacation?

◆ How will your relationship change with this group if you go or do not go on this trip?

◆ Because you volunteer with more than one organization, where will you put your emphasis in the coming months? How does that impact your decision?

And in between she sat quietly and listened to Lydia talk out her own answers. She was surprised by the result.

In less that five minutes Lydia said, "I know what I'm going to do! I think the trip with the students will be just the right thing for me this summer." And everyone got back to work.

Some of her other friends had said, "Yes, you should go," and some said "No, you should not go," but neither answer satisfied Lydia until she made a decision herself. She just needed a little help focusing and clarifying her own reasons.

The conversation Lydia had with Amy is a reminder that the PBC often already has the ability to come up with a solution to the problem based on her own ideas and experiences. The coaching conversation helps the PBC put those ideas together in new ways to produce new insights. The conviction in Lydia's statement also showed Amy that she helped Lydia much more by coaching than she would have by providing the advice she originally had in mind. This experience also helped Amy begin to understand that people are more satisfied when they arrive at their own answers.

Ask, Don't Tell

The answer the PBC generates for herself is better than the answer others give her, even if it's the same answer. This is because she now owns the information in the form of new synapses and neural pathways that will more likely prompt her to act than if she had been told an answer. Remembering this will help you coach more effectively when you are tempted to point a PBC toward an answer you have in mind.

Tips & Tools

To understand why coaching is so effective it helps to know a little bit about how the brain works. The brain typically stores new data in short-term memory, unconnected to related data we have already committed to long-term memory. Yet, the better the brain links new data with existing data, the more successful the people are in actually carrying out assignments. So how do you get people to link new data with existing data? By *asking* rather than *telling*.

If you tell an employee to do something, she stores the information in her short-term memory. The information gets stored as a discrete unit without the additional criteria for why it's a good idea or what the benefits are. The person doing the telling can improve the situation by adding all the additional information, but it will take longer to explain and the employee may not be ready to absorb all the details anyway.

Asking an employee a discovery question has a different impact than telling her what actions to take. In attempting to answer a discovery question the employee goes on a database search throughout her brain looking for all the pieces of information needed to formulate an answer. While on that search, she is looking for benefits of the task, what will make a good answer, why she should care, and what she can bring to the task from her past experience. When she arrives at an answer, it gets stored in short-term memory, but it's stored with connections to all the other data in her brain, making it far more meaningful to her. Once she acts on the data, it moves into her long-term memory.

Listen, Don't Talk

Another adjustment is to listen more than talk. This can be a surprisingly difficult shift for some people. Fewer words in coaching questions, encouragement, and direct communication—basically all the coaching skills described in the previous chapter—produce more space for the PBC's brain to fill in the blanks and go to work looking for answers.

Tips & Tools

Get comfortable with silence. Don't try to fill gaps in conversation with additional questions or advice. The only thing the PBC needs when he or she is silent is for you to WAIT: Why, Am, I, Talking?

If you ask a question and the PBC is silent for a moment, don't fill the silence with your own chatter! That silence means his brain is at work trying to connect all the pieces that will make up his answer. Just sit quietly and celebrate the fact that you got him to start thinking about the answer.

Rethink Your Value

Prior to reading this book, you may have felt that the value you bring to the people you interact with at work consists of the information you tell them. Subconsciously, you may be reluctant to coach them instead of simply giving them information because it would diminish your value to others. You need to adjust your thinking to recognize that you are definitely delivering value when you get the PBC to think new thoughts, come up with new solutions, and take new actions. That's more valuable than simply telling; you're increasing the brain power in the office!

By using a coach approach you get the PBC engaged in her own problem solving. She takes action and accepts responsibility for her own actions. While she is off taking those actions you can be making progress in other ways.

Getting to Know Your Coach Self

In coaching, as in all of life, your perspectives, worldview, and cultural underpinnings influence how you operate. It's important to learn how your background influences your coaching style. How can you do this? Think about a conversation you had last week then ask yourself: *How well did I listen? What were my thoughts about what I heard? Did I automatically look for what was wrong with what was said? Why? Did I have a knee-jerk reaction to something?*

Now consider how that conversation may have proceeded differently if you thought less about your reaction and listened with a *nonanxious presence*.

def•i•ni•tion

To have a **nonanxious presence** in coaching means to be focused on what is being said without constantly reacting, evaluating the content, and comparing it to what you would have said.

Your Reactions Reveal Your Worldview

How you react to others and what you'd like to say to them is part of your worldview. You won't always have the same worldview as your PBC, and that's OK. But it is important for you to understand how your worldview affects how you coach.

When you are coaching others, you are in a supportive role; the PBC is the focus of the conversation and sets the agenda. That doesn't mean that you can't skillfully redirect the conversation in order to stay on track, but it does mean you shouldn't automatically express your own views on the topic. You'll find opportunities where it will be OK to briefly share some of your own experiences, but you should do this only to help the PBC move ahead, or to continue to establish trust with the PBC.

Learning to be intentional about your responses to the PBC is part of being a good coach and will help you have the impact you want. You can guard against letting your worldview clutter your coaching by asking really clean, open-ended questions.

Your View of Work

There are many facets that make up your worldview. When it comes to coaching at work, a key component is your attitude toward work. Do you see it as an opportunity to work out your purpose in life? To joyfully celebrate and use the strengths you have? Are you excited about opportunities to accomplish the tasks you've been given to do? Or do you see work only as a means of providing financial resources to do what you really want to do outside of work?

To gain insight about your own view of work you can ask yourself these questions: *What would be the perfect job? What part of my current job is a perfect fit and what part is not? What part of my work is so important I would want to somehow make sure it continued, even if I moved to another job?*

Your answers to these questions should give you a good sense of how you view work. And if you're not careful, your view of work will seep into the coaching conversation in unexpected ways.

Suppose you are coaching a peer who values work far less than you. When the coaching topic turns to a problem at work how will you react? Your first impulse may be to think the PBC wouldn't have this problem in the first place if he or she were willing to work more diligently. Another option is to listen intently, try to understand the PBC's point of view, and guide the conversation toward focus and action.

Consider the results of each stance. One closes off any further connection and shrinks the possible opportunities to coach him or her further—neither party gains from the encounter. If you remain open-minded, however, the resulting action may influence how the PBC views work in the future, earn you further opportunities to coach, and enable you to do your job better because the PBC has made progress. An unexpected and intangible benefit of this path is that your abilities as a coach improve as you develop new ways to connect with people who are unlike you.

Your View of People

What do you think about people—all people? In any area of conceivable difference, what do you really think? The list includes gender, ethnicity, language, nationality, skin color, appearance, job level, and financial status. Do you believe that life is enriched by differences, or do differences make you uncomfortable? Do you tend to label groups of people in prejudged ways, or are you open to working with people who have value systems different from your own—even radically different values that may conflict with your most deeply held beliefs?

Your role as coach is not to share your values with a PBC. You may help someone clarify his value system, particularly when his words and actions seem to be at odds with each other, but your role is not to tell the PBC that his value system is unacceptable. And if you have preconceived and stereotypical ideas about any group of people, that can and will affect the kinds of questions you ask and the responses you anticipate. Then, instead of listening to what is really said, you will be filtering responses through your own set of values.

Tips & Tools

Look for opportunities to coach people who are unlike you. This will help you grow as a coach and avoid the trap of assuming everyone you coach will operate like you.

Getting past the filter of our own worldview to really listen to the PBC is key to learning how to coach in a wide variety of situations.

Your Integrity

As a coach you may have some work to do in aligning what you say you believe with your actions. If there are discrepancies, PBCs will likely know it in a hurry. That hurts the trust relationship and may impede the PBC's progress. Consistency between your lifestyle and your value system makes for more productive coaching. Ask yourself the same questions you might ask a PBC to probe for disconnects between what you say and your actions. If there's a difference between your words and actions, ask yourself Which one needs adjusting? Or, put differently, "What is getting in the way of aligning my words and actions?" And a third approach: "What system can I put in place to notice when my words and actions get out of sync"?

To illustrate these points, consider Bill's story.

Bill was a senior executive who embraced coaching, yet he found little time to coach his employees. He was so busy that he wasn't getting his own work done and wasn't helping those who worked under him to move ahead. And he felt like he wasn't doing all he could to contribute to the company's progress.

Almost every time his employees heard him speak, he talked about the need to be clear and concise, to be focused on protecting their time and schedule to stay on task. Bill had regular coaching sessions with a peer in which he realized that he was not doing what he was asking his employees to do. He had become a slave to a calendar that was out of control. He was spending all of his time in meetings, many that could function just fine without him.

After he discovered the disconnect he began to regain control of his time. He became more focused, more productive, and gained credibility with his employees. He was able to coach others more effectively around this topic. Similarly, your ability to coach others will be impacted unless you address the topics that are impeding your own progress.

Your Mental and Physical Health

Coaching is hard work. Listening takes a lot of effort. And matching coaching skills to the needs of the PBC is demanding. To be your sharpest and to give your best, you need to take care of yourself. Being fully present in the coaching conversation requires your full attention. Lack of sleep or exercise, poor eating habits, or unreasonably long work hours can all impair your ability to coach well.

Don't think of taking care of yourself as being self-serving; instead, think of it as self-preserving. Keeping yourself healthy physically and emotionally is necessary to help others through coaching.

If you don't take care of yourself, you'll pay a toll in your own life and in the lives of those you coach. You will not make progress in your own life, and you won't be giving your best to help others make progress.

Getting Buy-In Makes Coaching Excellent

In order for the coaching process to work, you need the PBC's willing participation. In other words, he or she must agree to being coached. Getting some form of agreement is an important step to getting him or her to do the brainwork necessary to have an "aha" moment. And you must get that agreement even if you use coaching skills in your job without actually calling it coaching.

Think of those people you most often interact with at work who will likely present coachable moments. If you had all the answers for them yesterday but today you have only questions, what do you think their response will be? Probably confusion. Or worse, lack of trust. Yesterday, they could trust you to have answers for them. Today's questions will seem like a test. They will assume your questions are leading to the answer you would have given them, even if you did your best to not ask a leading question. When you make the shift to seize those coachable moments, be sure to gain their agreement to operate in this new way.

Here are tips for how to do that:

You could start the conversation with "I just read this book about coaching, and I think it might be a good way to find the best solution today. It involves me asking you questions to help you formulate new thoughts on this topic so you will know the next steps to take. I believe you might have a better answer on this topic than I do. May if I ask you a few questions to help get at answers you might have?"

Another approach would be to say to the other person, "You are the expert on your job/situation. I have an idea of how we can tap into that expertise and make real progress. Let's work together in this conversation to draw from your expertise and look at this challenge from a different perspective."

Whatever you say to set the stage for this different type of conversation, be genuine and communicate how much you believe in the person's ability to come up with new insights and take new actions.

Coaching Everyone Who Is Coachable

You may be wondering how you can know whether someone is coachable. The following is a simple assessment of how coachable a person will be. Determine how well each of the following statements apply to a person to gauge his or her *coachability:*

def•i•ni•tion

Coachability is a combination of willingness, readiness, and respect for the coaching process. People go in and out of coachability based on their personality and circumstances.

❏ The person has potential but has maxed out on current resources.

❏ The person demonstrates a desire to continue growing in his or her current job and beyond.

❏ The person has goals and is willing to make life changes to meet those goals.

❏ The person is action-oriented and continues to make forward progress.

❏ The person implements change well and is often the first to attempt new processes and learn new skills.

❏ The person learns from others and uses new information to continue to grow.

❏ The person thrives when given new, challenging assignments.

❏ The person has difficulty balancing work and personal/family time.

❏ The person has been doing the same thing the same way for too long and definitely needs a boost to move out of stagnation.

❏ The person has good ideas but has difficulty moving from idea to implementation.

If three or more of these descriptions fit the person you are considering coaching, you can rest assured that coaching can help that person. The more of the statements that describe the person, the greater the need for coaching and the potential benefits. If you can't determine whether the statements do or do not describe the person you're considering coaching, maybe you need to spend a little more time getting to know the person before beginning to coach him or her.

Switching Hats

What if you still need to give the answers sometimes, telling instead of coaching? After all, that may be your job. No problem, you can switch hats. Just be aware that if you constantly go back and forth between providing answers and asking questions, you can create a lot of confusion. Here's a simple solution: just tell the person which hat you have on at the moment and why you've picked that hat.

Here's an example of switching hats in action:

You are a salesperson, and you are meeting with a customer over lunch. Your customer tells you that she has a challenge with her job, and you are pretty certain that one of the products your company offers could solve that problem. You want her to lead her company to buy your product, but you realize her decision will be more powerful if she is convinced that the product is the best by coming up with that insight on her own. You just switched hats to coach.

You start the conversation with a coach approach. To get her to focus, you begin by asking, "What's the most pressing problem we need to deal with today?" When she narrows the topic down, you ask, "What are all the ways you can address that challenge?"

She will list lots of parts to the solution, including your product, company procedures that need to change, and websites to be updated. A variety of tasks and products can contribute to solving the problem. The problem is that she is assuming your product will do some things that it can't. So you ask her if you can break in to this brainstorming phase to offer some information about your product. You just switched hats from coach to sales rep.

The customer now knows more about the product and how it can fit in the whole solution. You want her to take action. You put your coach's hat back on to finish the conversation. You ask what specific actions she will take and when. Hopefully buying your product is in the list.

Switching hats doesn't have to be a big deal. It can appear seamless to the customer.

Evaluating Your First Coaching Conversation

After you've wrapped up your first coaching conversation, it's time to evaluate your role as coach. The following questions will help you think through what went well, what didn't, and what you should do differently the next time.

Questions to Ask Yourself About the Process

Connect: *What evidence shows you made a solid connection with the PBC? How well did the PBC's responses indicate a good connection?*

Focus: *Which of your questions prompted focus? Was a clear focus achieved?*

Discover: *Did the conversation create new insight? Did the PBC report a new "aha"?*

Act: *On a scale of 1 to 10, how committed do you think the PBC is to the action he created? How specific was the action? Did the PBC establish a target date for completing the action? How well did the proposed action align with the focus of the conversation?*

Evaluate: *How well did you set the stage for the PBC to evaluate the results of her actions? What specific questions allowed that to happen?*

Questions to Ask Yourself About Your Coaching Skills

Listening: *How much time did you spend talking compared to the PBC?, How often did you start to formulate another question before the PBC finished answering?, What were the indicators that the PBC felt like you were really listening to him?*

Questioning: *Which of your questions could have been improved? Did you ask any closed-ended questions,* stacked questions, *leading questions, or lengthy questions? Did you rephrase any questions too quickly?*

def•i•ni•tion

Stacked questions are questions that are asked one right after another, before the PBC has a chance to answer the first. Asking stacked questions results in confusion because the PBC won't know which question to answer.

Identifying Keys to Effective Coaching

As you develop as a coach, your coaching techniques will become more nuanced.

Stay in the present by listening carefully to the PBC, observing both what's said and what's not said. Make sure you don't hijack the conversation to take it in a direction not intended by the PBC. It's the PBC's agenda, not yours.

Look for opportunities to be coached yourself. You will become a better coach by being coached by others. You can swap coaching conversations with a peer who is also trying to do her job better by coaching others. Listen to her questions and note how they bring new insights, focus, and turn you toward action. Your own positive experience will have you seeking out coachable moments with others.

Be creative as you look for ways to coach others. It could happen on the fly during coffee breaks, in team meetings, during brainstorming sessions, or even walking with someone from the parking lot into your building.

Progress You Can Expect

You will see forward progress for yourself as you coach others; and the more you coach, the more confident you become. You will develop better relationships as colleagues and customers feel valued during the coaching process. You'll achieve a higher trust level with colleagues and customers because they will begin to understand that you are working on their agenda, not your own. You'll have more repeat customers, more colleagues partnering with you, and more loyal employees because they trust you to have their best interests in mind.

You'll also develop more clarity in your own role in the company. This clarity can increase your productivity as you move toward working in your zone. An overall sense of collaboration will prevail in the team or division because coaching is all about bringing out the best ideas.

The Least You Need to Know

◆ Everyone in business can use coaching skills.

◆ Your worldview influences your coaching.

◆ Taking a coach approach doesn't mean you have to stop answering questions or mentoring. You can switch hats to suit the need.

◆ With your heightened sensitivity to coachable moments, you'll find more ways to help others by using coaching skills.

Chapter 6

Coaching Peers No Matter What Level

In This Chapter

- ◆ Recognizing everyday coaching opportunities
- ◆ Showing peers that coaching works
- ◆ Improving peer communication through coaching
- ◆ Making the coaching relationship clear

If you're like most people, you interact with your peers more than anyone else. This is good news for anyone interested in being a coach, because coaching is a peer-to-peer relationship, which makes it perfect to use with—you guessed it—peers! You might wonder: aren't your peers the ones you compete with for the good assignments, recognition, and promotions? Why then would you focus on helping them succeed?

There really are many benefits for you as you coach your peers, whether they are on the same team or in different parts of your company. The benefits are not always obvious, but they do yield positive return on your investments of time and energy.

Initiating Peer Coaching

Maybe before you invest your time and energy you need a little motivation. Here are some immediate reasons to coach your peers:

◆ Their success translates into your success.

◆ Their wasted time, energy, and incompetence can likewise translate into more work for you.

◆ When peers want to whine you can commiserate or, worse, whine together; but these time-consuming habits don't move anyone forward. You can be more efficient by spending peer time helping them be productive. Listening takes time, but with coaching, even in a brief period of time, you can turn the listening time into productivity.

◆ Developing a coach approach for problem situations will likely also shorten the amount of time spent talking about problems, and increase the amount of time spent making progress and taking action.

◆ Coaching builds trust, which is always a good thing when it comes to working with your peers.

Getting Buy-In from Peers

The goal of peer coaching is to help your peer get focused. But as noted in Chapter 5, that won't happen unless your peer buys into the process.

Tips & Tools

The progress that results from a coaching conversation is the best marketing tool for more coaching. Give "free samples" often to show peers the value.

For peer coaching to work, you must first truly believe that your peers are intelligent and resourceful. Then you must be persistent in helping them acknowledge their intelligence and resourcefulness as you begin to look for coachable moments. When a peer sees that you have his best interests at heart, that you truly want him to succeed, he is more likely to trust you when you see a coachable moment and offer to help.

Defining the Relationship

Often a coaching opportunity comes along with someone you already know fairly well. Notice in the following example how the peer coach asks her friend if she can help by using her coaching skills. Put yourself in Bev's shoes.

Keisha and Bev are peers at work who know each other pretty well. They no longer work in the same department but they enjoy interacting with each other while walking down to the cafeteria to get a cup of coffee in the morning. That stroll takes about 10 minutes each way.

Today, when Bev asked how Keisha was doing, she said: "I'm behind schedule. Yesterday was not very productive, and I'm not looking forward to today because it might be more of the same."

Bev immediately recognized that this might be a coachable moment. She already had a connection with Keisha, so she decided to take the opportunity to ask Keisha's permission to coach her. So Bev said: "You know, I've been practicing coaching skills recently. It sounds like coaching might be helpful in your situation. May I use this tool while we talk to see if it can help you get unstuck?"

Communicating Well

Notice that the peer who did the coaching in this situation responded with concern to her colleague's problem. She listened to the situation, and she offered to help. Because Keisha knew Bev already, trusted her as a friend, and genuinely needed help, she agreed to the offer. By doing so, she also bought in to trying to see her situation from a new perspective and finding new actions that would likely lead to forward progress.

Once a peer agrees to being coached, it's time to ask a powerful question. When a peer seems stuck, here are some possible lead-in questions you can adapt to your situation:

- ◆ Have you tried looking at this problem from a different angle? What different perspectives might you try?

- ◆ What can you do in the first hour today to get the momentum going? Then you can deal with the tougher challenges later. What will you need to do to protect that time?

- ◆ Who can you collaborate with to help you get unstuck?

Use the answers to keep the conversation focused on the PBC and his or her possible forward action. Back to our example, Bev spent the trip to the cafeteria getting Keisha (the PBC) focused and the trip back getting some actions set up. Now that's a productive coffee break!

Managing Progress and Accountability

When managers coach people under their supervision, the employee being coached is likely to follow through on action if only because they are dealing with their boss. But a peer-to-peer conversation won't carry that same weight, so you must end your coaching conversations by making sure that the PBC is truly committed to action.

Here are some questions to ask at the end of your conversation to encourage the PBC to take action:

- How will you know you're making progress?

- What systems do you need to put into place to measure progress?

- How will you know that you've succeeded?

- What will you do when you find yourself going off track?

If you sense that the PBC is just being polite and isn't really planning to do what he or she says, you can ask: "What's the likelihood that you'll actually do this?"

> **Another Perspective**
>
> David Allen's *Getting Things Done* (Penquin Group, [USA] Inc., 2003) is full of suggestions that people can use for managing their own progress and accountability. Check out www.davidco.com for lots of tips.

If your peer has indicated that coming up with new ideas is easy but actually following up is the challenge, you can ask: "What system do you need to put in place to make sure you do it?"

Be sure not to get sucked into being the accountability system for them. That will create a codependent relationship that is counter-productive to coaching conversations.

Refrain from checking up on the people you coach. Things could change drastically between when you talked and now. Those actions identified during the last discussion may have become invalid the very next day by market changes or any number of things.

Assume the PBC is a capable person. He makes judgment calls on a daily basis about what to do or not do, so actions that come from coaching should not be treated any differently. If he wants to update you, let him bring up the topic of his progress.

Team Members Coaching Team Members

You'll find the benefits are multiplied when you coach peers on your own team or work component. Any forward progress the peer makes is forward progress for your team as well. Coaching a team member toward greater productivity means other team members don't have to pick up the slack.

Build Trust

The positive results of ongoing peer coaching can have a snowball effect. Team members who are helped by peers are more likely to reciprocate by coaching or in other ways. They may even give you credit for helping them move forward. Team cohesion and mutual trust can improve. Coaching is a trust-building method in the workplace.

Unfortunately, coaching team peers also carries more risks than coaching people who aren't on the same team. Team members, unlike your coffee buddy, may be less willing to trust you. Your coffee break friend likely sees little risk or threat in talking with you about his or her challenges, but a team member may sense more risk talking to you about problems.

Make sure the PBC understands that your questions are intended to provoke discovery. If your peer trusts you, he is more likely to see that you are both working toward the same goal: team success. What you say should communicate to your peer that you understand that everyone makes mistakes, including you, and that another person, including you, may be stuck next week. That's just how it works on a team.

If you are sincere and your peer sees that, he will see that when you interact with her you have the her best interests at heart, as well as the best interests of the team, of which you are a part. Then the PBC may think, *Well, I haven't looked at the problem from the boss's perspective, or the customer's, or the competitor's views.* He may have an "aha" moment that helps her get unstuck.

You can overcome peers' sense of risk taking by building trust in advance. By affirming their work and consistently seeing the best in your peers rather than judging, you will earn their trust so that you are more likely to get the opportunity to coach in the first place. Keeping all your conversations in confidence, not just coaching conversations, will promote trust when it comes to coaching. Offer to coach before an opportunity for coaching arises: "I'd like to help you by coaching and would like the opportunity to be helped in the same way." Admitting that you also need coaching shows a sense of humility and builds trust.

Be prepared to work harder to make a coaching connection with a team peer. Just because you are on the same team doesn't mean you have an automatic connection. If you see a team peer who could benefit from coaching, begin to work on a trust relationship before asking for the opportunity to coach.

Try Another Point of View

You'll also have to concentrate on your listening skills and ability to focus on the needs and viewpoint of your peer. Because you are already intimately familiar with the team process, hearing a different perspective can be difficult. As a coach, you must put aside what you already know, just for this conversation, to help your peer move forward.

If you fail to see things from your peer's perspective, you may add to the confusion instead of moving the team forward. If the PBC doesn't understand that your questions are intended to bring new insights, she

> **Another Perspective**
>
> In their book *Made to Stick* (Random House, 2007), Chip Heath and Dan Heath refer to the "curse of knowledge": knowing too much about a topic can impede your ability to view it from another's point of view. Peers coaching peers are prone to this.

may think you are blaming or interrogating her. Your entire motive may be misinterpreted.

For example, you might ask your peer, "How can you look at your challenge differently?" If the PBC has a negative, nontrusting mind-set, he may think of you as a competitor. If he does, instead of an honest answer, he may feel that he needs to impress you and the boss that he is better than you. That's not a surprising response from a person who feels insecure about being stuck and wants to keep it secret.

Tips & Tools

Spin don't grind. When you're biking and start up a steep hill, you shift to a lower gear so that you pedal faster with less effort. In a coaching conversation, you may need to "match the terrain" by setting the pace of coaching to allow for new challenges. You may need to back off on the intensity of coaching toward rapid progress when your peer hits a steep hill and coach toward slower but steadier progress.

Managers Coaching Managers

Much of what was said about team member–to–team member coaching in the previous section also applies to manager-to-manager coaching, but some additional factors are at play. When managers are involved, you have leadership and personality responsibilities to deal with on top of the issues already discussed.

The scope of impact is larger. Any small changes a manager makes as a result of coaching may affect more people. A coaching topic discussed between managers may lead to an opportunity for the manager being coached to use similar coaching skills with his subordinates.

Consider this scenario:

At a weekly staff meeting Chad and a peer manager, Bill, began discussing work status. The two of them continued the conversation in the hall. Chad learned that Bill was concerned about how to continue to meet deadlines with two vacant positions. He needed to focus on filling positions at the same time that he continued making progress on projects. The problem was complex.

Recognizing a coachable moment, Chad asked Bill's permission to coach him. When Bill agreed, the following coaching conversation took place:

Chad: What's the biggest challenge for you right now?

Bill: I feel like I'm being stretched in many directions, and employees are not stepping up to the additional challenge.

Chad: Of these two problems—being stretched and getting employees to step up—which do you want to focus on now?

Bill, stating the immediate need as he saw it: Getting help from employees.

Pause. Let's review this conversation in terms of the coaching steps again from Chapter 1: connect, focus, discover, act, and evaluate. What has Chad done in the coaching conversation so far?

Connect. They continued the conversation outside of the meeting and Chad asked permission to try coaching.

Focus. Chad asked a couple of questions to get Bill focused. First was "what's the biggest challenge?" followed by "which do you want to focus on?" Notice that Bill's answers are dictating the flow of the conversation, but Chad has to keep in mind where they are in the conversation path so that they actually get to the action phase. If Chad had asked for more information about Bill being stretched in many directions, it would have taken the conversation in a very different direction.

Discover. Now that Bill has chosen a focus, the next step for Chad will be to ask questions to help Bill discover new insights for dealing with his employees. Unpause.

Chad: What can you do to get your employees to step up?

Bill: If they could just see they have more potential than they think, they can handle more than they are currently handling.

Chad: What can you do about that?

Bill: Hmm … ['aha' happens] … I could coach them.

Pause. This "aha" happened pretty quickly, and often it happens that way, especially if the PBC is very coachable. Sometimes it takes a series of questions for an "aha" to happen in the discover phase of the conversation. It happens pretty frequently that PBCs have multiple new thoughts. In the case with Bill and Chad, Bill might also realize that he could use coaching with his employees to get them involved in finding a solution to the personnel crunch.

If so, Chad could ask, "When might you start that? Who would you work with first?" From this point on, action steps will easily follow.

Tips & Tools

If the questions you are asking don't produce new insights, ask: "What is another angle we can use? This line of questioning is not producing anything." Otherwise, the lack of insight will have the PBC doubting the value of coaching.

Executives Coaching Executives

Coaching between executives builds on the peer coaching of team members and managers, but is once again more complex.

Executives are so busy leading their own organizations that the time they spend with peer executives is infrequent. They have to make each moment count. In addition, executives are competing for limited promotion opportunities. It's harder for them to take time to coach a peer, because they ask themselves, *Whose interest is being served by this?*

When a fellow executive is faced with a challenge, a peer can ignore the need, give advice, or coach. Coaching is the only option that acknowledges that the peer executive is brilliant, honors the executive as the expert, and expects the executive to find a solution because she knows her own organization so well. Therefore, coaching may be the best way to interact with a peer executive. Opportunities may arise more often than you think, and coaching each other may be best way to manage that peer relationship.

Coaching between executives may build trust at a higher level. To make peer coaching between executives work, the connection step has to be solid before you can ask a question to promote discovery. Think in terms of very brief interactions. You may only have time for one powerful question in a coachable moment.

For example, you might ask: "Who are your allies? How can you leverage them in this situation?" Or you can collapse your coaching moment into one powerful question by asking, "How can you leverage your allies?" The faster pace suits executives better. He will think about both of the above questions even if only one is voiced.

Here are some more examples of powerful questions to use with executives:

♦ What resources can be used to overcome these obstacles?

♦ What new strategy would match current market conditions?

♦ How will this decision affect your future standing in the organization?

♦ How does this align with your vision for your organization?

♦ What are the weakest parts of your strategy?

♦ If you stay on your current path, where will that take you?

Cross-Organization, Same-Level Peer Coaching

What's the value of coaching a peer who's not on your team? Coaching a peer from another part of your company gives you practice and builds your confidence for using coaching with people on your team or places where it is more obvious that there would be a benefit.

The dynamics change a little when peers are not in the same department or team but work in same company at the same level. The coffee buddy is one example. Perhaps you have the same job or function but work in different divisions of the company. You interact, but not in same line of command.

For example, you may be accountants in different divisions or regions, or you may both work in different areas of HR. The directors of two labs can coach each other. Or a veterinarian medical lab assistant in an animal hospital may have a friend who is a human diagnostic lab assistant in a hospital.

To develop a coaching relationship with a peer in another area, you'll need to take steps to form a relationship with him or her.

There are benefits to coaching peers with whom you do not interact on a regular basis. But there are also downsides. Because you do the same job, you may assume that you know the answers to his or her challenge. You may be tempted to tell an answer, ask a leading question, or assume a certain path is not right so you don't explore this area.

To combat these temptations, you must adopt a mind-set that you don't know the answer. Strengths and weaknesses for each peer are different, situations are different, and employees and bosses are different. This is an important lesson in humility.

Listening well and coaching someone can set the tone for your own day. You'll find that coaching others helps you see your own job from a different perspective and gives a greater sense of productivity in your own work.

The Least You Need to Know

- ◆ Before you coach anyone, you need agreement from the PBC.

- ◆ Coaching a peer doesn't need to take a lot of time.

- ◆ Coaching a peer always has benefits for the coach, though some situations may offer more benefits than others.

- ◆ Peer coaching becomes more complex as you move up the corporate ladder.

Chapter 7

Coaching People Who Work for You

In This Chapter

- ◆ Knowing when to coach and when to direct
- ◆ Developing coaching as a leadership tool
- ◆ Using coaching to mobilize others
- ◆ Keeping employees focused on forward progress
- ◆ Coaching at various levels of work supervision

What do your employees do when you're not around? Hopefully they are productive and motivated, but are they following the plan you have in mind? How can you keep them focused on the key goals when you're busy elsewhere? Do you always feel the need to be looking over someone's shoulder?

Most bosses have wrestled with these questions to some degree. Your job is to get people in motion. If you feel you always need to be in control you might be like a puppeteer whose marionette stops moving when he or she puts down the strings.

You can do your job better by thinking of your role as helping the people who work for you develop their brains. Coaching is a tool you can use to promote insights in the people who work for you so they continue moving forward when you are not around.

Getting Started

How you present the idea of coaching to your staff can determine the ultimate success of the program. Here's a conversation you might have with your team:

"Thanks for making this meeting a priority. I'd like to discuss an idea I have for making our organization more productive. After learning about coaching I'd really like to use it in our interactions. Instead of me always providing information and solving problems, coaching works by asking questions to tap into the knowledge you already have and drawing ideas and solutions from you. Perhaps the best way to understand it is to see it demonstrated. Is there anyone who has a recent challenge they would feel comfortable talking about in front of the group?"

At this point you explain the ground rules of coaching: listen, don't judge, and maintain absolute confidentiality. When a team member volunteers, they'll likely say they don't know what to talk about. To help find a topic, you ask, "What's an area where there's a gap between where you are and where you want to be?" Then the employee will probably list several topics. You can follow the phases of a coach approach outlined in Chapter 1 to finish the conversation and get the PBC (person being coached) to establish an action.

Next, ask the team "What did you notice about this demonstration?" They will probably mention the fact that there were lots of questions, you didn't provide any answers, and an action was established. Model coaching skills by asking the team what they see as the potential benefit of coaching. You can also explore any downsides employees bring up, but be sure to make clear that coaching is meant to be an empowering process, and its benefits will likely outweigh any downsides.

Finish the meeting by asking how and when you can get started with coaching. You might say, "What do you need to think about in advance to make your first coaching session productive?"

How to Know When to Coach

Coaching is only one tool in your managerial tool kit. And just as you wouldn't use a hammer to saw a log, you don't want to use coaching when a different managerial tool is more appropriate.

So how do you know when to use the coach approach with your employees? In the beginning it helps to keep in mind some characteristics that indicate a person is a good candidate for being coached:

- ◆ The person is resourceful and willing to think in new ways.

- ◆ He or she may be stuck and need help with brainstorming or encouragement.

- ◆ The employee can be trusted to act appropriately and has enough independence to do so.

- ◆ The solution to what the employee is stuck on is within his or her control.

When do you decide to leave the coaching tool in your toolbox and pick a different tool? Do not use coaching when the challenge is beyond the scope of the employee's abilities or the employee has performed so poorly that he or she can't be trusted to take responsible action—this includes employees who are close to being fired. In this case, the employee must be told what to do until he or she reestablishes trust. For more about determining when a person is coachable, see Chapter 5.

Common Coaching Scenarios

Here are some common topics coaches encounter and questions you may find helpful in those situations. Not all questions will apply in every situation, of course, but they can be a springboard for coming up with additional questions.

Assigning a New Project

When you've given an employee a new assignment, take these coaching steps:

◆ Explain the results you want to see in this new assignment.

◆ Ask the employee what ideas she has for getting started.

◆ Ask what new skills or resources she needs in order to do this assignment. How can she get those?

◆ Ask her what obstacles she can anticipate.

◆ Ask her when he can submit a detailed plan to incorporate these ideas and others.

Getting an Employee Back on Schedule

Here are some questions you can use when you are helping an employee who is stuck and/or behind schedule:

◆ What is another perspective you could explore on this topic that you have not yet examined?

◆ Who do you know that has dealt with a similar problem successfully?

◆ What are some ideas you have thought about trying but didn't?

◆ What would you do if you knew you couldn't fail?

◆ Given the resources we have, what can we reallocate to achieve your goal and that of the team?

Coaching Cautions

Don't let your ego take over when an employee responds to a coaching question with, "But your answer would be better than mine because you are the boss." Repeat your question with genuine belief that his or her answer will lead to progress.

Helping Employees Get Along with Each Other

Try these questions when an employee has a challenge with one of his or her co-workers:

◆ What are the benefits of your co-worker's perspective?

◆ What strategy can you use to show your perspective in a better light?

◆ How have you solved this type of problem before?

◆ What would successful resolution look like?

Staying Focused on Progress

People want to focus on moving forward in their work, but sometimes they just don't know how. It's the difference between real progress and effort expended. Effort expended does not always equal real progress. You can ask coaching questions to get at those differences. As progress is made, remember to celebrate even small achievements by asking ...

◆ What intermediate target dates need to be put in place to measure your progress?

◆ How much progress is enough, by when?

◆ How can you make progress with less effort (or expense, or a smaller team)?

◆ How will you know when you have arrived?

◆ What will be the trigger to know you should choose a different strategy?

Choosing Priorities Well

As the manager, you have to determine what will have the maximum impact. Coaching questions can help people sort priorities so they can focus on the return on investment (ROI).

Having clearly set priorities is the key to gaining focus. The priorities of the manager and the employee may not be the same. The following coaching questions can help expose priorities:

◆ How would you recommend the priorities be set for this project?

◆ How will you measure if the effort you are spending is worth it?

◆ What are all the factors that go into the investment?

◆ What are your expectations about the return, financial and intangible?

◆ What is the return you will get for this investment?

◆ How will you reset the priorities if the ROI doesn't happen as anticipated?

Leading vs. Coaching

A traditional view of a strong leader is one who gives direction with great confidence; someone who wins people to his or her point of view and vision. But leading doesn't always have to be strongly directive. Coaching, rather than telling, can be a very effective leadership tool as well; one that will help leaders develop other leaders.

Leadership and coaching have some common objectives:

◆ Getting people to the finish line.

◆ Inspiring people to action.

◆ Holding the vision to get there.

◆ Creating an environment where employees can bring all their strengths to the table.

◆ Advocating differences while creating community.

◆ Staying focused on results rather than effort.

Some of these ideas are inspired by the 5 Best Practices in the "Legacy Leadership" leader development materials produced by CoachWorks International (www.legacyleadership.com).

None of the elements of leadership require telling, but telling is one of most manager's immediate responses in order to accomplish the objectives. You can get to the goal just as successfully by coaching, but you'll need to make some attitude shifts of your own in order to use coaching instead of telling. Consider these attitude adjustments:

Assume your employees have untapped potential and it's your job to draw it out. You can say, "I've seen your work, and I believe you have more abilities than you see in yourself. I want to help those emerge."

Model drawing out the best from your employees and expect them to do the same with others. You can say: "I've noticed that when I listen more than talk and ask questions to help you draw out your best we get great results. I want to keep doing that and encourage you to do that with others."

Prepare yourself for your employees to excel beyond your own abilities and seek ways to make that happen. You can say, "You're going to do greater things than I've done."

You'll be more likely to earn the respect of your employees when you coach them rather than simply tell them because when you coach someone you are saying you believe the employee has good answers for the problems at hand.

Utilizing Coaching as a Leadership Development Tool

In addition to looking for coachable moments, look for these ways to develop leaders:

◆ Give new assignments and then coach around them to bring out untapped potential leadership.

◆ Look for new teams that an employee can coach.

◆ Look for opportunities where employees can get just-in-time learning and coaching for a challenge they are facing.

◆ Coach through situations that will cause them to use a variety of problem-solving skills.

◆ Ask them what coaching questions they can ask of others.

◆ Coach employees when the results are disastrous in order to identify lessons learned and put systems in place to avoid similar results in the future.

Another Perspective

"You will never stub your toe standing still. The faster you go, the more chance there is of stubbing your toe, but the more chance you have of getting somewhere."
—Charles F. Kettering (1876–1958), founder of Dayton Engineering Laboratories

Mobilizing Others

Being an effective leader requires motivating others into action. Building momentum so the people you lead are mobilized is key. Your ability to mobilize them is directly related to how well you get them to plan and set goals. Here are some coaching questions you can use around planning and goal setting:

◆ What steps do you need to take to achieve your goals?

◆ Are your goals SMART (specific, measurable, attainable, realistic, and timely)?

◆ What milestones do you envision along the way?

◆ How will you know when you are successful in reaching your goals?

Try this: pick a project that is beginning soon and use a coach approach as the team is beginning the planning phase. Coach them in the development of their plans and notice the differences, if any, of their behaviors throughout the course of the project.

Keys to Coaching for Managers

When you start looking for opportunities to coach the people who work for you, you will start seeing them everywhere. For each of the keys to a coach approach, here are statements to listen for and questions to ask.

Connect

Determine whether the connection between you and your employees is strong enough for coaching. They need to be able to trust you enough to admit they are stuck or don't have an answer. Notice what your employees are saying when they are fully on board with you so you will hear when they are not and know how to make adjustments.

Ask:

◆ What can we both do to strengthen our connection?

◆ What topics are easier to connect on than others?"

◆ What strategies have you used with other bosses to strengthen your connection?

Focus

Notice who among your team tends to focus naturally and who requires additional assistance. As your employees use strategies for focusing that consistently work, listen for ways that they share that knowledge with their colleagues. Encourage them to develop strategies for focus as a competitive edge for your business.

Ask:

◆ What department functions/processes distract you from focus?

◆ What actions can be taken to eliminate those distractions?

◆ What is your focus for this week?

◆ What system do you need to put in place to stay focused on your annual/quarterly objectives?

Discover

Pay close attention to the cognitive preferences of team members. This will give clues to how they think and behave that will help in developing discovery questions.

Ask:

- ◆ What angles have you not explored yet?

- ◆ Who else can you involve in the solution?

- ◆ What resources may exist but are underutilized?"

Tips & Tools _____

A free self-assessment tool for cognitive preferences is Mindframes, available at www.initforlife.com. Use the tool yourself to learn about cognitive preferences and use what you learn to "speed read" the people who work for you.

Act

Listen for willingness to take action. Pay attention to how much risk the employee is willing to take as compared to the level you prefer your employees to take.

Ask:

- ◆ What new actions have you determined to take, by when?

- ◆ On a scale of 1 to 10, how committed are you to taking this action?

- ◆ What would have to happen to make your commitment level higher?

- ◆ What impact would taking this action have on the rest of the team?

Pay particular attention to whether the actions the employee is deciding upon were generated out of new discoveries or if the employee would have taken the same actions even if they hadn't been coached. If the latter, then you know that coaching isn't bringing about new insights for the employee; he or she is just being cooperative. Once you are aware of this, you can address it and find out what changes need to be made.

Tips & Tools _____

Listen for "weasel words" (maybe, probably, intending to, hope to, will try to, etc) when your employees are identifying the actions they plan to take as a result of coaching. Identify the words and ask: "What would have to change to get you to take these weasel words out of your action plan?"

Evaluate

Listen to see if your employees are taking full responsibility for evaluating their own results or if they are expecting you to do that. It may take some effort on your part let go of the sole responsibility for evaluating results. Your role can shift to the evaluator of the evaluations. Listen for your employees' willingness to look objectively at their own results.

Ask:

◆ How will we as a team know that you have been successful in your actions?

◆ What systems will you put in place to alert the team at the first sign of trouble?

◆ What problem-solving strategies will you use to correct your course midway?

◆ How will you celebrate your success?

Adapting Your Coaching to Different Roles

Not all relationships between employees and people they report to are the same. The dynamics change depending on the role each person plays in the company. For instance, the relationship between a top executive and one of his mid-level managers is different than that between the top executive and one of the corporate board members. Depending on the relationship, you will want to emphasize certain phases of the coach approach more than others. The follow sections offer some guidelines.

Team Leader Coaching Team Member

Generally a team leader has no positional authority, no authority to hire or fire. That lack of hiring and firing authority means that the team leader needs to spend lots of time on the connect phase for coaching to work.

Manager Coaching Direct Report

The emphasis here is on the discovery and action phases. Managers are hired to make sure employees are following through on actions. The traditional way managers deal with employees who report to them is to tell them what to do, but coaching promotes discovery of new untapped potential and ways to use it.

Executive Coaching Manager

The executive should emphasize focus. Executives want everything done yesterday so they send messages that everything is important. When everything is important, nothing takes priority. By emphasizing the focus phase with managers, they can determine what has priority and creates the most forward progress.

Board Member Coaching Executive

The emphasis here is on checking results, the evaluating phase. This is the role of board members. Coach the executive to calibrate next actions for even better results.

The Least You Need to Know

- ◆ Each level of a boss coaching subordinates emphasizes different areas of coaching.
- ◆ All one-on-one coaching relationships are peer-to-peer.
- ◆ All coaching conversations are need-driven and action-oriented.
- ◆ Opportunities to coach the people who work for you are everywhere—all you need to do is seek them out.

Chapter 8

Coaching Work Groups and Teams

In This Chapter

- ◆ Understanding groups and teams
- ◆ Dealing with issues of trust, communication, and accountability
- ◆ Coaching teams to find solutions
- ◆ Recognizing and dealing with team focus challenges
- ◆ Multiplying benefits, actions, and, if you're not careful, dysfunctions

You already know that coaching helps individuals realize their full potential, but what about when you have more than one person involved? Coaching works just as well, if not better, when you coach more than one person at the same time. The skills involved are the same, but dealing with multiple people makes the task more complex.

How to Tell the Difference Between a Group and a Team

You may coach groups or teams. "Group versus team" is a common coaching *distinction*. They're not quite the same. So the first order of business is to determine if the people you plan to coach a group or a team.

def•i•ni•tion

Distinction is coaching jargon for a process of exploring the nuances behind a PBC's (person being coached) choice of words and using the underlying meanings to promote discovery. It goes well beyond just noticing that different words are used. You'll know you're a coach when you start saying, "tell me about the distinction between X and Y".

Because teams and groups have different characteristics, you'll need to be able to distinguish between them in order to adapt your coaching techniques to them. The following table shows some basic distinctions between groups and teams.

Groups vs. Teams

	Group	Team
Purpose	Have an affiliation because of a common job, usually have individual purpose	Have been placed on the team to achieve a goal together
Size	2–100s	Ideal is 6–8
Expected Participation	Members can keep going when someone is absent, not dependent on full attendance in group functions or in coaching; those who are there benefit.	Every member is needed and has a purpose on the team; if even one person is absent from team functions or coaching, something is missing; those who are there feel the absence.

	Group	Team
Expected Outcome in Coaching	Each person receives individual values, identifies individual action items that benefit them individually.	The team receives value, and action plans are created as a team to benefit the team; actions may be divided but are intended to achieve the team goal.

Examples of groups at work include people who ...

◆ Have the same job description (managers, programmers, accountants, secretaries, etc.)

◆ Work in the same division of the company or region of the country/world.

◆ Are interested in doing their job better by coaching others.

Examples of teams at work include:

◆ An account team responsible for a specific set of objectives for the year.

◆ A project team chartered to develop a new product.

◆ A marketing team working toward launching a new brand.

Sometimes determining whether people form a team or a group is difficult. What about the executives for a geographical region of the world? Are they a group or a team? The distinction isn't simply the label *team* or *group*. How the people operate in conjunction with one another is the determining factor.

Sometimes collections of people were put together to function as a team, but they actually function more like groups. That's where the coaching work comes in and can be a real benefit.

Coaching Cautions

You may be tempted to push a group toward becoming a team. A good coach will allow the members to decide this for themselves.

Get the people you are coaching to determine which format—group or team—would serve them best. It's better for them to make this decision on their own and then you can coach them to be great, regardless of the format they choose.

Steps for Coaching a Group

A model for group coaching follows. This is not the only model for group coaching, just an example.

Connect. Take a few minutes to check in with the participants. Ask the group to share their recent successes with each other as a way celebrating. Ask what challenges they are facing individually. Look for themes in their celebrations and challenges.

Focus and Discover. Ask permission to work on a challenge that would be common for most of the participants, either something most of them are currently, or soon will be, facing. In this model you are beginning the focus phase by keying in on a topic that could benefit all participants.

Based on that choice of a broad topic to begin the focus, ask one person to be the main recipient of your coaching questions while everyone else listens. Along with the choice of topic, choose someone who is coachable, the more coachable the better. Proceed to coach the main person through the rest of the focus and discover phases of the conversation.

Ask everyone else to listen closely and answer the same questions for themselves but replace whatever is going on with the main person with their specific topic. Inform the group in advance that everyone will be expected to identify and share an individual action plan with the rest of the group.

Act. Near the end of the session, ask everyone to share one thing he or she discovered and one action he or she will take. Verbalizing these things will reinforce that value was received by all even though only one person was speaking.

Evaluate. End by asking each person to determine how he or she will evaluate the success of his or her projects. You can ask one or two people to give examples of how they will evaluate their actions so that everyone gets the benefit of the ideas that are shared. Often, in subsequent coaching sessions, the celebrations and challenges that participants share come from this phase.

Benefits of Coaching Groups

Coaching groups yields lots of benefits for both individuals and the company. The following sections outline the biggest benefits to the business.

Generating More Solutions Quickly

When you coach a group of people you generate more ideas in a shorter period of time. You can coach a group successfully in an hour, even less if the group is really coachable.

During the discovery phase of a coaching session, you might ask something like, "What are all the options for addressing your challenge?" When you are coaching one person, the response you're likely to get is, "I don't know." In fact, that might be the reason the person is stuck.

During group coaching sessions, when you get to the discovery phase and ask the question, "What are all the options for addressing your challenge?" The person still might say, "I don't know." At that point you could ask everyone else in the group to brainstorm options.

In this way, everyone hears everybody else's suggested solutions for the challenge at hand, but chances are, at least some of the options apply to other challenges as well. That makes a group coaching session a great place for hearing lots of options in one conversation that might apply to multiple challenges, and the ideas were generated in the amount of time that it takes to have a group coaching session, likely only an hour.

One of the reasons people get stuck and stay stuck is they are overly critical of their own ideas. They invent reasons in their heads for why their ideas will not work. Some of that evaluation process is accurate, and sometimes it is not accurate at all. Because everyone in the group is asked to develop his or her own actions while listening to the coaching questions, the number of ideas for action will be at least as numerous as the group. If great solutions are brought up in the action step of a group coaching session, the participants will likely log those ideas and use them as soon as they are applicable.

Some questions you may ask to help team members see how to use the new ideas include: "How can you take this concept and apply it in other ways?" and "What part of this solution works in your own situation?"

A group coaching session is a safe place to voice ideas because no evaluation or judgment comes from the participants. Each person's ideas are valid for his or her own situation. Participants may even hear the ideas they dismissed for themselves last week; but now that they hear their idea voiced by others, they realize that it's not such a bad idea after all. And they might hear a variation on the idea that is the very tweak needed to make the idea work.

Building Productive Momentum

Coaching groups helps you do your job better because each person receives the benefit of connecting with others in the group. Group members get the benefit of a greater volume and higher quality of ideas because of listening to one another in group coaching. The opportunity each person has to focus, discover, and act as a result of the group coaching session helps him or her move more quickly toward solutions.

Fostering an Appreciation for Coaching

The best way for someone to know that coaching is beneficial to the organization is to experience it personally. This process happens more quickly when multiple people are present rather than a one-on-one coaching session. Some skeptics who would never think to participate in an individual coaching session are willing to participate along with others in a group. It's a safe way for individuals to observe what coaching is like without being put on the spot, but they still need to participate in identifying discoveries and actions so they experience the valuable benefits of coaching for themselves.

Participating in a group coaching session can have the impact of transitioning people from coaching skeptics to coaching fans. Following a group experience, individuals might even ask you for individual coaching conversations.

Steps for Coaching a Team

Here's a model for a coaching conversation with a team. Again, it's not the only way to coach a team, but it's a good example.

Connect. The purpose of the connect phase is to maintain a level of openness and trust between you and the team so new insights can be developed in the discover phase and real forward progress will come with actions that are identified.

For a team, this step can be done by a brief check-in before getting down to the business at hand. When a team is newly formed, however, this step may take more time.

A key to connecting with a team is improving the quality of your listening. Be sure to listen to each person individually. Listen to see if they are really a team or if that's just what they call themselves. Pay attention to their tone, attitude, and spirit. Listen to see if they are all speaking the same language—both literally and figuratively.

Encourage the team to draw on the strengths of all the individuals on the team. Also encourage team members to identify and acknowledge the strengths they have as an entity.

Focus. This is probably the hardest phase of a team coaching conversation because you are trying to coach an entity, called a team, but is actually made up of multiple people with multiple perspectives and opinions. Don't be surprised when you ask, "What do you want to focus on today?" if you get as many different answers to that question as there are members of the team.

Tips & Tools

Teams work best when they embracing differences. A metaphor that really promotes discovery for teams is that of the human body, which is made up of many parts that have different functions but which also functions as a whole.

Here are some ideas for getting the team focused on a single topic: have the team prioritize the list in order of greatest benefit to the organization. Ask: "How would our executive leadership prioritize this list?"

Many organizations have a set of three or four key performance indicators they use to assess the health of the business. Ask team members which item on their list will produce results that will most improve their key performance indicators.

If you find this phase taking longer and longer each time you coach this team, ask members to develop criteria for choosing a coaching topic that can be used each time you meet. You can even ask the team to do that work before you begin the coaching session to save more time for the discovery phase.

Discover. The goal of this phase is to get team members to collaborate. You want them to have a collective "aha" that everyone can see is a new insight that will address the team's focus item.

Collaboration differs from cooperation. Cooperation is when a team member decides to defer to another member. A common thought process among teams at work is that successful team participation is a series of giving in to the wishes of others on topics that are not your primary concerns so that they will defer to you when topics arise that matter most to you. Cooperation only produces results as good as the person who suggests the idea.

In collaboration, team members build on one another's ideas, and the resultant discovery is greater than the sum of the parts offered by each individual. When collaboration is at its best, no one is sure how to give credit to individuals because the solution is based on everyone's participation and contribution.

When you're coaching a team, collaboration is the goal. If you don't hear collaboration, you can ask, "What perspective do you need to take as a team to be able to collaborate?" You may need to ask the same question more than once.

Asking powerful questions is more involved when you are coaching a team. You may find that you have to ask the question multiple times to make sure that you elicit the variety of perspectives present in the room. Formulate your questions in a way that is specific to one person but applies to all.

Don't be surprised if the team members start to ask questions of one another. In general, that's good because that's what you want to happen when you are not around. But you'll need to help the team stay focused on the problem at hand.

When one team member has a new insight, ask him or her to share it with the rest of the team. It may be appreciated as a new awareness that will move the whole team forward. In this way the whole team stays together in the discovery phase.

Act. Just as in any other type of coaching, the ultimate goal is action. As a coach, it's your job to make sure everyone has something to do when he or she leaves the meeting.

Action items need to be listed and assigned. Teams have a tendency to assign action items to the manager or team leader. Your role as coach is to spread the responsibilities. If actions logically belong with one person because of his or her job description, ask, "What can others do to support this action?" or, "What else needs to be explored so that everyone on the team participates in the action based on today's discoveries?"

Assign action items to only one person even if it will take the participation from more than one to get the job done. If you put two or more names on an action plan, the likelihood that anyone will complete the task decreases drastically. Here's a way to handle that: have the team identify one person as its leader on an action and others as the supporting cast.

Tips & Tools _____

Formal systems of tracking projects can help a team assign and track action items. The system should be simple and easy to keep current.

Make sure the owner of each action item willingly accepts that ownership and was not forced to take it on. If the action is forced on someone, he or she is less likely to follow through. Also, if it was forced, there are likely obstacles that need to be discussed as part of the coaching conversation.

Evaluate. Make sure the team knows that it needs to evaluate the results of its actions. The team leader or manager can take the lead on this phase.

If the actions identified are just creating more busywork, the coaching conversation has not provided enough value. Coaching is only valuable if it helps the team move forward more effectively and efficiently. Ask the team to develop criteria that can be used to evaluate progress. This can be done after each session.

After one to three months of team coaching, the team can look at where it was before starting to work with a coach and compare that status to where it is now. If the team can't see significant progress, team coaching is not accomplishing what it should.

After the project has been running for the estimated time required for completion a more thorough evaluation can be done to determine if coaching helped the team achieve its goals. The result of coaching should also be compared to results coming from other methods (consulting, status quo team process, etc.) to see if the return was great enough to consider continuing. It does not serve anyone well to assume coaching will be beneficial without actually evaluating the results.

Coaching Team Dysfunctions

Teams often get stuck when they take on large, complex projects. But often the most serious obstacles are not due to the complexities of the projects, but because the teams themselves are dysfunctional.

Tips & Tools

Patrick Lencioni's book *The Five Dysfunctions of a Team* (Jossey-Bass, 2002) provides a great structure for noticing the dysfunctions teams need to address so they can move forward. The Five Dysfunctions of a Team online assessment at www.tablegroup.com/dysfunctions/ assessment is a great tool for helping teams pinpoint where they should start the process of overcoming their dysfunctions. It offers a detailed report of your team's strengths and weaknesses.

Here's one way of dealing with dysfunctions as a coach:

◆ Observe the team and determine the dysfunction that seems to be holding it up the most.

◆ Ask questions in the coaching conversation that will help the members discover their dysfunction and shed light on the actions they need to take to improve their team dynamics.

Focus the team on making progress on healthy team dynamics. Doing so will be just as valuable as progress on its goals, if not more so.

If you see: Lack of trust

Ask: How often do you admit mistakes to each other? What would have to happen for you to feel safe admitting mistakes with your team?

If you see: Fear of conflict

Ask: What are the benefits of conflict? How will you handle disagreements?

If you see: Lack of commitment

Ask: What are the most important goals for your team? What is the process for communicating goals or changing them?

If you see: Avoidance of accountability

Ask: What are the performance standards for your team? How will you communicate to each other when performance standards are not being honored?

If you see: Inattention to results

Ask: What are the current inhibitors to putting the goals of the team above individual goals? How and when will you eliminate those barriers?

Getting Started with Team Coaching

Teams need to have operating guidelines, sometimes called codes of conduct or team behavior contracts. Whatever you call these guidelines, because multiple people are involved, team members need to be on the same page with regard to how they will operate.

If an existing team doesn't already have something like operating guidelines, help members through the process of establishing them.

When coaching teams, point out when team members are not living up to the guidelines they have established for themselves and insist that they keep the guidelines updated so the team remains productive, effective, and efficient.

During your first coaching session with a team, be sure to set the time frame for the coaching interaction and the goals that need to be achieved during that time. Just as with individuals, the goals need to be SMART (specific, measurable, attainable, realistic, and timely).

Also be sure to set the expectation that progress continues on the project between coaching sessions, and that team members will begin to coach themselves between team coaching conversations. When this starts to happen, you will notice that the topics for discussion become more significant and the team handles the easier topics between sessions itself, saving the more complex issues for when it has a coach with them.

Benefits of Coaching Teams

Several benefits of coaching teams have been mentioned throughout this chapter. Here are the main benefits in summary.

Making Significant Progress Together

Significant progress comes from focusing everyone's full potential in the same direction instead of multiple directions. Coaching is a tool that helps teams focus.

Addressing Crippling Issues Immediately

Teams become dysfunctional and are slow to make progress when they don't address the key issues blocking their forward progress. When issues aren't addressed in a timely fashion, they can fester and keep the team from making progress. Coaching is a tool for making sure this doesn't happen.

Creating Results Machines

In a manufacturing process, machines keep the assembly lines going. The benefit of a machine is that it can replicate results. When it comes to the contents of the brains of team members, wouldn't it be great if a machine could keep the assembly line of new ideas running smoothly?

Coaching helps team members lay out a process to predictably produce new ideas to achieve the organization's goals. A team that has been coached on a regular basis starts to do the coaching process for itself in many ways. When that happens, the team becomes a results machine. Team members start to learn what issues tend to trip them up, and know they must address those issues before they block progress.

Coaching will also lead the team to learn to tap into the full potential of each team member and, therefore, have a chance to tap into the full potential of the team.

Tips & Tools _____

When members of teams that have been coached together are assigned to new teams, they want to operate at the same level of peak performance so they take those concepts with them. That's how the impact of coaching is compounded throughout the organization.

The Least You Need to Know

◆ Teams and groups differ in their work relationships and purposes.

◆ Coaching teams and groups multiplies the benefits in less time for the coach and the people being coached.

◆ Coaching teams is like coaching individuals, but is more complex.

◆ Participating in a group coaching session can have the impact of transitioning people from coaching skeptic to coaching fan.

9

Coaching Multicultural Groups and Teams

In This Chapter

- ◆ Working harder and smarter with multicultural teams and groups
- ◆ Making clear that expertise lies within the person being coached (PBC)
- ◆ Handling differences among cultural groups
- ◆ Resolving clashes in timing and communicating

As the world shrinks in perceived distance between global markets and businesses, a commitment to working with people from other cultures becomes essential.

Doing anything with multicultural groups or teams can be a challenge unless the team is committed to understanding one another and making progress together. Coaching is a great tool for working with multicultural teams because it orients around the PBC's agenda. This approach honors the cultural perspective of the PBC. But it also means you will have extra work to do when coaching a group or team representing a variety of cultural perspectives.

Everything in Chapter 3 on creating a coaching culture in an organization and Chapter 8 on coaching teams and groups applies in multicultural situations, but even more focus is needed when people on the team come from different cultures. The good news is that once you master coaching multicultural teams and groups, you can coach any group or team.

Keys to Understanding Cultural Differences on Teams

To coach multicultural teams or groups, focus first on developing skills to coach individuals from one or more cultures different from your own. Even when only two different cultures are involved—yours and the PBC's—you have several new factors to consider in your coaching conversation. And keep in mind that some cultures may take longer to warm up to the topic of coaching itself.

Coaching people from different cultures has some similarities to coaching people with different worldviews from your own. If you pay attention to the assumptions you make, then it doesn't matter whether you're coaching individuals from one or multiple cultures. Let's look at an example of how clashing worldviews can be overcome through skillful coaching.

In Austria, Claire was preparing to meet with a recently formed task force made up of several people who worked for the company. Task force members were from offices across Western Europe. Claire had been placed on the team because of the expertise she brought to the group. As she prepared a presentation for the first meeting of the task force, Claire confessed to Amie, the task force leader, that she was stuck.

Claire: I have a feeling this meeting will not go well.

Amie: What leads you to that conclusion?

Claire: Oh, you know how the Italians are. They don't listen.

Claire was convinced the meeting was in jeopardy because she had decided that all Italians were the same. But she had actually never met any of the Italians on the task force. Instead, she had stereotyped all members from one country.

Another Perspective

In his book *Coaching Across Cultures* (Nicholas Brealey Publishing, 2003), Philippe Rosinski refers to the process of leveraging cultural differences as "mining for the treasures in other cultures." Coaching celebrates the differences of perspective that come from a variety of work and life experiences.

Amie had been using a coach approach with her team, so she asked, "May I coach you to help with your presentation?"

Claire was happy to have the help. Amie asked, "What is the evidence that these particular Italians will not listen?" Claire had none. So Amie asked, "What do you need to learn about these specific people in your meeting?"

Amie saw from the beginning that Claire had some unfounded prejudices she needed to overcome in order to do her work well on the task force. Rather than point that out to Claire, Amie let Claire discover her own prejudices. This shift in Claire's views helped her have more productive interactions with her colleagues from the Italian branch of the company. She also learned that fears of her own inadequacies and fear of failure in this high-level task force were driving her prejudices. Fortunately she had coaching help before the task force began its work.

The conversation between Claire and Amie is an example of coaching one team member. In this case coaching was easy because Claire admitted that she was stuck. She came to realize her lack of progress was caused by her preconceived notions about working with a particular cultural group.

It's important to be aware that team members will be making similar assumptions about their colleagues from other culture, but most team members will never voice those assumptions. Language barriers, time differences, and other cross-cultural differences will be even more difficult to overcome when unspoken generalizations, stereotypes, and assumptions are informing decisions. For example, some cultures value punctuality above all else, and employees might even get fired for tardiness. In other cultures time is approximate and flexible. Relationships or simply enjoying the moment are valued far more than meeting a deadline. When people from two such cultures must work together, clashes are bound to occur. You can help avert some of these problems by bringing differences to light in coaching sessions rather than avoiding them. When differences are acknowledged, most teams work together and find that they actually have a lot in common; they find ways to get the job done—not in spite of differences but by putting their differences to work for the good of the group.

If you are preparing a team to work across cultures you can ask: "What are the most common cultural clashes we're likely to have in this group?" By looking at some of the most common areas of cultural misunderstandings, you can prepare everyone in advance to deal with them.

A basic coaching skill is understanding that the answer, the strength, lies with the individual. A good coaching question for someone who will be working cross-culturally is, "How can your team's diversity of backgrounds be used for the good of your organization?" Coaching a multicultural team to come up with a list of benefits of working together will help them focus on the positive aspects of their diversity.

Coaching Teams: One Culture vs. Multiple Cultures

Let's go through the five phases of a coach approach and identify the differences between coaching a team drawn from a single culture as opposed to coaching a team where members are from multiple cultures. Consider some challenges that might arise.

Connect. You may need to spend more effort and time on connecting when you and the team you are coaching have cultural differences or if there are cultural differences among team members. The purpose of the connection phase is to develop enough trust that the PBC is willing to search his or her brain for new insights. As you model a trusting relationship by demonstrating to team members that you have confidence in them, they will begin to share ideas; as they do, they will get to know one another better.

Spend extra time in coaching individual team members outside of team coaching sessions to get a better idea of what helps each individual move forward. Doing this before team sessions or concurrent with team sessions can increase the team's efficiency because you will be able to ask more pertinent questions of the group as a whole. This process works well for any team, but it is even more beneficial where communication is prone to being derailed by cultural differences.

To help you connect with the team, ask yourself: *What have I learned from coaching individuals from different cultures? What has worked well to establish trust on multicultural teams before? What are the barriers to connecting?*

Focus. Some cultures prioritize differently. The key is to watch for this and not make team members feel that one culture's priorities take precedence over everyone else's. Ask questions specifically to bring out the differences: "Where do they need to focus? and What's are the priorities?" If team members are having trouble agreeing on how to focus, use that as the topic of the first session. Ask:

◆ How will you choose focus topics for coaching?

◆ What process will you use for settling differences of opinion?

◆ What criteria will you use?

Discover. There is greater challenge in helping teams discover new insights when their perspectives are informed by different cultural experiences. The best approach is to ask very "clean" questions. Stick to concise, non-leading, open-ended questions that will unlock new insights. Individuals create new insights based on what they already

Coaching Cautions

Metaphor is a great tool for promoting discovery, but keep in mind that some metaphors don't translate well into other languages. For example: "a perfect storm" may translate into "a beneficial rainstorm" for someone who isn't familiar with the term's accepted meaning in English.

know as well as how that knowledge is sorted and associated for storage in their own brains. This may be different for different cultures. Be ready to adjust your questions to acknowledge potential differences. When one person comes up with a new answer, have that team member explain it to the rest of the team. Ask, How can you convey the new idea in a way that everyone on the team can understand it?

Act. The main outcome of coaching is action; however, the term "action" may have different meanings in different cultures. A big new insight usually means action will follow, but this might not be automatically true in all cultures. Some cultural norms require the employee to check in with his or her boss before taking significant actions. The strongest commitment some team members will be able to make is: "I will check with my boss." In that culture, the person's willingness to check with his or her boss is a commitment to action.

Check for agreement on issues like these: How much action is enough? What qualifies as action—doing something or thinking about it? A lot of these differences can be handled by sticking to the solid coaching technique of asking for specific action, completed by a specific time, by a specific person.

Evaluate. If you ask the team how it will evaluate the results of its actions, you may hear as many different perspectives as there are team members. You may be asked to specify what you mean by *evaluate*. Because evaluation is a regular part of the coaching process and team members are likely to be asked to evaluate on a regular basis, your time is well spent in making sure all team members have a common understanding of what is meant at this stage of the process. This clarification helps the team (as well as individual members), even when you're not involved.

Each team member will need to feel comfortable with the evaluation process. If team members see the evaluation process as being imposed from another cultural perspective, they will feel devalued and have more difficulty translating and implementing the evaluation process on their home turf.

Evaluation is most effective when started early and used as an ongoing process throughout the life of a project. From the very beginning ask how the group will evaluate their progress. Ask:

- ◆ What are the evaluation criteria?

- ◆ Who on the team would be best suited to evaluate?

- ◆ How will results be measured?

- ◆ What will be done if the results don't meet the standard?

- ◆ How will progress be tracked?

Coaching Culture vs. National Culture

Think of coaching a multicultural team as approaching an iceberg. No matter how hard you look, you see only the top 5 to 10 percent of it. No one person can ever really know all the characteristics of all the cultures represented on a multicultural team or group. The leader (or even team members) can try to avoid the worst pitfalls by learning all they can about the cultures represented, but they can't know everything. Coaching is an excellent tool to take that responsibility off the leader. When group members are expected to leverage the strengths of their cultures, all cultures are honored and respected.

How does a coaching culture help deal with cultural differences? Here are some common answers: Coaching doesn't automatically assume a response is right or wrong. Asking questions instead of providing information honors all cultures. Questions promoting focus on issues at hand help defuse conflict by taking attention away from cultural differences.

Another Perspective

The book *Kiss, Bow, or Shake Hands: How to Do Business in Sixty Countries* (Avon, 2006) by Terri Morrison, Wayne A. Conaway and George A. Borden, will help you navigate cross-cultural business relationships.

People usually love to share their culture with others. Asking people questions about their culture not only gives you information, but also helps team members become comfortable with a process that affirms individuals, their strengths, and their potential. When members are comfortable with one another, they can more easily work to a solution when the inevitable disagreements arise because they can think through the problem in a coach-approach culture—a culture they hold in common. As team players think like a coach, they'll welcome input from all members rather than wanting one culture to bend to another.

Keep in mind people are also inconsistent in their cultural behaviors. This, of course, further complicates cross-cultural understanding. Take expatriates, for instance. In Seville a coach worked with a team comprised of Americans, Spaniards, and American ex-pats—people born in the United States who had lived in Spain for many years. The long-time, ex-pat Americans had largely conformed to Spanish customs and culture, but sometimes they reverted to their native customs and culture. Their cultural flip-flopping confused the coach and other team members. Sometimes their responses to questions seemed almost contradictory. They had adopted the Spanish culture but not fully. They were difficult to read because their responses were unpredictable and you never knew whether you would see U.S. culture, Spanish culture, or a mixture of the two.

In such situations the person may not even be aware he or she is shifting between cultures. Your best approach is to clarify that person's responses. No person's answers are completely predictable, but when people send inconsistent cultural messages, they simply add to the confusion.

Language Tips

Although communication is more than words alone, words are the main ingredient in team communication. Here are some ideas for making your words count while using a coach approach.

Use Their Words

It's a good rule of thumb as a coach to use the PBC's words. And it's even more important when coaching multicultural teams. Consider these examples of coaches using the words of a team member:

Example 1:

Team member: Our biggest challenge is with the facilitation process.

Coach: What would it take to make the facilitation process go smoothly?

Example 2:

Team member: We are no longer a successful team.

Coach: How would each of you define success?

Notice that in each example the coach didn't ask a yes/no question about whether they thought they were successful or even working like a team. The coach just used the PBC's words but shifted the conversation just a bit to get everyone involved in a more productive conversation.

Here's another example:

Team member: We would be further along if all team members were contributing as they should.

Coach: How far should you be by now? What is the team process for addressing lack of necessary progress?

Again the coach not only used the PBC's words but redirected the comment to get everyone involved, back on track, and in a direction that could make progress.

Meaning vs. Understanding

It's important to understand the distinction between *meaning*, which is the intent of the speaker, and *understanding*, which is how well the listener grasps that intent. The gap between what the speaker meant and what the listener understood is something coaches have to deal with all the time in coaching teams, whether multicultural or not. However, communication gaps may show up more often and with greater intensity in multicultural teams. Hone your coaching skills when you face this situation and you'll be a better coach with any team.

def•i•ni•tion

In this chapter **meaning** refers to the speaker's intent while **understanding** refers to the listener grasping the intent of the speaker.

Let's look at the situation in which a PBC is not really clear of her intention so it's hard to figure out what she means. The coach can't be sure of what is going on in her brain. You just know what you heard and know it was confusing to the team. In this case the coach can ask:

◆ What are you intending to communicate?

◆ What's the key message you want to convey?

◆ What details would aid understanding?

These questions can help the PBC get clarity and at the same time help the team grasp the PBC's meaning.

In another example the PBC is clear on what he wants to get across but is using words or phrases that lead to misunderstanding. The coach may ask:

◆ Can you say that another way or rephrase it because it seems they're not getting what you're trying to communicate?

◆ Can you give another example?

◆ Could you simplify that?

If the speaker is clear and the team understands him correctly but they don't agree with him, the coach can ask the team: "What do you need to do next in order to move forward?" A team can move forward on a topic even without having complete agreement from *everyone*. The key is to have the team decide how much agreement they need to progress. For the coach this situation is much the same for any team—multicultural or not—facing a disagreement.

Tips & Tools

To get someone to simplify what they are saying, ask: "How would you explain this to someone you are sitting next to on a plane?"

In many cases the PBC knows quite well what needs to be communicated and presents it in a way that would be clearly understood by someone sharing his or her experiences or cultural background. Misunderstanding crops up when team members from different cultures don't quite grasp the intent. The coach can ask the speaker to restate his or her point but say it from another person's perspective: "How do you think your teammate would say this?" You can ask the other members, "What did you hear?" This can give the speaker an opportunity to listen to how his or her words are being interpreted and rephrase them if necessary.

Occasionally a subset of team members may need to use native language to confer in order to reach agreement on a topic. To facilitate this, the coach may ask: "Would it be easier to get your thoughts together in your first language then update us?" Listen for agreement and resonance during the side conference but don't waste time by asking for interpretation of everything that was said. You don't need to know all the details as long as the ideas they present are understood by the team and help the team make progress.

Listen to the team to see if they all agree on the statement of the challenge, the candidates for focus, and the suggested actions.

Get Team Members to "Interpret" for One Another

Avoid the temptation to become the interpreter for the team. When you observe miscommunication, ask team members to help one another understand instead of offering your own interpretation. Having team members interpret keeps everyone engaged rather than allowing members who are less conversant in the base language to drop out. When everyone is involved in ensuring that clear communication is taking place, no one is marginalized; no culture or language is diminished.

Yes May Not Mean Yes

In some countries "yes" may actually have one of several meanings: "Maybe."; "I heard you, but I don't know yet if I agree."; and "Yes, I am willing to share that information with my boss; but, of course, I don't have the authority to agree or disagree." "Yes" may be the only face-saving response in a particular situation. Don't assume you know what "yes" means.

Instead, to make sure you know what the speaker intends when he or she says yes, ask questions about next steps and actions.

"Yes" is just an example of a word that can have multiple meanings, depending on context and culture. Many words have similar nuances. Using a coach approach gives you an advantage because you can use questions, action, and the person's own evaluation process to clarify the nuances in meanings.

Be Concise

The more concisely you phrase your questions and comments the better. An economy of words reduces the opportunities for misunderstanding. Concise questions are also less likely to be leading. And because you probably don't know everything about every culture represented, being concise helps you avoid the risk of being culturally offensive. Team members may answer with their own cultural bias but you want to keep that bias out of your questions as much as possible.

> **Coaching Cautions**
>
> Avoid long-winded questions. Long questions narrow possible responses. Shorter questions allow broader thinking and thus help promote discovery.

Logistics

Just making decisions about the team's schedule can bring to light differing cultural values. What time will you start in the morning? How long will a coaching session last? How late will the team work? How long will they break for lunch and at what time?

While your concern may be limited to the coaching session itself, the team may need coaching to resolve issues regarding time. By now you've probably guessed that the first thing to do is to ask the team about this. As you work with the team to establish relationships, you can address logistical issues as well. Plan to allow enough time early in the process to address such differences. It will save headaches later.

Time and scheduling are not the only logistical issues you'll need to address. Cultural differences can also impact the *pace* of coaching sessions and team meetings.

Some cultures move deliberately and methodically while speed and conciseness are valued most in others. And you'll find other cultures at every point in between. You'll need to establish a pace that doesn't put the rapid pacers to sleep or make the more deliberate group feel frantic.

def•i•ni•tion

Pace in a coaching conversation refers to how much "slow motion" (every thought is voiced) or "fast forwarding" (some thoughts are skipped because they seem obvious) goes on between the coach and PBC(s).

Some cultures still enjoy a siesta, taking the early afternoon off but coming back to work much later into the evening. Some cultures are used to short workdays, and others wouldn't feel that they had done a day's work unless they put in nine or ten hours. People who are used to taking a nap, however willing they are to work through the afternoon, may not be very productive at times when they are normally asleep. Let the group find ways to take advantage of different styles of pacing.

In some countries everyone works through breaks and lunch, but in other cultures just talking about work during a meal is absolutely taboo. If you plan a working lunch, you'll lose respect among those team members. Because one of your goals is to build relationships, you can use mealtimes to help team members get to know one another. That's one example of using differences to meet goals. Team building is also work, but it doesn't have to feel like work.

Cultural differences of time are important. They involve the rhythms of life. Some team members may be dealing with time zone adjustments, eating different food, and speaking in a non-native language. Scheduling and pacing are important issues for the group to resolve. Don't ignore them, set your own schedule, or go with the largest or host group. Get the team involved to find a solution that works for all.

Business Protocol

When you work in your own culture, you often take for granted issues that must be resolved before multicultural teams can be effective. In some cultures the oldest person, the senior man, or the most educated male must speak first. In such a culture, building relationships means finding out who is the oldest and who has the most titles or degrees. In other cultures, asking someone's age is considered rude. In one country men and women are treated as equals while in others men still take priority.

When you ask a question, and some people don't respond, it may be because they are waiting for others to speak as a part of their cultural protocol. These same people may think it rude when young women speak before waiting for all the men to speak first.

Ask:

- Who can lead?
- Who gets to speak?
- How are priorities set?
- What other protocol issues might you expect?

The answers to these questions can help your group resolve differences before they impact productivity. Your initial coaching can focus on bringing these differences to light.

Values

Do you value agreement more than progress? Relationships more than profit margins? Some cultures value connecting with people more than meeting deadlines.

Here is an example of a clash of values: Gabriella is a scientist at a large U.S. biotech research company. She grew up in Brazil and values friendship very highly. She has established several close friendships among the staff and other scientists. If someone stops by her lab she is likely to stop everything she's doing, focus solely on her visitor, and have a pleasant and lively conversation until the visitor takes his or her leave.

Gabriella's approach to work is viewed by some other scientists as unprofessional or too casual in this highly competitive atmosphere. This has led some team members to feel she is not contributing enough. In a meeting on progress benchmarks the leader picks up on an atmosphere of conflict and asks: "What issues are beneath the surface?"; "What are the sources of friction here?"; and "What are the issues with our progress?" He asks one of the team members to explain his point of view objectively, without judging or blaming. Eventually it surfaces that Gabriella routinely works into the evening because of her husband's schedule and has been meeting or exceeding all her benchmarks.

The point is to identify whether there is a real impediment to progress or not. It may be that the conflict arises because the team members are simply taking different approaches. The key is for them to realize that the work is still getting accomplished no matter what the approach. The coach can ask: "How much progress has been made related to plan for where you wanted to be at this point? What next steps need to be taken?" This takes the focus away from how individuals operate and brings it back to productivity.

Challenges of Coaching Multicultural Teams

As you prepare to coach a multicultural team, you need to be prepared for differences. But how well members come together and work together will also depend on other variables, such as how long they've worked together and how integrated they have become. The more spread out members are, the more technology comes into play to make coaching productive.

Consider this example: two teams—one from Korea and one from the United States—were assigned to work on a project for their company. Although most of their work was done through conference calls and e-mail, they came together for one face-to-face meeting.

The team leader wanted to use coaching throughout the meeting. At the beginning of the meeting, he asked for a volunteer to partner with the coach to demonstrate how coaching works. The woman who volunteered to be coached chose to talk about a problem with a co-worker who was unknown to everyone else in the room. During the course of the coaching conversation, a question caused the woman to become very quiet; she was clearly on the verge of tears. The coach realized that expressing emotions publicly could cause her to lose face in her culture.

If you are coaching and bring out something that goes against the PBC's culture, it's not up to you to decide how to move forward in the conversation. If you sense a problem, stop and ask the PBC if he or she wants to continue the conversation. The PBC may or may not want to continue down this path. When the coach offered to stop the demonstration the PBC chose to continue because the insights she gained were so important to her. She later told the coach that the cultural norms that discourage expressing emotion publicly are "part of the old ways of doing things; I want to be part of the new way of doing things."

Here's another example of a culture clash and what a coach can do to help:

A team from a home office in the United States was working with a team from one of the company's manufacturing locations in Mexico. The team from the United States felt superior in every way. They were from the home office, located in a large city, with easy access to everything they needed. Whether team meetings were held in the United States or in Mexico, members from the home office wanted to dominate and control the meetings. Their attitude was get in, deal with any issue quickly, and get out. They ignored many cultural norms of their Mexican co-workers. While they thought they were an elite team of trouble shooters, they looked more like bulls in a china shop to the Mexicans.

The Mexican team members felt devalued and angry. The coach recognized this immediately. The northern partners either didn't see it or didn't care. The coach knew this culture clash needed to be addressed, and each team member needed to respect all other team members before real forward progress could take place.

Even though the coach was from the United States, she remained consistently neutral as she worked with the entire team. She asked powerful discovery questions to try to get past cultural differences so the team could focus on the collaboration and business matter at hand. She listened for lack of trust and avoidance of conflict. And eventually they were able to talk about their cultural differences, to see strengths in one another, and to work together out of a coaching culture of respect.

Business Rewards of Coaching Multicultural Teams

The tendency in businesses is to whittle away all the differences to get down to a common denominator so cross-cultural teams can be productive. In so doing companies may have shed all the best characteristics of the team. Coaching can bring out and celebrate the differences.

For instance, a coach can help a company use cultural differences to address customer patterns and buying behavior. By focusing on untapped potential, a coach can help team members discover and leverage their strengths to benefit the business. And as relationships strengthen among team members from different countries, they will find synergy and generate new ideas as they blend and mix multiple cultures.

The Least You Need to Know

- Teams can be coached to resolve multicultural differences.
- Leverage multicultural perspectives for the good of the organization.
- Coach teams to treat all cultures equally.
- You may need to resolve differences in communications and logistics before teamwork can progress.
- Establish a coaching culture to enable team members to work beyond their national cultures.

Part 3

Coaching in Specific Occupations

After Tony had experienced coaching from others and tried it with his peers, he began to learn how coaching is adaptable to many specific situations and roles. He saw that coaching can be used by people in many types of occupations in various industries. He learned that he could coach people he worked with both inside and outside his own company.

People generally appreciated the personal interest and attention and the way coaching helped them gain new insights and move forward. He saw coaching work with the sales team, the marketing team, with service providers, and support personnel. And in every case he found that the person being coached was capable of so much more potential than he might have originally thought. Coaching seemed to turn on a light inside a person. He found coaching to be as personally rewarding as it was beneficial to those he coached.

Part 3 focuses on how coaching can benefit those in various roles and occupations, sometimes in unexpected ways. Coaching as a marketing tool? Coaching customers? It isn't as far-fetched as it sounds.

Chapter 10

Coaching as a Tool for Sales

In This Chapter

- ◆ Key coaching skills for sales conversations
- ◆ How to adjust your mind-set to the customer's agenda, not yours
- ◆ A coach approach to dealing with objections
- ◆ Coaching for different types of sales scenarios

Coaching is a great way to approach a sales conversation. In fact, a coaching conversation and a sales conversation are very similar. Let's compare.

During a coaching session the coach listens to the PBC (person being coached), focuses the conversation, discusses options for action, and then has the PBC commit to that action. During a sales conversation the sales rep listens to the customer, focuses the conversation on how his or her products and/or services will be of value to the customer, discusses features and options that can be purchased, and then gains the commitment of the customer to take the action to buy the product.

The key difference between the two conversations is how each step of the conversation is actually achieved. As we have seen in earlier chapters, a coaching conversation requires a different mind-set. In the case of sales, you have to shift to thinking of your customer as the expert. Sales customers are the expert in their environment, their budget, their team, and even their problem—that situation that won you the opportunity for a sale in the first place.

With the mind-set that the customer is the expert, you can use the basic coaching skills of listening, asking questions, focusing the conversation, creating new awareness, and gaining commitment for action. The critical path to success in a coach approach to sales is dependent on how well you listen, understand the customer's agenda, and keep the customer focused on his or her goals.

Characteristics of a Sale

To some extent, a sales process is similar no matter what you are selling. Here are some characteristics all sales have in common:

- A customer with a need or a dilemma

- A choice of potential solutions to the dilemma

- A goal to get the customer to choose your product as the solution

- A need to distinguish your product from everyone else's

- A more solid sale if the customer believes your product is the best solution

- An ultimate goal of closing the sale

As you incorporate a coach approach into your sales calls the preceding characteristics are not going to change. While determining how to coach the customer, keep these factors in mind while trying to orient the conversation around the expertise of the customer.

Over the course of this chapter, we'll look at how coaching can enhance the elements common to all types of sales as well as the distinctions that occur in a variety of sales roles.

The Customer's Agenda

OK, you do have an agenda: you want to sell products and you want your customers to be impressed with you, the product, and the company. You want them to be so pleased that they keep coming back for more. However, when making a sale you want to focus on your *customer's* agenda. His agenda consists of his spoken and unspoken goals, his preferred way of solving his problem, and his sense of ownership of his decisions and actions.

Focusing the conversation on your customer's agenda will give her a greater sense that the conversation is all about her and for her benefit. To give you a better sense of this, let's look at what a sales conversation would be like without applying a coach approach and then with the shift to a coaching mind-set.

Without Coaching: You make assumptions that if a customer comes to you he wants your product.

With Coaching: You make no assumptions about a customer's needs until you help her determine where she is and where she wants to be.

Without Coaching: You go into a canned speech about products and options and ask, "Which one do you want?"

With Coaching: You thoroughly explore the client's specific needs before presenting options that meet those needs. Then you turn the conversation back to him for choosing next steps.

Without Coaching: You focus on how quickly you can make the sale.

With Coaching: You focus on the best timing of the sale for the customer's needs and keep a long-term focus on her agenda to get repeat sales.

Without Coaching: You focus on convincing the customer to spend as much as possible, without regard for his current needs or budget.

With Coaching: You focus on coaching the customer to spend the amount she really needs to spend to achieve her goals.

Without Coaching: You narrow the focus of the conversation to only the products you offer.

Coaching Cautions

When you switch to using a coach approach with a longtime customer, be sure to explain that the purpose of your new approach is to help him or her discover the absolute best solution.

With Coaching: You broaden the view to a total solution. This may require the customer to buy parts of the solution from you but other parts from other companies.

Without Coaching: You are satisfied to only talk about your product and make a sale.

With Coaching: You are satisfied only when customer is satisfied and his problem is solved.

Uncovering Your Customer's Agenda

There are several ways you can find out more about your customer's agenda to use during the rest of the sales conversation.

Ask the customer to describe the big picture. Get the customer to talk about the dilemma in terms of how it fits into the larger picture of her operation. Listen for what's most important to her as she describes the situation. Work with the customer to get her to list all the steps needed to achieve her total solution. Seeing the big picture with clarity will help her understand how your product can fit into that picture. A coach approach facilitates her coming to this realization on her own without you telling her.

Ask the customer to describe his ideal solution. As you move into talking about solutions, ask him to describe his ideal solution. It might also be helpful for him to describe good, better, and best solutions. Ask him how he will know when the problem is totally solved. Have the customer list his criteria for choosing a solution. If he doesn't have this list, help him develop it. Ask the customer to prioritize his desired features so he can have a sense of what is most important to him and what is just optional.

Notice how much a coach approach to sales focuses on customers clarifying where they are, where they want to be, and what steps will get them there. As they gain clarity, they'll have a better sense of whether your product is the solution they are looking for. That won't happen magically. There's more. But this level of clarity is a key step in a coach approach to sales.

Selling with a Coach Approach

If you work in traditional sales, you contact client companies on a regular basis to sell them a variety of products. You may contact them in person, via phone, or even e-mail. You may be selling any number of items: clothing, books, foodstuffs, auto parts, and so on. In any case, you are interested in making as many sales calls as possible to meet your sales quota on a regular basis; the greater the volume, the better.

In order to see the impact that a coach approach can have on traditional sales, let's look at an example.

Ted is a sales rep for a large Midwestern wholesale greenhouse firm that wants to sell spring bedding plants to Diane, a regional purchasing agent for a big-box retailer.

In working with people like Diane, Ted typically recommends a standard package of products that he considers a good mix for retailers. His lineup includes multiple varieties of marigolds, petunias, and other plants. He sees his job as convincing Diane that her only decision is to determine how many units are needed to supply her 47 garden centers.

Ted's cookie-cutter sales pitch was pretty direct: Tell me how many stores you have, and I'll tell you how much you need. Ted wasn't in this alone. His marketing department had designed a one-size-fits-all display system he talked up to all his customers. It matched the one-size-fits-all plant mix and delivery methods he tried to sell.

But Ted's cookie-cutter plan, nor that of his company's, hadn't been working as well lately. He decided to shift the conversation to focus more on Diane's agenda. Listen in on this conversation.

Ted begins: Thanks for taking time to meet with me, Diane. I'd like to discuss how our product line worked for you last year and show you our spring lineup. We have some great new geranium varieties I think will be popular this year.

Diane: We had good sales overall, but some plants received mixed results. And we also have some concerns about the delivery system.

Ted knew his plants. But he began to focus the conversation from Diane's perspective and asked which plants had sold best, which yielded the highest margin, and how sales varied in the different stores.

This was taking a little longer than just asking which package she wanted, but Ted was learning more from this short conversation than he'd expected. And, more than that, she seemed really engaged and interested in talking to him. He thought this chat might have potential for more sales so he kept going in this new direction. He asked what she needed in terms of display, delivery mode, and timing. He had in mind his standard plan A or plan B. Diane's response was neither of those: "We would like to have plants delivered every four days this year instead of once a week. I think that would help us keep the plants looking better."

Ted knew he couldn't automatically promise Diane that his company would customize her purchase to the extent she indicated, but he wanted all the input from her before he turned to selling his company on meeting Diane's need. So he said, "We would like to make this work for you if possible. What else do you need to achieve the profit you want from our plants this season?"

Diane was ready with her list and a little surprised to get a chance to share it. *Could Ted do this?* she wondered. *If so, he would get her business every season.* With this new approach, he had his work cut out for him, but the extra revenue would help him convince his team that change was a good thing.

Listening to Customers

You already know that listening is key to any coaching conversation. What do you listen for while coaching in a sales conversation? Here are some key things to listen for and actions you can take when you hear them.

Pay Attention to Full Engagement and Resonance

Listen for full engagement in the conversation rather than politeness. Is the customer saying maybe when she really means no? Test out your observations. Ask what can be done to gain her full engagement in the conversation.

Notice whether the conversation is really resonating with the customer. If so, move to gaining commitment to action more quickly. If not, remind the customer that you want this conversation to really be about her agenda and ask how the conversation could be reoriented.

 Tips & Tools _____

It is not a given that customers will be coachable. Use the criteria in Chapter 5 to check their coachability. If they are not coachable, you can easily shift back to a telling mode.

Mirror the Customer's Language

Pay attention to the words the customer uses to describe his situation and the ideal solution. Use his words as much as possible throughout the conversation to demonstrate that you have really heard him.

Find Out Who Has Authority to Decide

Listen for whether the customer has authority to make the buying decision. If she doesn't have the authority to decide, she will likely be using phrases such as "we will be meeting next week to propose a solution," or "we're gathering data for a presentation." If you hear phrases similar to this, you will know someone else is the real decision maker.

Because you would prefer to be coaching the decision maker, you can ask, "How would the decision maker describe the big picture dilemma? Prioritize elements of the solution?" This will help you have an indirect coaching affect on the decision maker as the insights gained from these questions become a part of the presentation to the decision maker.

If the answers continue to be, "I don't know, I'll ask," suggest that you include the decision maker in the conversation. Who knows, you might get the opportunity to use a coach approach with them as well. It's worth a shot.

Focusing on the customer's agenda and thoroughly listening to him or her will establish a firm foundation for getting closer to the sale.

Get the Customer to Talk Goals

A good way to keep the conversation focused on the customer's agenda is to get him to clearly articulate his goals. Many coaching conversations, whether in a sales conversation or not, address a person's goals and what steps he can take to get there. Because your job is to sell, let's look at how to talk about goals. Eventually, there can be a convergence of your customer's goals and yours.

Tips & Tools

Don't be surprised if the customer cannot state his or her goals immediately. Start with short-term goals and work your way to longer term ones.

There are several ways to facilitate the goal setting part of the sales conversation. The most important thing is to be genuinely interested in your customer's goals. Trying to convince the customer he or she has the wrong goals is not going to be a strong strategy for making the sale or winning loyalty.

Focus the conversation on the customer's goals rather than selling a particular product. In the earlier example, Ted did this by asking Diane what she needed to achieve the profit she wanted. Once your customer states her goals, link the rest of your conversation to them. Ted could have continued with "What mix of plants, delivery system, and timing will help you get there?" Your objective is two-fold: you want the customer to get what she wants and you want her to buy it from you.

Ask the customer how your product would fit with what he already has. This can help him see what additional steps he needs to take to solve the whole problem. The more he sees a total solution, the more he will appreciate working with you.

Sometimes, of course, your customer's goals don't include your product. If you force a product on her and it doesn't meet her goals, you may have created customer service challenges for your company that might ultimately eat up any profit from the sale. A coach approach to sales would involve finishing the conversation with the customer being really clear and committed to her next steps, even if her decisions don't involve your product. This attention to her agenda may buy you another sales opportunity in the future. Ending the conversation abruptly once your product is not in the mix is likely to have the opposite result.

On the upside, you may discover that the product you're hoping to sell may help the customer achieve a goal you never imagined. If so, you'll be able to use this information in future sales conversations with other customers.

Ultimately, you want the customer to perceive that you've helped him move toward his goal and not that you merely sold him something. This will produce greater product satisfaction and contribute to brand loyalty. After he's had a chance to use the product, be sure to ask him how your product has helped him move toward his goals.

Coaching Cautions

Don't correct the customer when he or she extends the application of your product in new ways. This is a great example of new insight that you are trying to bring out.

Dealing with Objections

Dealing with objections may be the part of sales that you dislike the most. It can feel like you are badgering the customer by having a comeback for each objection. But overcoming objections is such a big part of a sales job that some companies require their sales team to go through annual objections training classes. There is a better way.

Orienting around the customer's agenda and using coaching throughout the sales process will likely limit objections in advance. By having a coaching conversation with the customer, you are really addressing the objections all along the way rather than waiting for them to build up. This can have the impact of making the overall tone of the conversation more positive.

The salesperson who has coached the client throughout the entire buying decision will encounter fewer objections because the buyer owns the decision he or she has made. When doubts do arise, you continue listening and asking questions. By this time the customer is looking to you to help find solutions and ways to overcome problems. You won't have to keep selling; you'll be partnering with the buyer in problem solving.

Several years ago, a corporation began the process of creating a coaching culture. During the process, some of the sales executives realized that coaching could be used in sales conversations and decided to train the sales force in basic coaching skills. Team members were not as convinced that coaching would actually work for them when they were dealing with customers. They were accustomed to being the experts. They understood what their product would do, and they saw their job as convincing the customer that what they had to offer would do what the customer needed. How could shifting from telling to asking give them any credibility at all? They were skeptical at best.

One of the sales team members, Joe, began asking the potential buyer about what he wanted to do with the product. After looking at the features offered, it became clear that in one area, the product wouldn't fit well with the customer's needs. The buyer expressed doubts, finally saying that, in fact, the competitor's product would accomplish the need better on this one point.

The sales staff squirmed, but Joe kept asking questions. He asked about other needs and product uses. On all other points the buyer found that the product was a better fit. Joe kept asking questions. "Well, if this product would fit better in all these other areas, what would you do about the characteristic that doesn't meet your needs as well?" The customer began to figure out adjustments that could be made. He decided that this product would be the best overall fit. In fact, he would make the purchase if Joe and others on the sales team would agree to coach other people in the company about using the product.

If a salesperson had convinced rather than coached the client to make the purchase, the result could have been customer disappointment, great expense in customer service, a bad reputation for the seller, and no repeat business. Coaching addressed all the buyer's issues from the very beginning. A coaching approach minimizes further costs and complaints and leaves the buyer believing that he made the right decision with both product and supplier.

Objections don't disappear entirely in a coach approach, but the tone changes when the buyer and seller are seeking solutions together. You may lose the sale when the customer finally gets clarity. But your mindset has to be that if you had actually made the sale it would have been expensive in terms of customer service or other problems. Despite losing one sale, you may lead the buyer to come back for other products and refer you and your company to others because you treat customers with respect.

Closing the Deal

Coaching is about action. Every time you coach you want there to be an action. Every time you make a sales call you want there to be action. In this regard, coaching fits really well with sales. In addition, a coach approach to sales has the customer accepting full responsibility for deciding to buy your product.

Here are coaching questions to use when closing the sale:

◆ What next steps do you need to take to purchase our product?

◆ What approvals do you need to make this sale complete?

◆ What obstacles might prevent you from purchasing our product?

◆ What strategies could you use to overcome those obstacles?

◆ When can you take delivery of the product?

Coaching for Specific Types of Sales

The sales techniques discussed up to this point in the chapter apply to sales of all types. Now let's look at some specific considerations for five of the most common types of sales.

Five Common Sales Roles

So far this chapter has focused on traditional sales, in which a sales rep makes calls on a client company to offer any number of his or her company's products such as manufactured parts, foodstuffs, clothing, electronics, books, etc. In addition to traditional sales, there are four other common sales roles. Identify your type from the following list:

Complex Sales. In this case, there may be months between the first conversation and the actual sale, and many people are probably involved. An example would be the sale of large IT systems.

Retail Sales. On the other end of the spectrum, there is often only one brief conversation between the salesperson and customer to make a retail sale. An example would be selling department store merchandise.

Customized Sales. Somewhere between complex sales and retail sales is a customized sale. In this case, there are lots of options or features for the customer to choose from. Some of those choices may have to be adjusted based on availability. An example of this type would be residential real estate sales.

Customer Service. Even though it happens after the initial sale, customers connect the service they receive with the product they've purchased. Their opinion of that service has so much of an impact on future sales that those interactions are considered the first sales call for the next purchase. An example would be a technology product's help desk.

Complex Sales

A sales team from ABC Company sells wireless networking equipment, servers, software, and installation services. The team had been working with a state university system (15 universities across the state) to set up hotspots on all their campuses. ABC has everything State University is looking for except that State University's legacy equipment doesn't work well with one of the products.

The sales team planned a coach approach to this complex sale. From the first meetings between buyers from the university system and the sales team, the focus has been on the customer and the goals of the university system. Instead of starting the first meetings with "Here's what we can do for you," the sales team started by asking, "What do you want to accomplish with this new setup?"

The team knew how to keep the focus on State U's goals and objectives. Team members asked: "What would the ideal outcome look like? What experience do you want to create for students and faculty?"

The university representatives liked this approach. It helped them focus on the students' needs and consider how the universities could move forward with a new system in place. And because the sales team was so oriented to the universities' needs instead of just pitching its product, team members created a great foundation for the relationship between ABC Company and State University.

The sales team continued to keep its emphasis on the customer's agenda by helping solving the universities' problem in creative ways and coaching the customer's decision makers as a team. In subsequent meetings, the sales team discovered that a couple of the components of State University's legacy system were going to conflict with the new software and hardware that ABC Company proposed. This could have been a deal breaker.

The leader of the sales team decided to coach the university IT staff to look at all the options. She asked, "What are all the ways this conflict in technology might be solved?" Together they listed several options including not using ABC Company's products at all. This was a little unnerving, but she kept going.

During this brainstorming session, one person from the IT staff suggested that they purchase one component from a competitor to ABC Company that would provide the function needed for the total solution; it would work well with the rest of ABC's solution, and the university could implement the whole solution they articulated in the first meeting. For the implementation to succeed completely, someone from ABC might need to coach the implementation team at the university.

So many people were involved in this sale at ABC that they feared they'd drop the ball somewhere and send a mixed message to State U. The team leader of the sales team decided to have regular coaching sessions with the key people—sales reps, account reps, contracts, accounts receivable, installation, and customer service—involved over the months while the sale was being worked out.

The team leader coached them at each meeting on staying focused to deliver the solution that would meet the customer's goals. They often started their meetings by asking these questions:

◆ What's the most important topic we need to handle today?

◆ What is most pressing issue from the customer's perspective?

◆ What is our biggest obstacle to closing this sale?

◆ What are all the ways we could eliminate those obstacles?

◆ What needs to happen to solve this unique challenge that we've never thought of before?

◆ What new actions need to be taken, by when, and who will take the responsibility to make sure it happens?

What can we learn from the sales team at ABC Company? Here are just a few lessons:

Because complex sales require more time, think in terms of a series of coaching conversations. Each conversation should focus on forward movement and conclude with a commitment to action.

Complex sales require coordination of more people. You'll want all the members of the customer team to feel as if they've all been coached. You may also have opportunity to coach members of the customer team jointly. For this, see Chapter 8 on coaching.

Use peer coaching to make sure all members of the sales team are moving forward as one. See the Chapter 6 on coaching peers for guidance on how to do this.

Retail Sales

Retail sales are generally a one-time coaching interaction. If you are a sales clerk behind a counter or you frequent the sales floor, retail sales follows an abbreviated coaching format. The thing to remember is that the customer is the expert and he is looking at your merchandise to see if, in his expert opinion, your products will be the best for what he wants.

The key step is to create awareness. You've had plenty of training on how to connect with customers. If he makes eye contact with you, you might have a chance to use a coach approach. If not, he is not interested in your help.

For the small percentage of those who do make eye contact and want to connect, you can try these questions:

- How can I help you streamline your shopping today?

- What types of products would you like to check out (try on, browse through, etc)?

- What are all the options you are interested in learning about (or seeing) today?.

In retail, the interaction will be brief. Think of your role as aiding an expert to broaden his or her awareness.

Customized Sales

Customized sales are characterized by having lots of options and involve products that you can't just buy off of a shelf. Residential real estate sales is a great example.

To see the role coaching can have in customized sales, let's look at the scenario of a couple who is shopping for a house. The couple probably has some idea of all the features they would like to have in their new home. You as the salesperson will keep the customer needs in the fore-front while looking for listings to show the couple. Their dream house may not currently be for sale in their desired city so there will need to be trade-offs.

Here are some keys to using a coach approach to real estate sales. These concepts also apply to any sale that involves choosing from many options to create a customized solution for the buyer.

> **Another Perspective**
>
> Suzi Pomerantz, MCC, executive coach and author of *Seal the Deal* (HRD Press, Inc., 2007), says, "If you think of sales as the vehicle that propels business, relationships are the engine and you are the driver."

Connect: Spend time getting to know the couple, the family members, and the situation that is prompting the move. When you take time to connect customers feel respected and listened to.

Focus: Ask the couple to prioritize the features they desire in their new home. Use their answers to narrow down the list of houses to visit.

Act: Prepare a package of listings that meet the couple's house selection criteria. Ask the couple to choose the houses to visit before ever getting in the car. In addition to narrowing the focus, this places the responsibility for the home viewings with the customer. That sense of responsibility contributes to the forward momentum needed for action, which in this case is actually choosing a home and buying it.

Customer Service

You may not even think of customer service as sales, but it is an essential part of the sales process. And customers do make buying decisions based on a reputation for customer service. Computer sales increase when customers can call in for free help. A store that has the reputation that no sale is complete until the customer is satisfied has loyal customers.

Here's a simple example to demonstrate what can happen when a customer service rep doesn't use a coach approach. The customer wanted book a suite in a hotel with spa services. So she called the hotel to make the reservation.

Hotel: How can I help you?

Customer: I'd like to book a room …. (interrupted by the next question)

Hotel: What date and how many nights?

Customer: I need to find out first if you have spa services in the hotel.

Hotel: I don't know, I'm at the national reservation office. Would you like to call the property and ask about spa services and call back?

Customer: OK, before I do that let me ask if you have a suite that would sleep three adults in separate beds.

Hotel: Our rooms only have two beds.

Customer: How many beds do your suites have?

Hotel: Some have one and some have two.

Customer: There are no suites with three beds?

Hotel: I don't really have that information, you'll have to call the hotel directly.

The customer service rep in the previous scenario only knew certain questions to ask and stuck to them. In this scenario, the customer would end up leaving the conversation with no room and a lot of frustration with the entire hotel chain, not just that one location. But it doesn't have to work that way. Here's what can happen with the same scenario and a coach approach.

Hotel: How can I help you?

Customer: I'd like to book a room but I have some special considerations that I need to check out with you.

Hotel: Why don't you describe what type of accommodations you would like and I'll try to help.

Customer: I am coming to your city with two other friends to get away for three days. One of the friends just had knee surgery and is still in a big cast. The ideal situation for us would be to have a suite with three separate beds and spa services there in the hotel. Can you help us out?

Hotel: We do have spa services in this hotel. We also have several sizes of suites that have two beds and a roll-away can be added. Would that meet your needs?

Customer: Yes, that sounds nice.

Hotel: OK, let me check the availability of the suites. What date would you arrive and how many nights would you like to stay?

In the first scenario, the customer service person was mainly listening for a pause in the conversation so that they could ask the next question in the script. The customer service rep in the second scenario listened to determine if the hotel had a room that would meet the customer's needs. Notice that he didn't have to listen to the customer's life history, he just had to listen for details that would help him know where to go next in the conversation. The conversation wasn't significantly longer and didn't take a huge amount of additional skill. This is the heart of a coach approach to sales when it comes to customer service.

Train your customer service staff to use the coach approach by asking questions to determine the customer's needs. Think of customer service as an extension to the coaching conversation that started at the time of the sale. Continue to partner with the buyer to meet the customer's needs.

The Least You Need to Know

◆ Applying basic coaching skills enhances your ability to make the sale.

◆ The shift to asking versus telling will engage the customer to own the decision to purchase your product and create brand loyalty.

◆ Objections can be minimized throughout the sales conversation by using a coach approach.

◆ A coach approach can be used with different types of sales conversations from the simplest to most complex.

Chapter 11

Coaching as a Tool for Marketing and Communications

In This Chapter

◆ Using a coach approach with marketing and communication

◆ Coaching people at trade shows

◆ Coaching in focus groups

◆ Developing customer appeal

If you work in marketing or communications, you can do your job better by using a coach approach.

You can use coaching to improve your networking and pipeline development efforts, produce more effective communications, and develop unique professional skills. This chapter shows you how.

Applying a Coach Approach to Marketing and Communications

A coach approach works well with marketing and communications. Here's an overview of how the phases of the coach approach can enhance your marketing and communications efforts.

> **Tips & Tools** _____
>
> Several of the concepts covered in other chapters of this book will help you improve your marketing and communication efforts: coaching your peers (Chapter 6), coaching your team (Chapter 8), and coaching the people you manage (Chapter 7). Some of the ideas from the sales chapter (Chapter 10), such as coaching customers, also apply to people in marketing and communications.

Connect. When marketing products and services are involved, you first want to *connect* with your market—to develop relationships, either in person or through communiqueés that are compelling and create a solid foundation for loyal customers. The connect phase in a coach approach is a perfect fit. It begins with understanding the agenda of the customer or potential customer (the PBC) and then helping them realize ways to make forward progress on those agendas. The key for you as a marketing and communications professional is to find ways to match your products and services with the PBC's agenda.

Focus. In marketing and communications you want prospective customers to *focus* on the challenges they have that your products will address. The focus phase in a coach approach gives you an opportunity to help prospective customers gain clarity on their situation. That clarity will move the customer toward action. Hopefully that action will involve them using your products or services.

Discover. The consensus in marketing and communications is you have to promote your product seven to eleven times before people really start to know about it. Why not use a coach approach in some or all of those promotions to prepare potential customers for action?

You want prospective customers to have new awareness of your products and services and get insights into how they can apply your brand to their needs. If they have never purchased your products before, the "aha" may involve learning of your products for the first time, learning all the ways they are helpful, and what they would have to do to leverage your products to their maximum benefit. That's a lot to learn and retain.

With a coach approach, the *discover* phase is all about promoting learning to a level that is customized to PBCs and prompts them to action. A coach approach acknowledges that insights gained from powerful discovery questions are retained longer because the information originated from the PBC and not an external source. This coaching skill is a perfect fit for the objectives of a marketing and communications professional.

Act. You are setting the stage for *action*, the purchase of products and services. When you are focused on introducing products to people who are unaware of your company and product line, people who have recently tried your products, or people who have been loyal customers for years, you still have one major objective: to get them to buy, buy again, buy more, or buy related products.

Your efforts are successful only if eventual action follows. A coach approach is incomplete without action. All the previous coach approach phases are implemented to prepare the PBC to take action. Coaching in the marketing and communications context involves making sure that all interactions call for the customer to take action and help make those action steps obvious and easy.

Evaluate. Your goal is to attract and retain customers. What if they have problems with the product or it's not working out to be as thorough a solution as they had hoped? You want to know about product shortcomings or lack of customer satisfaction so that you can do something about complaints or problems rather than lose those customers or have sales erode. Customer satisfaction surveys, "contact us" tabs on websites, customer service feedback, and many more vehicles have been developed by marketing and communications professionals to access information about unfulfilled needs and opportunities to remedy the situation.

Another Perspective

In her book *Seal the Deal* (HRD Press, 2007), Suzi Pomerantz defines marketing as the preparation that turns networking (relationships) into sales (implementation). A coach approach fits well with marketing as it prepares people for action.

With a coach approach PBCs are asked in advance to determine how they will *evaluate* the success of their actions. You can use this approach to get the PBC to self-evaluate so you can take corrective action before the customer decides the next buying decision will take a turn away from your company. Setting up in advance the opportunity to take corrective action is a matter of getting the customer on board with the evaluation process and making it easy for him or her to do.

Incorporating Coaching Concepts in Marketing

Now that you know how the coach approach applies to marketing and communications, here are some specific ways to incorporate a coach approach into your marketing and communications efforts.

Trade Shows

Your goals at trade shows generally include getting brand exposure, announcing new products, attracting new customers to your booth, differentiating your products from others, and developing leads.

You can use your listening skills from a coach approach to determine how to respond to those who visit your booth. Are they coachable? If so, use a coach approach; if not, use a different approach.

While at a trade show, listen for ...

◆ Genuine interest.

◆ Responses to discovery questions.

◆ Readiness for actions.

- An indication of whether the person is the decision maker or will have to check in with a decision maker.

- How your products fit with their needs.

- Shifts or perspective or "aha's" if you get a chance to coach the person.

- Genuine commitment to actions: are they ready to buy or trying get you to leave them alone?

If you sense that a visitor to your booth is truly interested you may try a discovery question. A single discovery question may be all one prospective customer can handle. With another person you may be able to have a complete coaching conversation that leads to concrete actions.

Consider these four examples of different kinds of coachable moments at trade shows:

When a truly interested person approaches your booth and is ready to take a next step: spend time connecting and try to discover the customer's goals. If the person expresses genuine interest in your product, shoot for more than just getting his card for your lead database; go for action steps that move him toward purchasing your product or service. Use a coach approach to move him further toward a purchasing decision than he might have expected at this trade show.

When you're talking with a person who can't decided between your product and a competitor's: coach them to develop a strategy for reaching a decision. Start by asking questions to get the PBC to focus on what information she needs to reach a decision. Listen for barriers or obstacles that need to be thought through before making a decision and address them. Use specific questions to help her gain clarity in order to move forward toward a buying decision.

When you encounter someone who likes your product but admits he is having trouble convincing the decision maker that your product is best: help the potential customer consider the choice from the perspective of the decision maker in his company. Questions you might use include:

- What does the decision maker think are the most important criteria for selecting a product?

- What objections has he voiced?

- What information do you need to address these objections?

- How can you convey this information to the decision maker with his perspective in mind?

When someone comes to your booth with objections to your product and they want to argue merits with you: listen carefully until objections are aired and ask questions to flesh them out. This moves the conversation forward, whereas a defensive stance might just escalate the tension. Use questions to determine the real purpose or goals of the person. After you've done this and they are still participating in the conversation, get them to identify a next step. Some people in this situation are coachable; others are not. How can you tell the difference without wasting a lot of time? Try out a couple of discovery questions. If they are willing answer the discovery questions, they are probably coachable. If they keep returning to objections rather than answering questions, they are probably not coachable, and you should switch tactics to telling.

Tips & Tools

People go to a trade show expecting answers rather than questions. Here are some ways to shift their expectations: instill a coach approach in the visuals at the display. For instance, ask a coaching question on your main banner at your booth. An exterminator's banner might read, "What bugs you?" At an electronics convention a banner might ask, "What irritates you most about your personal communication tools?" At a consumer trade show for travel services, a banner might pose the question, "Where in the world can we take you?" Try to communicate to customers that you will work with them to create a customized solution, rather than offer a canned sales pitch.

Focus Groups

Marketing and communications goals in focus groups are generally as follows: to interact with customers you hope are representative of many other customers, to learn reactions to current and/or future products or services, to find out how to do a better job of marketing, to get reactions to marketing strategies or the products themselves, and to discover needs for future products. Focus groups offer an opportunity to talk to customers directly, and that means you have a chance to coach those customers.

In a typical focus group, people come in, you ask them a lot of questions, and they answer the questions. They get free food and, hopefully, walk away with a pleasant experience. You get information. But the customer generally doesn't leave with anything of substantial value (maybe small gifts) regarding the products you are trying to sell. And you don't interact with customers in a way that moves them toward action.

Why not try to turn the experience into one of value for the participant so that you get better quality participation and information? You can do this by using a coach approach with the participants.

A focus group typically yields information about the impact of your marketing strategy. The extra advantage of a coach approach is that you learn more about the PBC's challenges and get a bigger picture of how your product fits into their business or consumer scheme. A noncoach approach to planning for a focus group is to decide on a rigid list of all the questions before anyone arrives and decide never to waver from them. Using a coach approach you would still plan your questions in advance, but you would also allow room for asking additional questions as the session progresses or shifts direction based on early interactions and answers. Allow for a dynamic conversation by being flexible and willing to change direction.

A common frustration among focus group participants is that presenters don't listen to what the participants say. Group leaders do not intend to be rude but often have already decided what they expect to hear. Participants often feel unheard. If initial questions don't make sense or work for participants, the process offers no room for shifting the questions to fit the participants' responses.

Coaching Cautions

Focus groups benefit the marketing team but generally not the customer. Be careful to develop coaching questions that benefit the participants as well.

Here are some questions for focus group attendees:

- What would you like to get out of the time you invest today?
- What new insights did you gain and how can you apply them to your own work?
- What will you do with what you've learned today?
- What actions can you take as a result? How will you know today was worthwhile?

Websites

Keeping a coach approach in mind as you develop web content will help you improve the visitor's experience. Try to incorporate into your website the coaching phases of connect, focus, discover, act, and evaluate.

A website communicates a tone, an attitude. What attitudes come with a coach approach, and how can they be conveyed in a website? Coaching is about orienting around a PBC's needs.

No single design or formula will automatically accomplish all you want to communicate in a good website. But using a coach approach will promote discovery and new insights for the visitor. The PBC not only gets new information but also is asked questions that promote new insights. New insight comes from a combination of what they already know and what they gain from the website. The result of that new insight is something that's customized for them and will help them as they move forward.

One sign of a good, coach-approach website is visitors feel like they are interacting, not just reading or scrolling for information. The website will offer answers to frequently asked questions and a variety of problem-solving solutions for common problems.

Tips & Tools _____

Some companies follow up after a customers makes a purchase on their website by e-mailing the customer a few days later and asking them if they received the service they needed. If not, the e-mail offers a phone number to call for additional help. The follow-up e-mail can also present information on specific resources to meet customer needs and invite them back to the website with a link to several pages. On those pages visitors have the options to move on, ask for more information, look at products, make purchases, send information to someone else, or to talk with a customer service rep.

Incorporating Coaching Concepts in Your Communications

Whether you're a journalist writing news stories, a publicist churning out press releases, a technical writer in charge of a computer manual, or an executive creating a PowerPoint presentation, you can do a better job with a coach approach.

As you prepare to create your document, get clear on what you want to communicate and consider what knowledge your audience brings to the topic. With these two pieces of information in hand, you are ready to create a customized learning experience for your audience.

Tips & Tools _____

Remember to strike a balance between sharing information and facilitating discovery for the reader.

Always invite participation. For example, stop periodically and insert questions about how the information may impact the reader. Or at the end of the article ask discovery questions. Another way to involve the reader is to start an article or presentation with questions the audience may want to consider while they read your piece.

Here are some questions and ideas for focusing on your target market in each phase of the coach approach. Use the model as a checklist for the next communication you design:

Connect. How do you communicate so that each listener/reader feels he or she has a direct relationship with you? You are credible and relevant. What are you doing in your communications to relate to the audience?

Focus. In written communications you cannot answer questions, shift your focus, or respond to the reader. You have to anticipate his or her key areas of interest. You have to choose your focus with the PBC's probable agenda in mind. Ask yourself before you write, *What are the most common needs, wants, desires, and questions of my intended audience?*

Discover. How do you create a customized learning process and generate new insights? Consider using a metaphor, story, or questions to get PBCs to arrive at their own answers. How can you make your communication a unique learning experience for a variety of customers rather than simply sharing information? Examples include sidebars with facts, frequently asked questions, a product tip or how-to, a need that your product or service satisfies, and a prominent box with contacts for more information.

The Least You Need to Know

- Marketing and communication professionals can do their job better with a coach approach.

- Coaching provides multiple strategies for working with trade show attendees.

- Plan your focus group marketing questions in advance but also plan to ask customized questions if the situation warrants it.

- A coach approach can be used in developing brochures and websites to create a more interactive feel and more positive response from customers.

Chapter 12

Coaching as a Tool for Human Resources Professionals

In This Chapter

- ◆ Coaching on two levels
- ◆ Coaching when others are the experts
- ◆ Using coaching for onboarding
- ◆ Training when you are not the trainer
- ◆ Empowering leaders through coaching

Coaching and human resources/talent management are natural partners because coaching is people-oriented, and human resources is all about people. HR professionals can become the experts at coaching by using it in their own work as well as by coaching others to use a coach approach. This chapter explores how coaching can be maximized through your role in HR.

Expanding the Reach of HR

Not only does coaching fit the work of HR specialists, but HR personnel are prime candidates for becoming coaches of coaches. For instance, assume a middle manager comes to you for all her HR needs—from recruiting to terminating and everything in between. This provides ample opportunities to coach her. Let's look at ways you might connect with her at each phase of the coach approach.

Connect. You can have a *Level 1* connection with this middle manager by directly coaching her. By doing this, you are not only connecting with her but are also modeling connecting for her. You want to establish a good relationship with this manager so you have a clear channel of communication for future coaching sessions.

def•i•ni•tion

Level 1 coaching is direct coaching with an employee. Level 2 coaching involves helping others improve their coaching skills.

At the same time you can also have a *Level 2* connection with the same manager, coaching her to coach others. You can encourage her to connect with her staff, her peers, and her counterparts in other divisions. Building relationships with these people allows for coaching in the future.

These two levels of coaching can be incorporated into every phase of the coach approach, as described below.

Focus. At Level 1, each time you get a chance to coach the manager you will help her focus on a specific topic. At Level 2, you can talk to the manager about her strategy for helping those who report to her get focused. In one session, for example, you might discuss barriers her team needs to overcome in order to stay focused.

Discovery. At Level 1, you can ask questions that promote discovery by that manager, creating new awareness for her. You may also be able to offer examples of how other managers have dealt with particular situations. Or you may brainstorm with the manager to help her discover ways to create a customized response to a particular situation.

An example of a Level 2 question is, "How much do you find yourself telling versus asking, and what can you do when you find yourself telling rather than asking?" or "What criteria will you use to determine when to coach and when to tell?"

Act. At Level 1, you would make sure the manager lists specific actions as a result of a coaching conversation. At Level 2, you could help the manager make sure she helps her employees set actions.

A coaching question to ask here is, "What are some possible inhibitors to making sure each conversation ends in action?" The manager might respond that she does not have enough time in a brief coaching conversation with an employee to get to the point of setting a specific, dated action. You might suggest she set a time limit for the conversation up front and reserve the last third of that time to discuss actions.

A typical problem is the manager has not spent time at the outset agreeing that she and the employee will work together to determine an action. A coaching conversation might begin, "We have 15 minutes. What can we do in this time frame?" And later, "We now have four minutes left, and we haven't yet talked about actions. What actions can you take?"

Managers, especially new managers, have a tendency to take on all of the department's problems as their responsibility. Sometimes they don't hold the person being coached (PBC) to action because they may say, "That reminds me that I still need to do X before you can do Y." As an HR professional working with managers to help them coach, you can say, "It's OK to recognize that you still need to take some actions, but don't omit the PBC's responsibility to take action."

Another Level 2 approach is to ask, "What is your main contribution to this organization?" Your goal is to get the manager to realize her main goal should be getting her people in action. Additional questions for this stage are in Appendix C.

Evaluate. At Level 1 you ask the manager, "What criteria will you use to know that your coaching is successful?" At Level 2 you ask, "What will you do to ensure that your staff members are evaluating their own actions to make sure they are successful?"

One benefit of coaching is to get employees to hold themselves accountable for their actions. This can result in employees holding themselves to a higher standard than if they were evaluated only by someone else.

When the coach is a manager, encouraging self-evaluation in PBCs sets up a potential conflict with the manager's usual role of being the one to evaluate the results produced by her employees. Keep in mind, however, that self-evaluation can be an ongoing process and take place in parallel to the manager's evaluation.

The manager might say: "How can I let my people self-evaluate? That's my job." To which you reply: "Both roles have value. You can get benefits from an employee's doing self-evaluation, and you will still have opportunities to do an evaluation." You can use this coaching question: "What will you need to do differently to create an environment where both types of evaluation work together?"

Tips & Tools

Spreading coaching around doesn't diminish your role as an HR professional in coaching. In your role you are always listening on two levels—to find coachable moments with leaders but also to discover coachable moments leaders might use and coaching them on how to coach.

Training and Development

Coaching is an ideal tool for employee training and development issues such as onboarding and leadership development.

Onboarding

Onboarding is a great opportunity to apply a coach approach. You can help develop people who are new to the company or beginning a new position. Your help acknowledges they are in a transition position (new to the job), they earned their placement in the position, but that they don't yet know the job. Transitions such as these offer a lot of potential for coaching conversations.

def•i•ni•tion

Onboarding is the process of assisting new, newly-promoted, or redeployed employees settle into their new positions.

People are more coachable when they are in new positions because they want to start out on the right foot and they are aware they have a lot to learn. Because coaching is a learning experience, they'll be ready to tap into a method that gives them new insights. Conversely, people who have been in the job a long time and think they already know the answers will be less coachable.

Coaching can build new employees' self-confidence quickly because it enables them to use their own expertise as a basis for action. The process can help ease self-doubts that lead to inaction.

Make it standard practice in your organization to coach new people twice a week for the first six months they are on the job. This could take the form of group coaching or a couple of one-on-one sessions with HR personnel followed by peer-to-peer coaching. Encourage new hires to serve as peer coaches when they feel they're ready.

Leadership Coaching

HR has traditionally helped business leaders by telling, yet they don't always have credibility with executives because they don't know the executive's job. Using a coach approach, you don't have to know how to do a person's job in order to help them do it better. A coach approach can help by putting the emphasis on getting the other person's brain engaged. HR's coaching contribution is to bring out the best ideas from the person who has the expertise. Consider this illustration.

Joe is a software development manager who has personnel challenges. In the past when he has approached HR with similar challenges, he hasn't gotten much value from the interaction. Joe's view is this:

> The problem is that HR doesn't really know what we do; and when they suggest potential solutions, they really miss the mark. They don't understand how programmers operate and they give solutions that just don't work in a programming environment. I'm having problems with my programming team staying focused. They have such crazy hours that it's hard to know what progress they're making. The last time I went to HR, they suggested that I have a status meeting every morning at 8 A.M. Half my programmers aren't even awake at 8 A.M. because they've worked until midnight. I don't see how HR can help if they make suggestions that just don't fit our work environment.

When Joe heard that HR was using coaching, he decided to give HR another try with his problem. Here's how the dialogue went:

HR: How can I help you today?

Joe: I'm having problems with team focus and knowing where they are on the project.

HR: What would be the most helpful outcome for you from this conversation?

Joe: I'm not sure I know what you mean by that.

HR: What do you want to walk away with?

Joe: I want some new ideas about how to interact with my team so that I'll know where they are and what progress they're making toward our goals. I'm coming to you because you are people experts.

HR: So where do we start?

Joe: I'd like to start by finding out where we are today, but I'd really like to have an ongoing process so that I always know where we are.

HR: How can you find out where you are today?

Joe: That's the problem. Getting that information is difficult.

HR: What's the key information you need to know?

Joe: I'd really like to know if we're going to make deadline, but my employees mostly tell me how hard they've been working. I don't know exactly how far along we are, how much work has been done, and how much work remains to be done.

HR: What questions could you ask your team in order to get the information you want?

Joe: I just realized that I've been asking what they've done this week when what I really need to ask is, What work remains to be done?

HR: Is it that simple? Do you just need to ask a different question, or are other changes needed to get to your goal?

Joe: I could actually ask them to suggest the best way to get that information to me.

HR: When can you use these ideas?

Joe: I can do that at a team meeting tomorrow.

HR: How will you know if this new plan is working?

Joe: I'll have to think about that, but it's a good question.

HR: What key insights and value did you get from this conversation today?

Joe: I couldn't see that I had been getting exactly the information I requested, but what I really needed to do was to change the question.

As a human resources professional, you become more credible if you ask rather than tell because you're acknowledging that the manager is the expert and you're using his expertise in helping develop a solution.

Developing Next Generation Leaders

Young people entering the work force today differ in significant ways from previous generations, and some of those differences make coaching an especially good fit. Generally speaking, they don't like to be told; they want to discover new information for themselves. They're skeptical; having grown up with multiple ways to take in information, they've learned that sources don't agree and they have to decide themselves which ones are credible and what they believe. They rarely believe in overarching truth but find truth in their own realities. They like processes more than single tasks. They analyze as they participate. They like to experience things for themselves rather than being told how to do things.

Coaching Cautions

Don't assume a certain age or experience level is needed to coach others. Some believe you have to have a certain volume of years and wisdom to coach. Sometimes, lack of experience in a particular area makes the coach more objective. Focus on asking great questions and inspiring actions that produce better business results.

These young workers will be tomorrow's managers. Here are some ways you can use a coach approach as you work toward developing new leaders:

◆ Use coaching to help current managers identify and develop future leaders.

◆ Encourage current managers to use coaching with chosen successors to help them think through how they will approach current challenges. Help them find ways to participate now.

◆ Coach outgoing leaders through their next steps, the incoming leader through the transition of becoming the next leader, and the team to adapt to new leadership styles. HR becomes the stabilizing factor in the process.

Dealing With Difficult Personnel Issues

HR personnel must be prepared to deal with issues such as sexual harassment, employee performance problems, and layoffs. The following sections provide guidance for using a coach approach with managers who are facing these difficult issues.

Employee Performance

Managers frequently turn to HR to help address the daunting issue of poor employee performance. In your role of coaching managers, you can help a manager find insight on how to motivate an employee. You might ask: "What are some possible reasons for the employee's poor performance? What other information do you need to know about this situation?"

Or you may be able to help the manager coach the employee. For example, you might ask a manager, "What do you think the employee needs to understand about this situation? What questions can you ask to help the employee see her performance problems?"

You might also coach the manager about how the nonperforming employee is impacting the entire team and how the remaining team members will get the component's work done when they are short one employee.

Layoffs

Representing HR, you may find yourself coaching managers and/or the laid-off employees. Where is discovery needed with either group? Employees may need help comprehending the impact and the options open to him. Some of this will involve telling, but asking a question like "What resources outside of the company do you have to help deal with this situation?" may spur thinking beyond the immediate. Managers may be most concerned with the dynamics of the layoffs so you might ask: "What do you already know about this process? What are your biggest concerns?".

Tips & Tools

If your company uses outplacement services, before contracting with them find out if they use a coach approach by asking prospective agencies the following questions: "What is your approach to working with employees facing layoffs?"; "What can employees expect to gain?"; "What strategies do you use to foster self-discovery?"; and "How would coaching fit with the process you use?".

Appeals

Both managers and employees often turn to HR when an employee appeals a management decision. For instance, if an employee is passed over for a promotion she believes she deserved, the employee might turn to HR for guidance on how to appeal the decision, and the manager might seek assistance in answering the appeal. Whatever your company's policies about handling these situations, you can use a coach approach to help both parties find resolution and move on.

You can ask the employee:

◆ What leads you to conclude the decision is wrong?

◆ How can you communicate with management about this?

◆ What options do you have?

Questions for managers might include:

- How do you think the employee views this decision?
- What is the best outcome from the appeals process?
- What actions will best prepare you for the process?
- What plans should be in place if the employee's appeal is successful?

Career Discussions

Many companies have a pretty traditional way of plotting career paths for their employees. An employee takes assessments and, based on the results of those tests, an HR person suggests that an employee is suited to a particular career area. The company suggests specific steps for the employee to take in order to move up that career ladder. Such processes are usually canned, one-size-fits-all approaches rather than customized to specific individuals. This is the way IBM once directed employees.

Recently, however, career centers at IBM and other companies have started using a coach approach to career development. Employees may or may not take all the assessments. The goal is to help each employee get a good grasp of his or her strengths, understand how to set long-term goals, and determine what next-step actions should be. The career-path process is no longer a prepackaged approach because everyone's needs are different.

HR professional face some career topics fairly routinely. Here are some coaching questions you may want to use in those situations.

Promotion Wannabe

An employee is up for promotion and is trying to decide if moving into management is the right choice for both short-term and long-term goals. Questions you might ask include:

- What are your goals?
- What can you do in your current job to make progress toward those goals?

- How can you tweak what you're currently doing to help with career goals?

- What do you know about being a manager that would indicate management is a good fit for you?

- Who knows you well that you could ask whether you would be satisfied in management?

To Leave or Not to Leave

An employee has been offered a job with another company. The money's good, but he's not sure he will enjoy working with the people there. You can ask:

- What elements have to be present in a job for you to perform at your peak?

- How many of those elements are present in the new job?

- What are some other things you need to consider in addition to the pay and the work environment and culture?

Coaching can help him clarify his decision; and if he decides to stay, he will be more satisfied that the decision was his and will likely be more productive than if he was "convinced" to stay.

Career Makeover

A manager has been at her job for more than 20 years and is contemplating a career change. She is fairly sure of what she wants to do but needs help planning a graceful exit. Consider these questions:

- What plans need to be in place to make a smooth transition?

- How will peers react, and how can you gain their support?

- What are some obstacles?

- Whom do you need to be developing to make a smooth transition?

Coaching can help smooth the way with succession planning.

Experts on All People Processes

In Chapter 3 you learned that it's important to have people processes that use a coach approach. You design people processes and change or enhance them over time so they integrate a coach approach.

Applying a coach approach to the people processes of recruiting and retention may very well attract potential recruits, especially young adults. Coaching both the hiring manager and the candidate can result in better decisions on both sides. Both get clearer on what they're looking for in a job. In addition, a coaching culture may help retain employees if they see value in being managed with a coach approach, especially if it is not used in other organizations they may be considering for employment.

> **Another Perspective**
>
> "I start with the premise that the function of leadership is to produce more leaders, not more followers."
>
> —Ralph Nader (1934–   ), attorney, author, and political activist

Coaching can also make it easier to deal with routine people-process tasks such as benefits administration, U.S. employment law compliance, vacation, payroll, and retirement planning. Consider this illustration.

Deepika is helping Tim think about early retirement from a construction firm where he's been a manager for more than 20 years. Tim asked specific questions:

- How does sick leave count toward retirement?

- How does vacation count?

- What percentage of full retirement will I get?

- What happens if I die before my wife?

- What dollar amount can I draw now?

- What is the projected amount if work for five more years?

Deepika could have simply answered Tim's questions or referred him to the FAQs and calculation tool on the company website. Instead she got

Tim to think more about the broader scope of what early retirement involved by asking open-ended questions:

◆ What's your situation?

◆ What do you want to accomplish by taking early retirement?

◆ What level of income would your wife need should you die first?

After Tim had answered those questions, Deepika offered to give him a more comprehensive answer that covered the range options he was interested in. She ran his numbers to give him specific information rather than allow him to leave with only partial information or an educated estimate from HR. After this conversation Deepika referred Tim to web pages that offered more detailed information related to his goals. In this customized approach Deepika was able to help him understand the big picture, his range of options, and answer his original questions.

When helping people through the company's people processes, encourage them to discover new insights about the bigger picture related to the topic. And keep the decision-making in their court to the extent that's possible—this will help the person own the decision and be more likely to follow through with action.

Coaching doesn't replace giving employees information they need, but you can look for coachable moments where there's an opportunity for someone to gain new insights and take actions. Help employees think one step beyond where they are currently looking. You might ask, "Once you take this action how will you deal with the next phase of this problem?"

Contributing to Business Success

As you establish HR as the place where people can get coaching and learn how to use a coach approach, HR can become a resource for excellence in coaching throughout the organization.

To spread the impact of coaching you can adopt a mind-set that says: *The more I coach, the better I can do my job; and the more I get others to coach, the better they do their jobs.*

Coaching Cautions _____

Don't assume that as coaching spreads in your organization your job will be diminished. The opposite is more likely to be true.

The Least You Need to Know

◆ A coach approach is a natural partner to HR's focus on people.

◆ HR professionals coach on two levels—directly with employees (Level 1) and helping them coach others (Level 2).

◆ Times of employee transition are excellent opportunities for HR to provide coaching.

◆ You can help HR become the source for spreading coaching throughout the company.

Chapter 13

Coaching as a Tool for Service Providers

In This Chapter

- ◆ Coaching as a bank account with deposits and withdrawals
- ◆ Providing services without providing all the answers
- ◆ Being the expert but incorporating the client's knowledge to form a better solution
- ◆ Improving patient care when doctors use coaching skills with their patients
- ◆ Talking to clients without talking down to them

As a service provider you are focused on meeting the needs of your customers. You can use coaching to identify your customers' immediate needs and determine how you can help satisfy them. Coaching also helps you to clarify the next steps to take with the customer. This chapter highlights the benefits service providers can enjoy by employing a coach approach.

Framework for Integrating Coaching into Services

Client relationships are like bank accounts you can make deposits to or take withdrawals from. Think of a deposit as sharing something about yourself; showing that you're interested in your clients; or giving them answers, discounts, or free services. Withdrawals include asking customers to overlook poor service; making them go out of their way to get to your place of business; having complicated websites for placing orders; not meeting expectations; or not being able to fulfill a request. ("I'm sorry, but my computer's down right now.")

Here's the sticky part: questions can often feel like a withdrawal to a customer, but questions are still key to the coach approach. Your job is to make sure the customer sees your questions as deposits rather than withdrawals. How do you reconcile this tension? Explain why you are going to ask questions, and ask permission before you begin. For instance, you might say something like, "I can answer most of your questions and I will, but I also think you may have some valuable ideas about how to use our services or the kind of solution you need that would help me provide you with the best possible service. Would it be OK if I ask you a few questions to help us discover possible solutions to this problem?"

> **Coaching Cautions**
>
> Don't forget the connect phase of a coach approach. Even the most powerful coaching question can seem like a withdrawal without first establishing a trusting relationship.

When continuing the conversation, be sure to give the client the credit for helping come up with the solution. It's perfectly reasonable to fear the client will determine he doesn't need you; to help mitigate this possibility, you can also ask him what new insights he gained during your conversation. The client will probably recognize your questions were key in helping the two of you find a solution.

Here's how the phases of a coach approach apply to the role of service providers:

Connect. Continuing with the bank account analogy, the connect phase of the coach approach is all about deposits. Service providers have to make a lot of deposits with a lot of people, because they never know who may later become a client or customer. Those connections create opportunities for new business.

Focus. Coaching questions can help clients focus on and clarify their real challenges. As a service provider you will benefit from this clarity because you will be able to tackle the real problem immediately.

Service providers may tend to only ask questions that lead people toward needing their services. A stronger solution involves encouraging clients to think about the bigger picture. Ask them, "What are your overall objectives, and how do you see our services helping you achieve them?" By encouraging big-picture thinking, you are getting clients to see the whole context and how your service fits into it. Try to create this awareness in the focus phase before narrowing to specific issues. This deposit provides a value to clients.

Discover. The purpose of the discovery phase in the service sector is to help clients gain new insights about the services you provide. What will they do as a result of the discoveries they make? When they have a new awareness, it will feel like a deposit in their bank account. If you ask questions that don't promote new insight, answering the questions may feel like a withdrawal to your clients.

Act. As you know by now, real coaching hasn't happened if no action is taken. Of course you want clients to hire you for your services, and you want them to take action on your advice. The strongest action is one that results from a new insight in the coaching conversation that neither of you anticipated. This will be the biggest deposit you can make in the action phase.

To make sure potential customers take action, ask coaching questions such as these: "What next steps will you take and when? What systems will you put in place to make sure this action happens on an ongoing basis [if appropriate]?"

Evaluate. The person being coached or PBC (the client in this case) is the one who evaluates the results of the actions. The service provider can set expectations and clients will need to periodically evaluate the results. This could take the form of a written survey or follow-up phone call.

When expectations have been met, it is like a deposit in the bank account. When expectations have not been met, it is not necessarily a withdrawal if you have created a relationship that fosters communication. If you have a good rapport with your client, you might be able to make adjustments to your work to meet the needs of the client before any damage is done. This adjustment in itself can be a deposit.

Coaching as a Tool for Specialty Services

Making people feel more independent is good for business. That may be a surprising and seemingly contradictory statement for service providers. How can this be true? The general mind-set of some service providers is to make people more dependent on them so the customers will keep coming back for more services. Such companies see helping people feel more independent as a threat to future business. But helping people become independent is like a deposit in your relationship with those clients. It makes you more credible and valuable in their eyes. For instance, a car repair business offers customers suggestions for how to prevent problems and prevent the need for a future repair. That creates customer loyalty. Loyal customers will continue go to that auto shop when they do have a problem, and they will refer others to the business as well.

Tips & Tools

If you work for a large company, think of yourself as a service provider to internal customers in other parts of the company.

In each of the job categories that follow, you'll find specific benefits of coaching for service providers. So what's unique about a coach approach if you provide legal or financial services or work in the health-care or public service arenas?

Lawyers

As a lawyer, you may be accustomed to having a client hire you to determine what needs to be done, telling the client the plan of action, and then proceeding to do all the work on the case. But a coach approach would include helping the client to take ownership of certain aspects of the problem. In a coaching relationship, you lead clients to set actions for themselves. The work becomes a joint set of actions that both you and your clients will take. Ultimately, when the legal work has been completed, clients will retain the information better and walk away with the ability to handle or prevent similar problems in the future. This will increase your value in their eyes.

For example, a tax attorney working with a small business client who has failed to file the annual forms required for the company retirement plan can help the client complete the forms, pay the penalty, and mail it in. But by coaching the client to set up a system where the forms will be filed automatically in the future, the lawyer is adding value to his or her services and helping the client avoid future problems and penalties.

With legal services, a coach approach may work if there is ...

◆ Already a good working relationship between the two parties.

◆ Some willingness on the part of the client to explore new options and create new insights.

◆ An atmosphere in which the client is willing to take action rather than simply dwell on problems.

These are indicators that a coach approach may work. If they don't apply to your situation, then it may be better to stick to a more traditional mode of operation.

Mediators

Mediators want to make sure there's a win-win solution to disputes. Their goal is to lead their clients to settle their disputes out of court. Mediators often say that one of their main goals is to get the two parties to talk to each other. A coach approach can facilitate that.

Mediators have to have a trust relationship with both parties. They need to make it clear they care equally about the interests of both parties. Real progress involves getting each party to see the issue from the other person's perspective, and a coach approach can help with that.

For example, your job in divorce mediation or between feuding neighbors is to get the parties to speak civilly to each other. When you ask coaching questions that promote discovery, you may help clients see each other's point of view. Coaching also encourages clients to come up with all or part of their own solutions. This will make the solutions more palatable than if you tell them what they should do.

Health-Care Professionals

The term *health-care professional* covers a lot of people, including family doctors, surgeons, hospital administrators, nurses, and pharmacists. One thing all of these medical professionals have in common is their customers are usually ill, in pain, or feeling vulnerable. Healthcare is so specialized that many people don't understand the language of doctors, nurses, or pharmacists. As a health-care professional, your challenge is to speak the same language as those you are trying to help.

Tips & Tools

Use a coach approach in your doctor's office, in all your patient interactions. Make sure everyone in the office, including receptionists, nurses, technicians, doctors, and insurance processors, adopt the coach approach.

One approach is to tell people what they need to know in language they can understand. This often comes across as, "I'll dumb it down so you can understand, but I'll just tell you." It's one-way communication.

Without coaching, a visit to a doctor means a quick examination, a prescription, and the patient is sent on his or her way. With coaching, a doctor asks: "What has worked best for you in the past? What types of treatments would you prefer to try first?" With a coach approach, doctors engage patients and acknowledge they can contribute to their treatment. After all, it's their body, and it only makes sense they have more information about it than anyone else. Acknowledging the patient's knowledge is congruent with a coach approach of assuming the answer lies within the PBC. A doctor won't ask a patient to make the diagnosis, of course, but a doctor working with a patient will come up with the best options for care.

Well-placed questions can uncover what has worked well in the past or what problems are present when using a specific treatment. A coaching conversation might help uncover information the patient might not otherwise think to tell the doctor. As a consequence, a coach approach might help physicians avoid mistakes and malpractice suits. Treating patients with a coach approach might also promote patient loyalty.

For instance, a patient with chronic or recurring sinus infections who is seeing a new doctor for the first time probably has a good idea of what his problem is and what type of medication usually cures the infection. The doctor may find that the patient is wrong, but assuming the patient has some knowledge will make for a better ultimate answer.

Another benefit of coaching is it can help patients gain new insights and set new actions to help prevent future health problems. A patient who participates in setting those actions will be more likely to own them and follow through.

Consultants

Earlier chapters made the distinction between coaching, which draws expertise from the PBC, and consulting, which provides expertise from the consultant. A consultant who coaches may seem like a contradiction in terms, but consultants can switch hats to coaching depending on the situation:

Incorporating coaching into consulting works well when the client is willing to collaborate in coming up with the answer. It works well when the client is creative and resourceful, willing to take actions, and can come up with actions based on your work. It also works well when the client has enough time, money, and people to participate in brainstorming sessions and come up with and do actions. It does not work well if the client just wants to pay you to solve a problem with little or no input on their part. They may be in a crunch and hire you to do it all, and in that case coaching is not a good option.

The level of customization in a consulting situation is a factor. If the client's problem is routine, then your standard approach is best. If it requires customization, then coaching works well.

To be successful using a coach approach in your consulting services you will need to become adept at switching hats from consultant to coach. For example, if you need to explain why you are asking a question rather than simply giving an answer, you can say, "My experience has shown that asking discovery questions results in a better overall outcome than just finding solutions based on my answers alone."

If the current focus is closely aligned with your expertise, then assuming you were in your coaching mode, you may say, "I'm switching hats now." If you're in a consulting mode and need to switch to coaching because you sense the need for the solution to be a blend between your answer and what they can contribute, say: "The solution here may benefit from both of our best thinking. Can I ask some questions to bring that out?" If you are going back and forth between coaching and consulting, you need to tell them in advance. They need to be prepared to participate that way.

Public Servants

Public servants may not think there are many opportunities to coach those with whom they interact, but you may find more occasions than you think. If you are an information provider, you have probably experienced having people call your office with only a vague notion of what they need to solve a problem, or they may not even be sure of the nature of the problem. A few well-placed coaching questions can help the caller clarify the need as well as promote new insights about how to deal with the issue both in terms of external help from your agency and things they can do on their own. For instance, a police officer might coach a business that has suffered repeated vandalism to be proactive to create better lighting and to begin a neighborhood watch.

Accountants and Financial Planners

If you are dealing with money matters as a financial professional, you can use many of the same coach-approach methods as other service providers. Here's one example:

A small business owner approached a new accounting firm to get a midyear tax estimate after having less than stellar results with his previous accounting firm. In the initial meeting the CPA gathered general information from the business owner about her business, but he also asked discovery questions concerning the owner's experience with the previous CPA firm, goals for the next few years, biggest challenges, and biggest accomplishments.

This discussion of the larger view of her client's company allowed the CPA to give better answers about how his firm could assist in more ways than just filing taxes. The client felt she got a lot of value from the CPA because she gained some new insights about future directions during the conversation. After careful study of the client's taxes, the CPA found an error in last year's tax filing that may save the business a few thousand dollars and also uncovered a tax deficit, allowing the owner to pay an estimated payment in order to save several hundred dollars at tax filing.

The more ideas and perspectives you can get from your customer, the better you can serve them. Even if they don't know anything about the finance world, with well-placed questions you can help them discover the nuances that will help you serve them best. Other coaching questions for finance professionals might be as follows:

◆ What do you hope to do with proceeds from your financial investments?

◆ What are you willing to do now for future results?

◆ What challenges can you anticipate when it comes to the way you deal with money?

◆ Who else needs to be consulted in your money matters?

Creative Services

Providers of creative services, from interior designers to graphic artists, can benefit from taking a coach approach to working with customers and employers even though the content of their jobs differs greatly. If your job involves creative services, coaching can help you work with customers to discover together exactly what would most satisfy the customer. This applies to all sorts of creative services, including landscape designers, interior designers, clothing designers, illustrators, writers, and graphic artists.

All of these businesses have a number of characteristics in common. All provide creative ideas and services, work directly with clients, and may have many clients who are unclear of what they want or need. Even though these people are creative, they have to please their customers, so knowing what the customer wants helps them create accordingly. Miscommunication can add up to a lot of wasted time, effort, and money. And because creative design is often subjective, pleasing the customer is essential. Unfortunately, consumers do not always know what they want. Coaching helps the designer and the customer speak the same language and discover together the desired result.

For creative professionals, the main benefits of coaching come during the focus and discovery phases.

You can use a coach approach with your clients and teach them to coach you to make it a mutual discovery process. The process is similar to peer coaching (see Chapter 6).

Here are some questions that you can ask your customers:

◆ How will my services best help you achieve your objectives?

◆ If you don't know what you want specifically, what is the essence of the service you desire?

◆ What responses would you like to receive once others see what I've provided you?

Coaching can also help designers and other creative professionals stay within a budget, meet deadlines, or deal with other limitations the client may have. Coaching in this context is definitely win-win. The working relationships are enhanced. Creative work is valued and appreciated. The customer is more likely to be pleased. The creative person is less likely to be frustrated. And the improved service leads to referrals and repeat customers.

Other Services

A coach approach may also help those in other service-related fields such as cleaning services, personal assistants, and personal shoppers. It can even help those in the new fields of home organizing and managing and those who design and create storage space in a home.

A business moving into a new office space in a new city needed a new cleaning service. They were not familiar with services in the area and just picked one from the Yellow Pages. The service had a standard list of things they did, and they did not ask the new customers what they wanted.

Employees and customers kept finding small irritants: the plants weren't watered. The conference rooms were not clean and ready when needed. Some areas were clean while others were dusty. Inconsistency was a real problem. If they complained and the problem was fixed on the next visit, a different one popped up that week. Each problem gradually chipped away at overall customer satisfaction.

The company was cleaning well in general, but they weren't paying attention to the individual needs of the client because they simply had not asked what the company wanted or needed. The client company eventually decided that constantly asking for do-overs wasn't worth the trouble. They canceled the cleaning service and chose another one.

The second service used a coach approach. The owner of the service asked to meet with the facilities manager and used coaching to learn what the customer really wanted:

- What are the most important things you want us to do?

- Which areas are most important?

- Which areas will your customers see?

- Where do you want us to focus our attention regularly?

- Which areas need attention less frequently?

- What was not getting done to your satisfaction with previous cleaning services?

If you are in a similar service industry, here are some tips you can use for incorporating a coach approach.

To connect with your customers, create opportunities to form relationships by offering to meet with client representatives. The cleaning service operates at night when employees are gone, but the manager came in during the day to meet the client's schedule.

You'll improve your focus when you find out how your client prioritizes. You can ask questions like the cleaning manager asked: "What is most important? What can you provide that will help them serve their customers better?"

The discover phase of coaching can foster new insights as you work with your customers. You want your customers to think of things they haven't thought of before, to think of specific ways you can meet their needs. You want them to think of what they need earlier rather than later. That way you spend your time on what they really need and you are more likely to please them immediately with what you do. You also want them to discover all the ways you can do business together rather than only one way you can help. Ask: "What are all the expectations you have for our services?" This discussion can lead to desired services that you are willing to offer. The cleaning company may not generally water plants, wash windows, or recycle; but through discovery questions the company and the client can reach an agreement from the beginning about these additional services and their costs.

Coaching as a Tool for Customer Feedback

If you are trying to get feedback on how well you served your customer, try a coach approach. It will be a second coaching conversation. The first one involved asking, "What do you want?" This one will basically ask, "How did I do?"

Coaching Cautions

Don't confuse customer feedback with the evaluate phase of a coach approach. Customer feedback involves the customer evaluating your services. The evaluate phase is about the customer (PBC) evaluating his or her own actions.

A direct question during a conversation works much better than surveys, which generally get a low response rate and often generate more complaints than kudos. Open-ended questions may get better answers, even if the responses are harder to compile or analyze.

A coaching conversation is, by design, flexible and customized to a particular situation. In a coach approach to customer feedback, you are looking for new ideas and insights for what might have helped you improve your service to this particular customer. Hopefully, what you learn in this conversation can be applied to other situations.

You can even respond to negative feedback by asking: "What ideas do you have to help us improve? What might we do differently?"

The Least You Need to Know

◆ Making people feel more independent is good for business, even for service providers.

◆ For service providers, asking questions can seem like a weakness, so questions need to lead to discovery.

◆ Lawyers can provide added value by coaching clients and leading them to take action rather than doing all the work themselves.

◆ From financial planners to cleaning services, a coach approach yields more satisfied customers.

◆ Coaching is a powerful way to meet customers' needs and win their loyalty.

Chapter 14

Coaching as a Tool for Support Personnel

In This Chapter

◆ Clarifying requests and getting help in doing your job

◆ Becoming more effective and efficient by asking the right questions

◆ Finding time to coach support teams

◆ Learning the value of coaching for executive assistants

Without support staff or administrative assistants, nobody else would be able to do his or her job well. These people do everything from running errands to making photocopies to completing routine reports. If your job is to support everyone else in his or her job, it probably seems like all the to-dos land on your desk! You can get your job done better by taking advantage of coachable moments with the people you support.

With a coach approach you can be more effective and efficient. You can gain a greater understanding of the assignments you are given and how they contribute to the success of the organization.

The result will be that you multiply the positive impact of your efforts by using the requesters' brain power whenever possible. Read on to see how coaching can help you be more efficient in your role as a support professional.

Who Can You Coach?

You may be surprised to learn that you can use coaching in a support role in many different ways. You serve as a communications and services hub for your department. In a large organization you may interact with large numbers of people, perhaps more than any other level of employee. Those relationships offer you numerous opportunities to coach.

People Who Request Your Services

You can coach people who request your services regardless of their level and despite difference in levels between you and the requester. This is how Jordan uses coaching in her job.

Jordan manages grants for an academic department at a university. Four professors called her on the same day asking for assistance with a new federal regulation regarding documentation for grants from the National Institutes of Health (NIH).

Realizing that if four professors had already called her, she would more than likely be hearing from more professors soon, she wanted to get a better sense of the scope of the problem and determine the best approach for efficiently communicating the change in regulation to everyone it would affect. Jordan called the contracts and grants office and asked for Amy, an employee in that office with whom she has a good relationship with her.

Jordan explained the situation to Amy and asked a series of coaching questions:

◆ What can we do to communicate to everyone what's needed to satisfy the new requirements?

◆ What systems can we put in place to learn about these new regulations quickly before they become a problem?

- What are all the steps in the process?
- What actions can we take to ensure the communications happen?
- What obstacles do you envision?
- How will we know when we have the right process in place?

Together Jordan and Amy brainstormed ways to solve this problem quickly and create an action plan to help head off similar problems in the future. They queried the grants office database to learn which faculty had NIH grants due for review soon and alerted them and their administrative assistants to the new regulations. Their success set a precedent for future collaboration when similar problems appear.

Your Team

Not all administrative support staff are part of teams, but in larger organizations teams of support staff often work together, perhaps with each one specializing in a different role. Coaching an administrative team is not much different from the process of coaching other teams (see Chapter 8), but the tricky part is having an opportunity for everyone to be together.

Support teams often have difficulty getting together for team meetings or anything else. Who would answer the phones? Instead of meeting in person, set up a coaching chat room. Conversations can happen in real time, or comments can be read later. Or set up a schedule in which a rotating shift of skeletal staff handles the phone while the rest of the team meets to coach one another on team challenges. Or group team meetings by role or topic: all the financial people, all the administrative assistants, and so on.

Coaching Cautions

Don't let your support team meetings turn into gripe sessions. Use these guidelines to keep meetings productive and focused on a coach approach: 1) Only discuss topics that are in your control to change; 2) Ask: "What actions can we take to improve the situation?"

What's Stopping You from Coaching?

What would stop you from using a coach approach? You may be worried about wasting time when you're already busy, wondering if a coach approach will only make the task take longer. A coaching conversation doesn't have to take a long time. It can be as short as one question.

You may feel that you can't approach someone at a much higher level. But coaching is not a hierarchal process. You can be sure to say "we" when proposing actions so it doesn't sound like you're asking the other person to do your job.

You may be hesitant because you don't know the person who controls the situation very well. Just introduce yourself, explain your role, and mention some of the people you support. Point out the common goal you both have in serving the needs of the company.

Tips & Tools

What can you do if you need to partner with an office in another state? You can use a coach approach very well on the phone. In fact, a lot of coaching is routinely conducted on the phone.

You may think that if you use a coach approach to get others to help create solutions, then people may think less of you. Stay focused on your overall objective of getting the job done. The more people see you got the job done, they will be less interested in how you did the job.

You may feel reluctant to coach people because you do not have the same expertise they do, and you may not understand their project or how to discuss it. You don't have to understand everything other people do in order to coach them; they just have to understand it. You need to understand your task and what they want you to do.

Coaching as a Tool for Action

Coaching is about taking action. In order to take advantage of that action, you have to look for coachable moments. Here is an example of a situation with coachable moments:

When someone asks you to do something, you want to get a good enough sense of the big picture to understand where this task fits. If you can, take a few minutes to ask these questions after the request is made: "Can you tell me more about all the things you'll need help with to get this project completed? What are the range of possibilities I can use in this task and still meet your needs?"

If you're wondering if the time is right for coaching, ask yourself the following questions and use this process to determine whether this is a coachable moment:

Tips & Tools

You may find it helpful to keep a coaching journal. You could log who's coachable and the types of coaching topics and questions that help most you in doing your job better.

How complex is this task? Are there multiple ways to accomplish the goal? If you think the job cannot be done exactly as requested, it may indicate the need to coach the requester. You need to find out in advance how to make decisions about the variables.

Do you have a relationship with the requester that allows coaching? If you know this person well and you trust each other, the questions will be seen at face value. If not, that person many think you are trying to get out of doing the work.

Does the time seem to be appropriate for a question? If someone is under stress or a deadline, the questions may not be heard as you intend them.

Would coaching help in the long term? A coaching question may not be needed specifically for this job but may help with later assignments.

Here's what happened with one receptionist: a visitor to the company has gotten a parking ticket. Nothing in her handbook tells her what to do in this situation. She needs to contact someone to clarify how to handle the matter.

Coaching questions can help a person establish a procedure to avoid similar problems in the future. She calls Dave in security who sets policies involving driving on campus. He tells her what to do. But she doesn't stop there.

Receptionist: While I've got you on the phone, do you have a minute to talk about this? I think we could put our heads together to prevent similar confusion on other topics.

Dave: Sure. I'd love to eliminate any confusion and get fewer calls to answer questions. Often I'm not in my office to help people, and then they get aggravated because they have to wait. What can we do?

The receptionist was ready with her questions. Here are the questions she asked Dave:

◆ What's the process for giving input on policies and procedures that may need to be changed?

◆ How are new procedures communicated?

◆ What steps can we take to improve the process?

◆ What could have been done to avoid the ticket? When can we get something in place?

def•i•ni•tion

Toleration is coaching jargon for enduring something that blocks progress. Once "tolerations" are removed the PBC often has "aha's" and makes new action plans.

Why would you want to be proactive? What's in it for you? You already have lots to do. Coaching in situations like this can save time in the long run and keep you from getting bogged down repeatedly in similar situations. Being proactive is a much more positive approach than *tolerating* a situation that constantly annoys or hampers your creativity.

Getting a problem fixed now can save you and the rest of your team down the road. If you use a coach approach, instead of making someone—Dave in this case—angry or irritating him with repeated problems, you may be able to build a relationship of trust with the person in charge (Dave) and lay the groundwork for later work together. Rather than escalating any tension over a problem situation, a coach approach defuses the situation and gives better results than simply complaining would.

You know you need to use coaching to be proactive when …

◆ People complain about things that zap time and energy. Ask the complainer: "What would be the ideal solution that would save you time and effort? What steps would we need to take to make that happen?" Using "we" implies shared responsibility. This is a coach approach, but it has to be right situation. You don't want to appear to be insubordinate.

◆ You notice you get the same requests from multiple people. Maybe you can take care of requests before they are made.

◆ You see a pattern of requests that come on a weekly or monthly basis. Use a coach approach to find out what needs to be done before those requests pile up.

Managing Time

Managing time effectively is one of the most common challenges for administrative assistants. Here are some coaching questions to ask yourself and each other: *What are the overall objectives? What have you done in the past that has worked well? What tends to get in the way? Are there better times of the day for certain types of tasks? What systems do you need to put into place to help? What are the consistent sources of interruptions and what strategies can you use to deal with them?*

Match the amount of time you put into a problem to the value it brings. You have a time budget. Getting some coaching can help you plan your time budget so you don't spend an hour on something of low value leaving you with only 10 minutes to deal with something of greater importance.

Managing Details

Handling the many details of a particular job is one of the main tasks of administrative assistants—it's what managers need most. Here are some questions you can ask yourself or other administrative assistants to be more effective in managing details: *What will help you capture all the details? Whom do you need to call? What kinds of details are likely to slip through the cracks? What organizational methods can you put into place to make sure you track all the details? What standard set of questions can you ask when you receive a request to make sure you get enough information to cover all the details? If you are not a detail-oriented person, what can you do and whom would you contact to learn from or get advice? Who is best at handling details in your group? How can you leverage that person's skills to help you do details better? How will you evaluate your results?*

Communicating with Internal Customers

It's not enough just to do your job. You need to let people know what you're doing, how you're progressing, what problems you've run into, and what help you might need. Here are some coaching questions to consider to ensure quality communication:

◆ Which groups of customers need to know this information?

◆ What strategies do you use for knowing how much to communicate and when? For example, if someone requests 10 copies of something, you say, "Done." If a task requires three weeks to complete, the amount of communication required would be very different.

◆ What modes of communication do your customers prefer? Is it different for different groups? Here's an example: managers may prefer to have all announcements condensed into one summary at the end of each week rather than several small e-mails during the week.

◆ How can you highlight the actions your customers need to take in your communications that will actually get them to do it?

◆ How are your communications perceived by others? How can you make them sound confident without being insolent?

◆ What can lead to misinterpretation of communications? How can you avoid this?

◆ What elements need to be present in all communications before they go out? What kind of model can you follow?

Following Up on Projects

How you are viewed and valued as an administrative assistant can be greatly impacted by how well you follow up on projects. This is more than just managing details. It's knowing when, how, and with whom to follow up.

What types of projects need follow up? Here are some discovery coaching questions:

- ◆ When does follow-up need to happen? (Example: you may need to follow up on a project a year later because it impacts an annual event.)

- ◆ What level of detail is needed? (Example: an annual event with stockholders requires a lot more detail than a one-time lunch meeting of four managers.)

- ◆ How will you know you're doing a good job of following up?

- ◆ How will you know the follow-up is complete? Different internal customers may have different requirements for follow-up reports. How do you manage that?

- ◆ What resources do you need to complete the follow-up?

- ◆ What problems have you run into in the past?

Executive Assistants

Executive assistants tend to run the show. They anticipate problems and needs before being asked. They are good at people management. But they can be even better at their job by using a coach approach.

Because the scope of their responsibility is broader, so are the consequences of their actions. Where administrative assistants execute the actions ordered by others, executive assistants tend to instigate action.

If you are an executive assistant, you have ample opportunities to coach by virtue of your position and the volume of work you manage.

The following sections give examples of scenarios executive assistants may encounter and coaching questions for each.

Managing the Executive's Calendar

The objective is to protect the executive's time, making sure that anything that gets added to the calendar is worthwhile and an appropriate amount of time is scheduled.

Coaching questions include:

◆ How does this potential meeting fit with the priorities of the executive?

◆ Who should be there to accomplish the task?

◆ Can this problem be handled by means other than a meeting?

◆ What needs to be in place to make the meeting productive?

◆ What potential conflicts may emerge?

◆ What are the executive's preferences about how this type of meeting is handled?

Dealing With People in the Organization

Your executive routinely interacts with a number of people. That means you interact with them, too. Here are some coaching questions to help you in dealing with the people you and your boss encounter on a regular basis:

◆ What practices do you need to establish that will help you communicate more effectively?

◆ What problems do you routinely face in communicating? What patterns do you see?

◆ How do you deal with people who are less than communicative?

◆ How do you protect the executive's time from people who just want to chat?

◆ How do you anticipate needs before they are voiced based on existing patterns?

How can you prioritize requests? For example, some people make lots of routine requests, and those requests move the business forward. That's OK. However, if those requests don't accomplish goals, you'll want to be aware of them and guard against them bogging down the team.

What are the key relationships you can cultivate and manage? You want to have relationships in place before you can coach those people when needed.

The Least You Need to Know

◆ Support staff members rarely have full-blown coaching sessions, but even asking one question can make a difference in clarifying a request for a task.

◆ Because coaching is nonhierarchical, support staff can coach anyone at any level if the situation is appropriate.

◆ Coaching is an effective time management tool.

◆ Executive assistants can use a coach approach as a tool for maximizing their effectiveness.

Part 4

Coaching Challenges for Specific Organizations

As Tony became more proficient at coaching, he found more and more ways to apply it. He coached his brother as he made decisions about expanding his small business. And he talked with his sister, a vice president in a large multisite business, about ways coaching could work for her as she related to people all over the world. He even found ways to implement coaching at church and in his Parent Teacher Organization. In the course of his volunteer work with a community-based nonprofit he began to see applications for coaching there, too. Tony clearly was sold on the idea, and everyone could easily tell that. His enthusiasm helped get the coaching ball rolling.

How can a small business use coaching to carry it through growth pains? Where is coaching useful in large corporations facing big changes? What role can coaching play in not-for-profit and faith-base organizations? You'll learn the answers to all these questions in this part of the book.

Chapter 15

Coaching Small and Family-Owned Businesses

In This Chapter

- ◆ Coaching questions and tips at each stage of development
- ◆ Coaching to help employees maximize profitability
- ◆ Dealing with growing pains
- ◆ Using coaching skills with suppliers and distributors
- ◆ Setting up a company with a coaching culture

A coach approach helps small business owners look up from their relatively limited perspective to see a bigger world and take actions to grow. Small business owners have limited resources, including people, time, energy, and money; coaching helps make the most of those limited resources. And coaching is a great tool for working with both suppliers and customers to maximize the benefit for all parties and solidify relationships that are key to the success of a small business.

Questions to Ask at Each Stage of Development

When you want to foster a coaching culture in a small/family-owned business, you need to answer the following questions during each stage of the business' growth:

- Who can be the coach, and who can be coached?
- What are coachable moments typical of this stage?

These two main questions crop up in each section of this chapter as we follow how a small business grows through the predictable stages of development.

Hobby vs. Business

Mark is a farmer who was looking for a source of income to fill in the gaps during the months where profit from farming was at its lowest. He dabbled in several different enterprises but none really produced the profit margin he was looking for to supplement his farm income.

At this point Mark's access to coaching was a book he had read about the power of asking discovery questions and a friend he had lunch with now and then who was a coach.

At one of those lunch meetings his coach friend asked him if he knew what level of profit he would have to make for his side business to provide the income he needed. Mark admitted that he'd never thought about that specifically, but he committed to coming up with an answer.

As a part of that dabbling, he stumbled onto the idea that he could package and sell athletic socks wholesale to distributors. Nearby mills produced athletic socks from unbleached yarn. They were shipping the unbleached socks to several other small processors to bleach them, press them, and package them. These processors would then sell them to distributors. After a bit of research, Mark decided that this could be a way to help out the local sock mill owners (because they would have a reliable local packaging and marketing agent), and it might be the very thing he was looking for to supply extra income.

During the early stages of processing and selling the packaged socks, Mark's business was not making much of a profit, which made the enterprise look more like a hobby than a business. He was able to use the business to justify buying new "toys" like cell phones, PDAs, website software, and just about anything else that seemed like cool technology. These gadgets didn't actually contribute to the profitability of the company, however.

Mark had so much to learn, processes to put in place, and improvements to make that someone looking from the outside in might wonder if it was a real business and if it was going to survive. The tide began to turn when his wife, who is also a great coach, asked him when he was going to get serious about turning the sock business into a significant source of supplemental income. When he replied, "I am serious," she asked, "What evidence leads you to that conclusion?" That was the coaching nudge he needed to move to the next stage.

Typical characteristics of this stage are ...

◆ Only one person is involved in the company.

◆ The person has a lot to learn about the market, the products and services, and himself as the owner.

◆ The person is typically enamored with the thought of having a business but not necessarily focused on profitability and sustainability.

◆ The owner is usually trying to do everything related to the business and is stretched thin.

Question 1: Who can be the coach and who can be coached?

At this stage, the company is so small that the answer to almost everything is "you, the owner." You're the only person around. But there are some creative ways to answer the question of who is doing the coaching and who can be coached.

◆ You, the owner, can use books and other similar resources to coach yourself.

◆ You can hire a coach, and you might even be able to find incentive grants, free coaching or other services to help your small business get off the ground. Most states have a chamber of commerce or an economic development agency to help small businesses get started. It's worth exploring.

Tips & Tools _____

When you are the only person in your business, look for a coach at local business networking meetings (Business Networking International, Small Business Association (SBA), Chamber, Rotary, etc). You might find someone willing to barter his or her services for services or products from your business.

◆ You, the owner, can take advantage of coaching services offered by bank officers who specialize in helping small business owners.

◆ You, the owner, can be coached on just about anything that is going on in the business at this point because you face many decisions and new experiences.

◆ You can coach suppliers on challenges they have in their own businesses. Both businesses will receive direct benefits and will develop strong relationships in the process.

◆ Similarly, you can coach your customers to be clear on their needs and overall goals to be certain that your products and services provide real value to them. This creates customer loyalty because of the fit of your products/services to their needs but also fosters strong relationships as with your suppliers.

Question 2: What are coachable moments typical of this stage?

Transition from start-up to profitability. The owner of a small firm is discussing the need to expand capacity of her business with a friend. The friend, using a coach approach, may ask: "What options have you considered? What are the criteria you will use to choose the best one?"

Developing plans for steady revenue flow. As co-owner you may ask, "What are the main bottlenecks? What signs do you see before revenue is about to drop? What strategies have helped you manage revenue in the past?" This may lead to a better balance of time spent on supplies, marketing, and managing.

Focus on margin from the beginning. A small business owner may have a problem knowing how to keep prices low to build a customer base for his finished product without substantially undercutting profits. A small business loan officer at the bank may ask: "How have you tried to trim costs in the past? Of those areas where have you found the most potential savings? How will you know you have reached your objective?" Good questions may bring out ways to trim shipping costs or help the owner decide what criteria will be used to set prices.

Me and My Tiny Team

At first, Mark's sock "team" consisted only of Mark and one part-time worker; but by the time the business was consistently profitable, his wife, Melissa, had joined the team. Mark and Melissa worked long, hard hours learning the process and the equipment and working out all the kinks of both.

Mark kept thinking about Melissa's question: *What's the evidence that he was taking the business seriously?* That question kept him focused on making progress with the business. Soon Mark had made enough contacts with suppliers of unbleached socks and distributors of socks to begin to turn a profit.

Coaching Cautions

Some days are just too filled with frustration and emergencies to allow any coachable moments. Don't force it. Wait until the stress subsides.

The additional demand caused Mark to hire a few more part-time workers. Some of them were reliable and efficient, but some were not. As Mark soon realized, growth causes more headaches.

One of the frustrations of this stage was that most of the workers were doing basically what they were told but not applying their own thinking to the processes. On several occasions, Mark would check on the part-time workers to see how things were going only to find that they were doing things in very slow or inefficient ways. When he asked why they were doing it that way, they would say that's what they were told to do. Mark felt that he had to be present all the time to avoid expense over-runs from employees not using their brains to make wise decisions. But being with the employees meant he was not able to do business development work of finding more and better suppliers and distributors.

Melissa, a peer and co-owner of the business, asked Mark how they could operate differently with their employees to get them to look for ways to be more efficient. This was a great coaching question. All Mark could think of, apart from watching them every minute, was to coach them.

Mark and Melissa became the first internal coaches for their small company. Some of the workers were uncomfortable with the coach approach and didn't know how to open up and respond. They felt like Mark and Melissa were checking up on them and they were afraid of giving the "wrong" answer. Other workers were coachable and were coming up with new insights and action plans.

Thankfully, part-time workers come and go. Over time Mark and Melissa were able to see common patterns of behavior in their employees who were coachable, and they started looking for those characteristics in the people they hired. These coachable employees became great coaches for one another, which allowed Mark and Melissa to focus on the bigger issues facing the future of the company.

Typical characteristics of this stage are …

◆ More people than just the owner are now involved, and their performance is critical to the success of the business.

◆ Profitability is becoming stable.

◆ Growth is more rapid.

Question 1: Who can be the coach, and who can be coached?

The owner can coach employees and vice versa. Because coaching is not a hierarchical process, it can go both ways. Example: the owner is stuck on how to obtain a piece of equipment at a reasonable cost. An employee may ask: "What are all the possible options? How will each of these impact production time versus down time? What are the benefits and drawbacks of each plan?"

Employees can coach one another. Example: when a serious accident with a forklift is narrowly avoided, the shaken employees sit down to talk about it. One employee asks the team: "What factors helped create this situation? What can we as a team do to create a warning system to prevent future problems?"

Question 2: What are coachable moments typical of this stage?

Resolving employee conflicts. When employees disagree over vacation time scheduling, the owner may ask the team: "What other options have you considered? What rules would you put in place to make sure everyone is treated fairly?"

Productivity and quality issues that emerge when more than just the owner is involved. While checking on the progress of an order an owner finds an employee is making more errors than expected in packaging the items. The owner may ask: "What do you need in order to increase your accuracy? Who can help with this solution? What are the obstacles to starting this new plan?" Because the employee arrived at her own solution she will be more likely to use the new insight consistently and even pass the idea on to others.

Dealing with rapid growth and accompanying change. As orders begin to pile up the secretary may ask the order fulfillment team: "What support do you need to be more successful? What processes do you need to put in place to be more effective?"

All the Officers Are Related

As the sock bleaching and packaging business grew, so did the challenges. The small company was running out of space to handle the volume of socks the business was processing. The equipment started to need more maintenance as it aged. Mark and Melissa brought in other family members to work part time and some to work full time. Each additional family member they hired had an opinion about how the business ought to be run and spent more time trying to help run the business than doing the jobs they were hired to do.

Time was being wasted in family disputes instead of being spent on handling the growing demand. Now they were in even worse shape than before hiring family members.

Coaching Cautions

Beware when coaching family members! What you intend as a question to promote new insight might be interpreted as bringing up conflict from the past. If this is a danger, preface questions with your purpose in asking.

As these challenges mounted, Mark and Melissa decided that an objective third party from outside the family might be a viable way to settle the family quarrels. They used the coaching services of the local SBA. The SBA offered a one-day seminar, Coaching for Small Businesses, which included a morning session on how to deal with small business challenges, an afternoon group coaching session, and six one-on-one coaching sessions on the phone over the three months following the seminar.

As a result of that experience, the business became successful at a whole new level. The main question that had been asked in the afternoon group coaching session was, "How will you anticipate and prepare for change to help your business thrive?" Before that day, Mark only thought about changing when things became so painful that something had to change for the business to survive. He had not thought about anticipating and preparing for change.

In the one-on-one sessions his coach had asked, "How can you leverage the most profitable part of your business?" Those two questions became the theme for this stage of the business.

During this time Mark and Melissa made a couple of really significant decisions. They expanded their facility to deal with greater volume. And they noticed that the distributors they shipped their products to were making a higher margin on their product than they were, so they became a distributor and enjoyed higher profits for several years.

They continued to foster a coach approach to every aspect of their business. When their suppliers were having challenges, they had coaching conversations with them, asking, "What do you need to focus on? Where can you find new ideas? What actions will you take?" They continued to use the SBA coaching services as well.

The primary characteristics typical of this stage are ...

◆ Continued rapid growth of the company.

◆ A growing customer base and more relationships to maintain.

Question 1: Who can be the coach, and who can be coached?

As the owners bring a coach approach to everything they do, they will model coaching for new employees who can also learn some coaching skills. If some of the new employees are family members then coaching can be tricky. Discovery questions can sound more like "trick" questions to which the owner already knows the answers. This can be mitigated by having a clear understanding of what coaching is and how it can help everyone do his job better. For instance, before she needs to bring up a problem topic the owner may state, "I would like to discuss the problem we had yesterday. I think you have some good ideas we can use. Do you mind if we have a team coaching session to brainstorm solutions and pick the best option?"

Question 2: What are coachable moments typical of this stage?

Family conflicts as the company grows and more people are involved. Over a meal the topic of unreliable suppliers emerges. Everyone has an opinion about the "best" solution and no one is willing to compromise. Tension mounts as no progress is made toward a solution. One of the family members may ask: "What are the patterns we see when suppliers start to become unreliable?" This may redirect the conversation to a more productive path.

Long-term planning to anticipate growth and prepare for it. During a meeting at the bank to discuss plans for a loan to modernize equipment the loan officer asks what processes are in place to accommodate growth. On the way back to the office this question kicks off an impromptu coaching conversation in which one of the co-owners asks: "What should our business look like in 10 years? What are the key things we should be doing now to make that happen? What obstacles are we likely to encounter?" By the time they arrive they have listed several actions they need to put into place in order to survive the growth they anticipate.

Bigger decisions related to expansion. Determining if franchising is a good idea, or keeping the business remain small? This is probably the type of topic where the owners look to external resources for assistance. In that case, a coach approach would be to ask the owners: "What are the risks involved? How can you evaluate your options?"

Founder Retires

Talk of retirement rarely came up at first, but it was coming up a lot lately. Mark and Melissa thought and talked about places they'd like to go and things they'd like to do if they weren't working all the time. But they also were reluctant to walk away from the business they had started. So they kept putting off their decision.

Tips & Tools

In small businesses, practically every experience is a new experience. If you don't know what next coaching question to ask, ask: "What should I be asking you?" You might be surprised how well this works.

Many of the ways business decisions were made were still in Mark's and Melissa's brains and were not available to any potential successors. They knew they had some work to do if they were ever to retire, but they were so busy they weren't making time to put their processes down in writing.

Mark went to lunch with his coaching buddy who asked, "When are you going to sell your business and enjoy the proceeds?" That was it, he talked to Melissa and they finally decided to sell.

Typical characteristics of this stage are ...

◆ The founder is often in denial that retirement is possible and doesn't mean death of the company.

◆ The founder wonders what value he has to offer if he is no longer involved in the company that has become his "baby."

◆ The business is still considered small but has gone through a lot of growth to survive.

◆ Founders are notorious for not developing successors. Even if the founder tries to do this, it is often met with resistance and denial on the part of the successor as well.

Question 1: Who can be the coach, and who can be coached?

The founder is one focus of this stage for both coaching others and being coached through the transition away from the company. For instance, the founder's son may ask: "What do you want your life to look like in five years? How should the company be handled by then?"

Hopefully the owner has been coaching a successor before this stage because it's definitely a time for that person to gain insights and create actions for dealing with the transition. To sustain the coaching culture that was built, the successor should continue coaching everyone as coachable moments arise.

Quest 2: What coachable moments are typical of this stage?

The future plans of the founder. At the age of 55, 15 years after starting up a small business, the daughter of the owner has expressed an interest in working with him and to eventually continue the business after he retires. He's delighted but it spurs the realization that he needs a succession plan if the transition is going to be smooth. His daughter coach may ask: "What would you have wanted to know before you started the company? How can you communicate those insights to me?"

Celebrate the contributions of the founder. The leader who is staying on to help run the company for the new owner may ask, "What are the key contributions that this business has made to the community over the years? What specifically did the owner(s) do that produced those results? How can honor the owner(s)?"

Making a clear transition to the successor. The owner may ask of each employee/family member: "What needs to be done to establish a solid relationship with the new owner? In this time of transition, what needs to continue, what needs to stop and what need to be started to set the new business up for success? What assumptions about the new owner are you making? How can you confirm (or let go of) those assumptions?"

Establishing the strategic plans and key relationships of the successor. The owner may ask the successor: "Who can be your allies during the transition time? What kind of support will you need?"

Company Is Sellable

Mark and Melissa hired a business consultant to help them price and sell the business. After years of having a coaching culture within their company, they were a bit disappointed when the consultant mainly gave advice and told them what to do rather than coach them through the process. The one helpful question the consultant did ask was, "What is special about your company that would make it attractive to a prospective buyer?"

Mark and Melissa wished someone had asked them that question way back when they started the business so they would have been more intentional about creating a sellable company. But even at this late date, they coached each other to determine what advice to accept. They were much more pleased with the way their coaching helped them than they were with the consultant they had hired. They developed an overall plan for selling the company and found a buyer within 18 months of putting it up for sale.

Typical characteristics of this stage are …

◆ Energy is given to valuation of the company, both tangible assets and intangibles of the brand and customer base. You might hold team coaching sessions on this topic to set criteria for valuing the business.

◆ Employee anxiety is high as employees wonder whether they will still have a job under new ownership. You may assure employees you will encourage new owners to keep the staff intact. Having a nonanxious staff is essential in coaching small/family-owned businesses, especially when it comes time to sell the business. Emotions can run very high. Team coaching sessions may help employees develop strategies for showing the new owners their value to the company or to evaluate whether they really want to stay in their current position.

◆ Reticence and even resistance of founder to stay focused on and move forward with the sale of the company.

Question 1: Who can be the coach, and who can be coached?

The owners will want to be coached through all the facets of the sale to feel confident they have acted wisely on each decision leading up to the sale. They may ask each other: "What problems will need to be solved before the company is ready to be sold?"

The buyer can be coached to ensure this is a solid move for her to make with this company, this market, and at this time. The owner may ask the potential buyer: "How does this business mesh with your other enterprises? What gaps would it fill?"

Question 2: What coachable moments are typical of this stage?

♦ **Employee excellence.** During the process of valuing the company for sale the owner will ask the employees for high-quality performance in order to fulfill due diligence requirements. The owner may ask: "What are all the details that need to be considered as we go through this process? What could prevent us from doing an excellent job?"

♦ **Concerns of employees once the potential sale is made known.** The new owner may coach the current employees by asking: "What options are possible to help merge the operations of this business with my other company? How would you handle this in my place?"

♦ **Future plans of the owners once the sale is complete.** One of the current employees who has become quite good at coaching may ask the new owner: "What is your process for long range planning? How would our input benefit you in this process?"

Think Big, Be Big

As long as the owner thinks of his business as small, it will remain that way. As you develop a coaching culture to help your small business thrive, keep in mind that perspective is a big part of what keeps PBCs stuck and conversely helps them get unstuck. A key perspective for small business owners to adopt as a backdrop to coaching is "think big, be big."

When the owner is coaching employees, you can ask questions that assume future bigness. When peers are coaching one another, you can ask what can be done to solve a current challenge and prepare to prevent the same challenge as the company grows.

Another Perspective

"The vision must be followed by the venture. It is not enough to stare up the steps; we must step up the stairs."

—Vance Havner (1901–1986), Christian evangelist

A serious inhibitor to small businesses' success is the fear of growth. With a coaching culture, the owner(s) and employees can constantly address this fear in small ways in each coachable moment so that it doesn't build into a crippling fear at some point in the future. Great questions for this would be: "What might be the negative consequences of growth?" and, "How can you anticipate those and mitigate them within your current plans?"

The Least You Need to Know

- Each stage of growth for a family-owned business has predictable coaching opportunities.

- Coaching family members takes special sensitivity because all sorts of baggage can arise.

- You can use coaching, even with part-time workers, to increase productivity, efficiency, and profitability.

- Coaching can help small businesses in all their phases of development.

Chapter 16

Coaching in Big Business

In This Chapter

- ◆ Taking advantage of your company's size
- ◆ Avoiding the tendency to make company-wide rules about coaching
- ◆ Building community with a coach approach
- ◆ Finding people across the company to coach
- ◆ Simplifying corporate communications with a coach approach

The bigger the company, the more complicated everything is. Your organization might be so large that the positive impact from coaching is imperceptible at first. However, with a few cautions and tweaks to the coaching process, you can amplify the impact of a coach approach.

The Pros and Cons of Coaching in Large Companies

As far as coaching is concerned, being big has a downside. People can feel lost. They sometimes have a hard time getting started because they feel they have to get executive buy-in to start coaching, and they may not know where to turn to get permission. The good news is that most of the content of this book can be done without permission from anyone other than the person you want to coach.

But being big also has an upside. A big corporation has the resources to put coaching in place throughout the business. As coaching takes root, it might take on different forms. In one part of the company peer coaching may be strong. In other locations managers coaching employees could dominate. This may seem counter-intuitive but grass roots efforts can really thrive in large companies, sometimes better than company-wide initiatives.

If coaching does take hold, people can develop expertise. They may specialize in coaching administrative assistants, coaching teams, or training managers to use a coach approach with employees.

Here are some tips for coaching in a big business:

Start small. Start where you are with the job you have, looking for coachable moments even if it involves asking a single coaching question.

Build community. You can develop your coaching skill and find more coaching opportunities by connecting with like-minded people, even if it's only one or two others. Build community of those who thrive using a coach approach and find ways to learn from one another.

Leverage communication. Look for economies of scale wherever you can. If your company already has processes in place about how to create *Communities of Practice*, internal blogs, or teleconferencing for meetings, then leverage those communication systems to keep the community learning together and to communicate the benefits you've seen with a coach approach.

def•i•ni•tion

Communities of Practice (CoPs) are groups of people who have an interest in sharing their knowledge and learning together. There are detailed suggestions for CoPs in resources on knowledge management —one example is *The Complete Idiot's Guide to Knowledge Management* by Melissie Clemmons Rumizen, Ph.D. (Penguin Group (USA) Inc., 2002).

Leverage training. Utilize your training department, if you have one, to teach a coach approach throughout the company. In most large companies there's a good chance that some form of coach training is going on, and the training division would know about it. Check to see how they define coaching. Is it more like content-rich coaching, framework coaching, or something else (see Chapter 13)?

Be flexible. As you start advocating a coach approach, look within your company to learn from other groups' systems, successes, and mistakes. Don't assume your own way of starting coaching is the only way. Be nimble and ready to change to other systems of training.

You can also learn from other companies. You may have more affinity with another company, and their methods may work better for you than other coaching initiatives in your own company. Don't be so closed-minded as to look only inside your own corporation.

Get more than one sponsor. If only one executive backs your coaching effort, you run the risk of losing executive support for your program if that person changes jobs. You'll need more than one sponsor who is willing to be an advocate until a coach approach just becomes a normal way of operating in your company.

Who Does What in the Organization?

You'll get better results from you coaching efforts if you put some effort into deciding whom to coach. Some people show great gains from coaching while others don't create many new actions or insights. The new insights—"aha's"—are at the root of the actions that yield results. So focus your efforts on people who are the most coachable. That's not to say that you can't use a coach approach in all aspects of your job, but be selective if there's a choice. All else being equal, select the person that's the most coachable (see Chapter 5 for more on identifying coachable people).

Who Already Knows the Answer?

Throughout the corporation you'll find a lot of untapped potential. Coaching is a great way to tap into that potential when you have, or can establish, the relationships you need.

How do you find those resources? Some companies have a knowledge management system to track who has specific strengths or experiences. If your company has such a system, use it to find out who has the knowledge and expertise to help you do your job. Then use a coach approach with them to draw them out. Here's an illustration.

Alex is in marketing and has a dilemma. He has an idea for a new marketing campaign for an upcoming trade show, but he needs help developing it. Alex would like to find people with experience in marketing who can help him flesh out his ideas.

Alex began by going to his company's knowledge management database to find some people. He got several names and thought about how he'd start a conversation with them. He identified himself and began: "I'm in marketing in another division. I found your name in the knowledge management database, and I think you might be able to help me with a problem I'm having with a marketing campaign for a new product. I don't want to take a lot of your time, and I'm also interested in making this benefit you as well."

Alex explained his dilemma to Phil, one person he had contacted in another division. Upon hearing Alex's problem, Phil admitted that this specific problem was new to him.

At that point if Alex had not been using a coach approach, he might have ended the call. However, Alex was thinking like a coach, and he realized that Phil had potential insights anyway.

Alex decided to plunge ahead by asking, "How would you handle this problem? What strategies would you use?"

Phil doesn't have to have had experience in this area to bring new ideas to the problem. Using a coach approach is different from just calling someone up who has been there, done that, and asking, "What did you do?" A coach approach can work with people who have not been in a particular situation. They still have ideas, perhaps better ideas or more broad vision than the person who has faced the situation and succeeded. The person who has dealt with the issue already may have too narrow a focus and won't present anything other than how he did it.

You may not want to do exactly what the person with experience did because your situation will not be exactly the same. Coaching helps you generate a customized solution to help you get your job done better than if you just found out how someone else did it.

Because Alex used coaching on a regular basis, he wasn't at all surprised when Phil began to have new insights that benefited both men in their work in different divisions. When they worked through one of Phil's "aha's," Alex responded, "Thanks for your help. By the way … what are you going to do with that new insight in your work?" With both Alex and Phil creating action plans, more is getting done in the company.

Seeing Beyond the Organization Chart

Encourage your colleagues not to be shy about coaching people outside their division or organization. That may be where some of the best coaching happens.

A pitfall to working across organizational lines is choosing people to coach is more difficult. But the benefits outweigh the potential downsides. People in other parts of the organization have different experiences and have been exposed to different ideas. If you feel stuck in trying to get new insights in your own area, get out of your rut and interact with those outside your sphere. Having access to so many people within your own company is a real luxury, and you will likely find just the help you need. People in small businesses would love to have the opportunity to tap into the ideas of people with different experience and knowledge, and you have those assets right in your own company.

Dealing With Reorganization

Some large companies seem to reorganize on a monthly basis. Sometimes employees have difficulty keeping up or even wanting to keep up with all the changes. Often the reasons for change are unclear. And no one seems to know why such drastic change has to happen so often.

If businesses take the trouble to reorganize, executives or managers somewhere have real reasons for change. They see inefficiencies they hope to eliminate through reorganization, and they have determined that the inefficiencies in the current system outweigh the inefficiencies that are bound to happen as a result of the reorganization. Management determines that change is really worth the inevitable downtime and low morale that often results when employees are trying to figure out new systems and relationships.

Coaching is a great tool to help employees understand the reasons for the changes, the anticipated benefits, and how to get the new organization up to speed as quickly as possible.

Consider this example: the specialty foods division of a large food supply company has three areas—new product acquisitions, restaurant business development, and retail business development. The lead managers from the business development areas noticed that they were behind schedule with customer commitments much more than before. The organizations had become more complex, and inefficiencies had developed over time.

The company had been through reorganizations in the past that failed to meet all of their expectations. Before making a radical change, the managers got together and decided to try a coach approach to making decisions about reorganization.

Bill and Debbie, the managers of the two business development areas, decided to coach each other about the problems. They decided to do some peer coaching to help each other gain the new insights they needed.

They started the conversation with the assumption that one of their areas needed to change to better adapt to the other area's way of doing things. They didn't know which should adapt, but each assumed the other's area would be the one to change.

Bill and Debbie needed to get focused in the conversation. One way to focus a conversation is to determine how big of a gap exists between where you are and where you want to end up. Once you know how big the gap is, you can start developing steps to get from start to finish. Bill and Debbie began by getting clear on all the details of their current situation.

In addition, they agreed that they would trade off the roles of coach and person being coached (PBC).

They went back and forth asking questions. Both listed several problem areas. They noticed that employees from the different areas within the division were wasting time trying to figure out who within the company they were supposed to be working with to deliver solutions and get the products to the customers. They also noticed that many of the problems were related to the distribution functions that existed within both their areas.

Once they got a handle on their current situation, they started to talk about what they wanted to achieve. Their answers tended to center around on-time deliveries, lower distribution costs, and accurate deliveries. They realized that neither of their areas were anywhere near where they wanted them to be.

Debbie and Bill decided to look into that function in greater detail. They concluded that both of their areas might need to reorganize in order to create a separate area focused only on distribution.

They considered the situation by asking each other these questions:

◆ What data exists to support the conclusion that a reorganization would make us more efficient?

◆ What criteria will we use to make sure this is a worthwhile move to make?

◆ If we do this, who needs to move?

◆ Who else will be impacted?

◆ What challenges will they face?

The answers to these questions led them to share their thinking with the product acquisitions manager, Jill. She had a few more questions for them before proposing the reorganization to the division president. The president approved the plan.

A coach approach can also help everyone survive the reorganization. Jill, who will be impacted less by the restructuring, offered to be a coach for the other two managers. She got them to brainstorm all the steps needed to make the reorganization a reality.

Here are some questions that can help in this situation:

◆ What are all the steps that need to happen?

◆ When do they need to happen?

◆ What is the best timing for the reorganization?

◆ When do you need to communicate to those involved?

◆ What are biggest challenges?

◆ What contingency plans should be in place?

◆ What is the time line to completion?

◆ What is the plan to minimize confusion and anxiety among the employees?

A coach approach is a valuable tool for thinking through organizational changes thoroughly before committing to them. Coaching also helps managers think through the steps of implementation. A refresher on a coach approach for all the leaders involved would be useful. This will allow managers who lead the rollout of the reorganization can coach peers and employees through the process.

You can supply leaders involved with a list of coaching questions they might use at different stages of the reorganization. Coaching can help reduce the anxiety and loss of productivity caused by employee uncertainty over new roles. And a coach approach gives everyone involved an opportunity to talk through these problems and determine what actions, if any, need to be taken. It might even help mitigate the endless reaction chatter that often accompanies reorganizations and help everyone get back to action.

Ushering in Mergers and Acquisitions

With mergers and acquisitions two or more organizational cultures are involved. With a merger the companies are trying to integrate the cultures. With an acquisition the cultures may remain more or less intact, but some degree of change is inevitable. Coaching helps employees get through these changes by focusing on drawing out the best of both cultures. Coaching says, "You don't have to be wrong so I can be right."

In a merger or an acquisition, lost productivity is inevitable because people must put effort into figuring out how to do their work in the new environment. Coaching gets people unstuck in this situation and validates what they already do. Coaching helps employees figure out how to leverage the newness for benefit (the very reason the merger or acquisition took place). And coaching helps people have new insights so they can combine what they know with people from the new organization to create synergy of ideas.

Maximizing the Impact of Coaching

Coaching can be used beyond just helping solve individual problems or team challenges. Where coaching is used routinely, it can help improve how people work together in general across the organization.

Simplifying Communications

The focus phase of a coach approach gets at the heart of any message that needs to be communicated. A large volume of words doesn't necessarily equate to communication that has a positive impact. You can use a coach approach to ask questions that focus on making concise communication have your desired impact. For more on how to deliver concise messages, check out this skill in Chapter 4. Also see tips for communicating in Chapter 11.

Focusing on Results Through Systems

Large companies tend to have more *systems resources*. A coach approach fosters the development and utilization of these systems because it focuses not just on today but also on the long-term impact of any action. A coaching conversation can surface the fact that a system resource glitch is actually the root of the problem.

def•i•ni•tion

Systems resources are a variety of tools designed to help replicate results by facilitating a standard way of addressing a certain situation. Examples are: a process, database, software tool or website.

Look for simplicity when you use systems rather than using them simply because they are available. Use the evaluation phase of the coach approach to ensure that the system remains valuable.

Stimulating Positive Culture Change

You are not going to change the culture of a huge corporation over-night, even if many people start using a coach approach to do their jobs better. What you can do is start with one part of the organization at a time.

Start with an organization that is very coachable. You can use the following Coachability Index for an Organization to get an idea of whether coaching will work well in a certain organization. You can answer these questions yourself, and you can ask leaders within the organization to answer them as well.

Even those organizations that score in the "not coachable right now" category tend to benefit from taking the assessment. They become exposed to what it takes for coaching to work well in an organization and they start to take steps that move them in the right direction. Next time they are ready to assess coachability, the numbers are likely to have changed.

Coachability Index for an Organization

Just about any organization can benefit from coaching. However, it is not for all organizations. With permission, the following questionnaire was adapted from Coach University's "Client Coachability Index." It can be used to determine if an organization is coachable.

Less   More
True   True

1 2 3 4 5   Managers of all levels of the organization are willing to support coaching through regular participation in individual and group/team coaching sessions.

1 2 3 4 5   This is the right time for the organization to participate in coaching.

1 2 3 4 5   The organization has a history of innovative thinking with regard to all business processes, not just personnel-related processes.

1 2 3 4 5   The organization is willing to focus on strengthening strengths of individuals and not on adding skills where there is no foundation of strength.

1 2 3 4 5   The organization has a reputation of delivering on commitments.

1 2 3 4 5   Time for coaching sessions is not an issue for the organization; coaching is seen as an investment.

1 2 3 4 5   The organization would be willing to put a "contract" in place committing to work with the coach, to support all coaching activities, and to make appropriate organization-wide adjustments that result from individual and group coaching sessions.

1 2 3 4 5   The organization is willing to look at any and every part of the business for improvement.

Less   More
True   True

1 2 3 4 5	The organization has a history of commitment to continuous improvement as evidenced by significant changes that have been successfully implemented.
1 2 3 4 5	The vision of the organization is well understood and embraced at all levels of the organization.
_____	Total Score

Scoring Key

10–20	Not coachable right now.
21–30	Coachable, but ground rules should be put in place and honored!
31–40	Coachable.
41–50	Very coachable; expect great progress with coaching!

Start with parts of the organization that are the most coachable. The positive impact coaching has in one part of organization will inspire staff in other parts of the organizations to want to adopt a coach approach as well.

Sharing Coaching Successes

In large corporation it's often the case that one area is unaware of the positive results of coaching experienced in another part of the organization. Use the size and communication resources of the company to share the successes you experience with a coach approach.

Coaching Cautions _____

Don't assume that others are aware of the good results that come from a coach approach. In fact, the larger the company, the more you can assume that people don't know about your success.

Here are some ways you can share successful coaching results:

◆ Examples of getting unstuck and moving forward on large projects with a coach approach.

◆ New systems that were put in place as a result of a coach approach that might benefit others.

◆ Client testimonials from sales that used a coach approach.

◆ Team projects that were highly successful as a result of a coach approach.

Creating Communities of Practice for Coaching

In a large company you have the benefit of connecting with others who are as interested in honing their coach approach skills as you are. You can start informally by writing an internal blog. Beyond that you can set up a monthly or quarterly conference call with people who are interested in using a coach approach.

When you talk, blog, or meet, what would you talk about?

Share successes, coach one another through challenges, and inform others of techniques you've tried that worked. And if you want to take it even further, your CoP could have a knowledge database where you collect helpful information about how to extend a coach approach to more people, more jobs, more processes, and more systems. You can even invite guest speakers from outside your company to come and inspire your CoP.

Here are some things you can put in your knowledge base for your community to improve your coach approach:

◆ Coaching questions that seem to work really well for particular jobs, divisions, markets, client groups, or levels in the organization. (See Appendix C for a starter set of these.)

◆ How-to information for measuring results of a coach approach that has been successfully communicated to executive leadership in your company.

- Sample operating guidelines for team coaching sorted by different types of teams unique to your company.

- Tips on advanced coaching skills.

- Synopses on the latest in coaching books, leadership books, etc.

If this sounds out of reach for your company, it's not as hard as it sounds. IBM Coaches Network is now a formal CoP that has grown from 3 members to more than 500 members worldwide. It started with a monthly conference call, a small internal database, and a leader who was passionate about fostering a coach approach in the company.

The Least You Need to Know

- Corporate-wide coaching initiatives generally do not work because of subcultures within the company; a small beginning works well.

- You can take advantage of existing communication and training systems to make them work for spreading a coach approach.

- You can use the wide range of corporate systems to evaluate coaching's success.

- Coaching offers an effective means of dealing with reorganization concerns.

Chapter **17**

Coaching Nonprofits and Government Organizations

In This Chapter

- ◆ Understanding the differences in coaching nonprofits versus for-profit businesses
- ◆ Strategic planning for nonprofits and governmental agencies
- ◆ Working with board members in nonprofits
- ◆ Developing a future story
- ◆ Writing grants with a coach approach

Some characteristics of coaching within nonprofits and government organizations overlap with common coaching basics and methodologies presented throughout this book, but some aspects are unique. One challenge is answering the question, "What are we trying to accomplish for whom?" Another important challenge for these organizations is the constant need to juggle precious limited resources. Coaching can be an affordable solution to many of the unique challenges these organizations face.

In this chapter we examine how coaching can help nonprofit and government agencies. You may think you don't have the financial resources for coaching, but coaching is a very low-cost way to improve work in nonprofits. Coaching is about mining for resources that already exist and aren't being used: in boards, in employees, in those who benefit from your services.

Key Coaching Topics

Coaches who have worked with nonprofit and government organizations notice that two main topics consistently come up as focus items:

◆ The need for more effective short-, medium-, and long-term planning.

◆ The need to stretch resources that tend to be limited.

Nonprofits and government organizations can often benefit by gaining greater clarity about the ultimate purpose for the organization. They need to align their plans, goals, and strategies around purpose. Coaching is an excellent tool to make this happen.

If your goal is to serve people, for instance, coaching helps you focus on that goal. If the goal is for the organization to remain financially viable, coaching can help there, too. Coaching can create good business results by helping you increase income, manage expenses, and make wise investments.

Tips & Tools

Habitat for Humanity insists that future owners actively participate in building their own homes. This creates a deeper sense of ownership and pride in the finished product. Coaching creates that same sense of ownership when people participate in decision-making, taking new actions, and self-evaluation.

Basic Planning for the Upcoming Year

A foundation is developing an after-school program targeted at neighborhoods where many at-risk children live. They have developed creative and innovative plans for helping kids become more successful. They learned a lot about what works and what doesn't in the first year. Now it's time to prepare for their second year of operation.

Stan, a board member, realizes they were fueled mostly by passion in the first year, but they need to focus on goals for this second year in order to keep on track. Stan is a vice president at a bank that has adopted a coaching culture. He offers to coach the foundation leaders and staff to help clarify their goals. He starts by leading them in goal setting for the near term, talking with Margaret, the director.

Stan: What do you see yourself accomplishing next year?

Margaret: We reached 100 kids in our program last year. We'd like to open up the program to more kids and offer them more activities next year.

Stan: Can you be more specific?

Margaret: Well, I'd like to see 300 kids involved. We had four options for activities they could do last year. We'd like to have more options, but we don't yet know who will run them.

Stan discussed the need to establish checkpoints to make sure they stay on track to accomplish their goals. After brainstorming for several minutes, they settle on tracking student enrollment and promoting growth by surveying the current students to find out why they got started in the program and what they like best. They also decided to follow up with students who dropped out of the program to learn how to reduce the dropout rate.

Nonprofits and governmental groups have a tendency to say, "I'm headed in the right direction." A coach approach is geared

Tips & Tools

A good rule of thumb in early planning is to work in a 3- to 12-month time frame. Being clear on goals, establishing milestones to track progress, and creating contingency plans for those times when milestones are not met are essentials in nonprofit planning.

to get you to the goal, not just aim toward it. The coach's role is to get the PBC to set goals, make plans, and identify actions that will achieve their plans.

Stan coached the director to determine how they'd know when they arrived at the goal and to evaluate how successful they were during the process.

The coach might ask these additional questions in the planning process:

◆ Which goals are within reach?

◆ Which are probably out of reach?

◆ What criteria set them apart?

◆ How will you know you're successful?

Looking Ahead Two to Three Years

About halfway through the year Margaret reported to the board the foundation needed more space and equipment because enrollment was rising slightly ahead of projections. During a coaching session after the meeting Stan asked Margaret several questions:

◆ Where do you see yourself in two to three years?

◆ What types of financial needs will you have during that time frame?

◆ What will your staffing needs be?

◆ What about space and equipment?

◆ What are some potential sources for providing for those needs?

◆ Who can help you obtain those resources?

◆ What obstacles may get in your way?

◆ What data do you need to make informed decisions about the future?

The process of answering these questions helped Margaret develop a three-year plan for growth. She realized that she didn't really know

where to find the information she should be assessing in order to anticipate needs and plan intelligently for the next three years. Many of the
questions that helped Margaret also apply to a government office to
help with strategic planning.

Coaching Cautions

If Stan came in and said, "Here's how you need to plan," and
based his advice on his banking experience, it would not be nearly
effective. Not only is planning at a bank different from planning an after-
school program, but coaching Margaret to come up with her own solutions is far more effective in the long run than telling her what to do.

Strategic planning helps prevent the need for asking for more money
every six months. Growing pains are common with small nonprofits
as they serve more people. Strategic planning takes out some of the
guesswork and provides information that can be used in soliciting funds
and writing grants as well as in the daily operation of the agency.

Leaders may be so involved with the daily operations, they don't look
up to see what's ahead. The benefit of using a coach approach is it can
remind you to take some time to look forward to the future.

Strategic planning is different from short-term planning in that you're
starting to get into less familiar territory. Whatever your vision for
the project, you can find multiple paths to reach your goal. Without a
two- to three-year year plan, your actions could seem disjointed. You
may try several different strategies and not settle on any one. A coach
approach can help leaders pick a strategy and stick with it.

In government offices the strategy may change as new administrations
are elected and policies change. Coaching is a great tool for dealing
with these transitions. Coaching helps people look at where they've
been as well as where they are going.

A coach approach has several additional benefits during times of transition. Coaching helps you keep tabs on where you are on the path of
transition, and it can help foster an attitude of rolling with the punches
to keep going.

Vision for the Next 10 to 15 Years

At a fund-raising banquet one of the major donors approached Margaret to congratulate her on the success she'd had over the last two years. He presented her with a check for a large donation and asked her where she saw the project going in the next 15 years.

Margaret said, "We want to keep doing the same good work." She later realized that she had no concrete long-term goals or visions beyond that. The donor asked her to think about what the future might hold and get back with him.

A couple of weeks after the banquet, Stan and Margaret met for lunch. Stan asked her how she thought the banquet went. Margaret said that she felt good about it but continued to be disturbed by the donor's question about plans 10 to 15 years out. "Should I have that kind of plan? It's hard enough to plan for three years. How do you plan for 15?"

Stan asked for permission to coach her on this topic and explained how helpful it would be to paint a picture of what the organization would look like 10 to 15 years down the road.

> **Another Perspective**
>
> In her book *The Path* (Hyperion, 1996), Laurie Beth Jones spells out a simple process that can be used to guide people through developing a compelling mission statement and vision for the future. It is a popular resource for nonprofits.

Stan begins: "I can see some benefits for having a vision of what you see the project doing in 10 to 15 years, but it's more important for *you* to see some benefits. How do you think a compelling vision of what the future could be might help you?"

Margaret thought about what life might be like in 10 to 15 years. Her future story included a vision about who they would serve, expansion into many more neighborhoods, details about the kinds of programs they would offer, and how the organization would be perpetuated when she stepped down.

As she began to share her vision, Stan said, "Think about what it will take to get there. What new parts of the project will be put in place to make that happen? We aren't talking about long-range planning. It's more like organized dreaming than it is planning."

Margaret got excited about her dream casting, something she'd really never thought about before. Before this conversation, she had not really thought about a future story.

You can use a compelling picture of the future with a coach approach. It can help you determine what steps to take and what steps to avoid, because when making decisions you can ask yourself, or the person you're coaching, *Does this action support my future or detract from it?* The story of your future can serve as both a compass and an encouragement if things aren't going well at the moment. Instead of getting discouraged, you can hold on to that picture and remind yourself that the problem you're currently facing is just a short-term glitch. The vision for the future is still intact.

Another Perspective

"The best picture has not yet been painted; the greatest poem is still missing; the mightiest novel remains to be written; the divinest music has not been conceived even by Bach."

—Lincoln Steffens (1866–1936), American journalist and author

Once you create a picture of the future, you'll probably find yourself making significant progress in that direction in only a few months or years. This forward progress would probably not have happened if you hadn't been prompted to envision the agency's life in 10 to 15 years.

Making the Most of Your Money

A key activity for nonprofits and government entities is to manage limited resources. It's easy for leaders and employees to develop a scarcity mentality, and it shows up in your attitude and impacts your work if allowed to run rampant.

Funding is a constant struggle with most nonprofits and government agencies. While coaching can't magically create new funding, it costs little to try and usually improves efficiency and results. Gains can translate into money saved or more success stories, which can be leveraged to bring in more donations or funding.

Coaching your team around the topic of budgets may generate new ideas for saving money. It certainly will get you further than any suggestion box ever did. Your team has untapped brainpower that coaching can harness to create synergy with ideas from other people.

Consider these related coaching questions:

- What are the major budget hurdles we can expect this quarter?

- What patterns of cash flow have you noticed?

- What patterns have you seen in donations from small donors? Large donors?

- What adjustments to our expenses are possible during slack times?

- What can we do to smooth out the effects of fluctuation in funding and expenses? Who can help us in this process?

- What actions should we take? How will we divide the actions among the team members?

- When can we expect these actions to be accomplished?

Coaching Cautions

Listen for a scarcity mentality in your coaching conversations. If the person being coached (PBC) is already convinced there will never be enough, he or she will have a hard time meeting his or her goals. The mental shift to "there is enough and it's a matter of finding it" will help tremendously.

Coaching could be used in fund-raising and conversations with major donors and foundation directors.

The Coach Approach to Grants

Grants are a major source of funding for nonprofits. The director of a nonprofit organization is often saddled with the responsibility of grant planning and writing.

The entire system of grants can be a daunting process. It is full of unknowns about the goals of the granting agency, the criteria for approval, and the myriad systems it uses to announce opportunities, accept applications, and make awards. What is the coach approach to getting and using grant money?

Coaching your leadership team or being coached can help you gain clarity on the process and not feel overwhelmed by it. Consider this illustration.

Dale, the director of a nonprofit retreat center, presented 15 different opportunities for grants to his board and staff. They brainstormed which grants they should apply for and what to write into the grant justifications. Dale's coaching questions included:

◆ What elements of these grants mesh with what we do?

◆ Which are congruent with our goals?

◆ What risks are involved?

◆ What will we need to change in our operations to meet the requirements?

◆ How far is this request from our normal operations?

◆ How can each one help us?

The team identified several of the grants as being out of the scope or purpose of the retreat center and decided to focus on the eight grants with the best fit. Then, as the team coaching session progressed, Liz, one of the team members asked, "How do we want to prioritize these?" She felt comfortable in asking a coaching question in the meeting because a coach approach prevailed throughout the organization.

Liz's question kicked off another round of discussion about how to approach the task of actually writing the grant proposals. The team sorted the grants by value to the organization and by deadline. Dale reminded the team of all the other work that has to keep going, and they began to flesh out ways they could prepare the proposals without negatively impacting their other work.

Ultimately they decided to use the services of a grant-writing agency to help. The level of detail they were able to provide to the grant writer helped keep those costs to manageable levels. Dale worked closely with the grant writer but still had time to manage the organization.

Managing grants can involve great levels of detail concerning purchases allowed under the grant, how spending is documented, and reporting required by the granting agency. The director of an organization is ultimately responsible for this work, but coaching his team can create new insights for how to manage these tasks efficiently and enable team members to plan actions to support the director in this effort.

The director can coach his accountant or financial team and purchasing person to develop processes that support grant management as an integrated part of their routine jobs. The director can get coaching from board members or the team on how to manage the proposal writing process.

The director might ask questions like these:

- How efficiently is the money being used?

- How is meeting the requirements of this grant impacting your work?

- What outcomes are we seeing that will help us evaluate future grants?

- What can you do to support managing these grants without negatively affecting the other work you do?

Circumstances frequently change between the time grants are made and the completion of the funding cycle. The needs of the organization may change significantly for many reasons, including loss of major equipment, vehicles, or personnel changes. Existing grants are unlikely to be flexible enough to allow the director to shift funding easily. So what can the director do?

If you are a board member for this nonprofit, you can coach the director on these problems using questions like these:

- How different are your needs now than when you wrote the grant?

- What are your options for dealing with the change?

- Who can help you clarify the options acceptable by the granting agency?

- How much leeway do you have in shifting funding?

- What plans do you need to put into place to deal with this issue?

The evaluation phase for grant funding is also important for nonprofits and government groups. Here are some questions you can use:

What can you learn from this experience to help plan for future contingencies?

◆ How well did you do in managing the grant?

◆ What will your report back to the granting agency contain?

◆ What criteria will you use in selecting future grants?

◆ What processes will you use in managing future grants?

The director and the team can be much more concrete in how to approach future grant opportunities if they carefully evaluate their past experiences.

It's Not in My Control

When you manage or work in a government office or a nonprofit agency, many things are out of your control. Funding is limited. Government agencies are constrained by guidelines and rules that are often more narrowly defined than in the business world. But people who work in these areas usually think they have far less control than they actually do. In reality, those who lead nonprofits and government offices have a lot of control.

Everyone deals with situations that are out of their control at times. You can use coaching strategies like those you would use when someone feels defeated or stuck by things not in his or her control. Questions include:

◆ What *is* in your control? (The answer can't be "nothing.")

◆ Who is in control? How can you talk to them?

◆ What can you say to them?

◆ What are their top priorities?

◆ If you were in control, what would you do? How would you operate?

◆ How much of those things can you do with the level of authority you currently have?

If you really have little or no control and have no prospects for gaining any control, you will feel invalidated and perhaps should not be in that position. As a manager in a government office, you may ask, "What level of lack of control would prompt you to leave?" This discussion may lead employees to realize they actually do have more control than they think they have.

> ### Coaching Cautions
>
> Asking an employee about what would prompt him or her to leave carries the risk that the person may actually decide to find another job. If this happens, it will ultimately benefit you because that person would not have been productive in his or her position.

Nonprofit and government employees may feel stuck in a system with few resources. Coaching can give hope. It's inexpensive, and it doesn't depend on approval from Congress or elected officials.

Mobilizing Volunteers

Nonprofits rely heavily on volunteers to achieve their goals. Challenges with volunteers include finding them, keeping them, and making sure they are doing good work. Leaders of nonprofits can use a coach approach to help get their volunteers to be focused and moving forward.

Here are some tips for using a coach approach with volunteers:

Introduce volunteers to the concept of coaching early in their involvement with the agency. One of your first coaching questions might be to ask them how their volunteering helps them achieve their personal calling.

Make it clear that you believe everyone has more potential than is currently being used and introduce the coach approach as a way to draw out that potential for the good of the nonprofit's mission. If your volunteers' participation is sporadic, ask: "What is inhibiting your participation? What strategy can you put in place to minimize the interruptions?"

If quality issues arise concerning the work of volunteers, ask them how they would evaluate their efforts and what criteria they would use to determine whether they were successful or not. Based on their answers, ask them what actions could be taken to improve results by one point on a scale from 1 to 10. Creating a climate of self-evaluation will help keep the quality level high.

Use the connect phase of a coach approach to get to know volunteers personally. Set a goal of coaching each volunteer on a regular basis. Based on the size of your organization, that might be once a week, month, quarter, or year. But in any case, spending time listening and helping them move forward in their own lives communicates they are valued. People who feel valued are more willing to join you in your mission.

Encourage volunteers through regular expressions of appreciation. These don't need to be big expressions as much as consistent expressions. Pay particular attention to encouraging volunteers who use a coach approach with the people you serve in the mission of your nonprofit.

Volunteers are an unpredictable source of help, but by coaching them you can increase their productivity and usefulness to your organization.

Tips & Tools

If your nonprofit is facing challenges in daily activities, don't forget to include volunteers in team coaching sessions.

Clarity on Constituents

Nonprofits and government groups commonly get fuzzy about whom they are trying to serve. This is especially true when the nonprofit was founded years ago to serve a particular need and lots of transition has happened through the years. Sometimes the need changes or may even disappear altogether (Have you heard of an initiative to help people in the United States with polio lately?) Agencies can lose sight of who they are trying to serve. A coach approach can be used to help you focus on the present and get really clear about the audience you are trying to serve and what will serve them best.

The people being served by nonprofit organizations and government agencies have untapped potential and might have many more answers than they currently realize. Coaching can help nonprofits that are focused on helping the homeless; people dealing with addictions; and abused, incarcerated, and needy people to help themselves.

Coaching is not the only tool nonprofits and government agencies have for helping people; it's just another one that can be used along with others. As you improve the results you are getting with the people you help, coaching will help the viability of your nonprofit. Coaching can also help elected officials and heads of nonprofits deal with challenges that come from the general public: town meetings, differences in public opinions, office management, public relations, campaigns, and strategic planning, to name just a few examples.

The Least You Need to Know

- ◆ Financial planning, funding, and responsibility are crucial to nonprofits even though the bottom line is not money.

- ◆ Coaching is a great tool for government employees going through transitions.

- ◆ Coaching can help government employees discover where they have control in a world that often seems to allow them little control.

- ◆ Coaching volunteers makes them feel valued.

Chapter 18

Coaching Faith-Based Organizations and Churches

In This Chapter

◆ Coaching volunteers in the church to make decisions and take action

◆ Shifting the minister's role from telling to asking

◆ Preventing minister burnout

◆ Learning from powerful questions Jesus asked

◆ Helping people grow at their own pace

Coaching is about connecting with people. Faith-based organizations want to connect with people. So coaching for excellence is as relevant for faith-based organizations as it is for any business. Just as coaching helps people at work do their jobs better, coaching also helps people improve their ministries.

Many of the topics already presented in this book also apply to faith-based organizations, but churches and other faith-based organizations benefit from some unique coaching approaches that may not be obvious. This chapter focuses on what's unique in coaching people in churches.

Ministry Leaders as Coaches

Throughout this chapter, "ministry leader" will be used as the generic term for pastors, board members, staff, elders, deacons, lay leaders, denominational leaders, leaders of faith-based nonprofits, and anyone else wanting to influence others in the life of faith-based organizations. Ministry leaders can benefit both by being coached and by coaching others. The following story illustrates both benefits.

Just about everybody, including the people in his church, other ministers, and denominational leaders, saw Matt Johnson as a successful pastor. Matt knows more about contemporary culture than just about any 40-year-old around. When he heard about coaching, he wanted to explore it by getting a couple of days of training. He hired a coach for several months, thinking it was worth the expense to experience being coached. He brought two topics to his coaching conversations: achieving life-work balance and maximizing sermon preparation time.

Another Perspective

Read *Christ-Centered Coaching: 7 Benefits for Ministry Leaders* (Chalice Press, 2006), by Jane Creswell for more information on the benefits of applying a coach approach to ministry.

Matt experienced a fair amount of success on these two topics so he decided to talk with his coach about a big challenge he was facing in the church, an opening of a pastoral position. He wanted to attract and select the person God wanted in that position. The process of finding this person was becoming increasingly stressful for Matt for two reasons: with the position vacant, Matt had more work to do, work that wasn't necessarily the best fit for him. And everyone in the church had an opinion about who should fill this position.

His coach asked, "What are the main challenges in filling this position?" Matt responded that a committee had the bulk of the work to do in finding the right person. The person the committee found would have to be approved by others in the church. Yet he still felt the burden because people were coming to him for answers.

As he voiced his answer, the "aha" came. "Hey, I could use coaching. I could coach the committee and other staff ministers about what they are doing. That way I don't have to have all the answers. And everyone involved will have responsibility for the work to be done."

The hiring team responded well to Matt's coaching. They also felt more responsible for the selection decision and were, consequently, more engaged in ensuring his success.

Even though the story is about a pastor, all ministry leaders can benefit from applying coaching skills to coachable moments. For ministry leaders, there is extra importance placed on seizing those moments because the new insights gained in ministry-related coaching conversations becomes a building block in the faith development of the PBC (person being coached).

Applying a Coach Approach to Ministry

Each of the phases of a coaching conversation has a unique application in ministry.

Connect. Ministers already tend to connect well with their parishioners. A different emphasis is needed for connection in coaching, though. When coaching is not the goal, the purpose of connection is to set the stage for the minister to tell someone the answer. The level of trust required for this type of connection may be at a fairly shallow level, just enough to keep people present to hear the telling.

With coaching, your goal is to draw an answer out of a person. That requires a different way

Another Perspective

"Coaching is a powerful way of relating that can have a positive impact for the kingdom of God."

—*Coaching for Christian Leaders: A Practical Guide,* (Chalice Press, 2007) by Linda J. Miller and Chad W. Hall.

of connecting. To be a coach you must be willing to accept the answers the person being coached gives. This willingness to accept the answers given and the discoveries people have requires a much deeper level of trust because the coach (pastor or other leader) must trust people enough to let them make their own discoveries. This is a biblical model, a model of how God trusts us to follow him of our own free will.

Example: a ministry team that you are a part of faces roadblocks due to a shortage of volunteers. In a telling mode, you would just determine how to solve the problem and inform everyone of your decision. In a coaching mode, you would solicit and accept the team's suggestions even if they were different from your preferred solution. During a team meeting you ask:

What are our major obstacles to getting enough volunteers? What is the perspective of the volunteer? What is under our control?" Discovery questions like these may lead the team to brainstorm ways to get more volunteers, trim noncore activities, or help make their existing workers more effective.

Focus. While businesses have a built-in focus—profit—many ministry settings lack clear focus. People will find a coach approach refreshing as you encourage them to place greater emphasis on focus and clarity. Focus is more than just creating a mission statement. It is a process of regularly blocking distractions to attend to core needs.

Discover. Expecting others to come up with answers to problems requires asking the kind of questions that prompt new thoughts, new perspectives, and new insights in the person being coached. In ministry the temptation is to ask leading questions, but that's manipulative and has no place in coaching. The discover step is critical in ministry coaching because people will refer to the discover step as where God speaks or where they learn something about God's direction.

Consider the situation where a young church member is deciding whether to pursue a career in ministry. Asking "What about this path appeals to you?" or "What discoveries have you made about yourself that inform this decision?" will elicit much more honest self-assessment and opening up than a leading question or advice about your own experiences.

Act. Coaching requires people to take personal responsibility to identify actions and actually follow through with them. This is no different in ministry, but it's not the normal way of operating there. Interestingly enough, ministries want to use volunteers, but the usual systems of telling require little or no personal action beyond just showing up for a specific task. Coaching is a way to get more people to take action. This step is so key to coaching in churches that we will specifically discuss mobilizing volunteers later in this chapter.

Evaluate. Make sure the person being coached is the one doing the evaluating, otherwise it will seem judgmental. The temptation in both ministry and business is for the person coaching to be the evaluator. It's even more important in ministry to get person being coached to check his or her own results so the coach is not tempted to judge.

Mobilizing Volunteers

Gina is pastor to college students in her church. She makes sure they have excellent Bible study, retreats, and other activities. She finds ways for them to connect to others in the church. And she gets students involved in volunteer missions and ministry both to reach out to others and to help them grow in their faith. Gina has found that through ministry students get a handle on what faith is from a practical perspective.

She began to notice, however, that the same set of students did everything, and those who volunteered were, not surprisingly, the best students. Because the point of the volunteer ministries is to help students grow in faith, if only a small number participate, only a few are growing.

Gina wanted to get others more involved, especially edge people, those on the margins. She noticed that her normal way of getting people involved was to beg and pester. She realized that she was repelling the very students she wanted to reach. In fact, because they didn't want her to ask them to volunteer, some had stopped coming to any of the student events.

She realized, through being coached, that she could use coaching with students to get them involved and, ultimately, to help them grow as Christians. As she began to talk with students and to look for coachable moments, she learned that those who were not volunteering were often dealing with study problems, roommate relationships, sororities and fraternities, and projects that weren't working. As she listened, students began to trust her and to talk about their faith. Without forcing the issue of volunteering or begging them to participate, the students often had the "aha" that one way they could grow in their faith was to volunteer to help with missions and ministries. As a result of her coaching, students focused on some issues, discovered their own resources to deal with them, and made decisions to take actions including volunteering for ministry.

Gina's coaching resulted in more students becoming involved because of their own "aha" moments rather than because they felt coerced. There is a connection between coaching people and letting them make self-discovery at their own pace. That foundation of self-discovery dovetails well with what a faith community is trying to do. In matters of faith, people are best left to their own pace, their willingness and readiness for understanding, and their level of personal responsibility for the actions they decide to take.

Consider these suggestions for mobilizing volunteers with a coach approach:

Get volunteers together for a basic coaching skills refresher. Have them pair up and coach each other for 10-minute sessions and then switch. This builds confidence for coaching others and shows how much coaching is valued in your ministry.

Before each volunteer project begins, remind the volunteers that they are gifted, intelligent, and have plenty of the answers that are needed for the projects. For example, if a volunteer team is planning a community-wide service project day, demonstrate the value of coaching by coaching the planning team as they gather information about the soup kitchens, food banks, and homeless shelters that will be served that day. On the day of the event, coach the volunteers to develop options for solving any of the challenges

Tips & Tools

Operation Inasmuch is a proven model for organizing community-wide service days. The whole process aligns well with utilizing a coach approach. Check it out online at www.operationinasmuch.com.

they may face. After the event, coach the various volunteer leaders to develop "lessons learned" from the experience that can be used for the next event.

Introduce the concept that the leader will ask discovery questions and ask for specific action plans based on new insights. This gains their agreement to participate in the coaching process and unlocks new insights. Always ask what the new insights were and what actions they plan to take.

Have a system in place for celebrating the progress that is made, always acknowledging that the ideas came from the volunteers and not the leaders.

Communicating a Compelling Message

Chapter 11 deals with the many ways coaching helps improve communication in business. This section illustrates ways coaching can help ministry leaders communicate—including creating and delivering a compelling sermon.

Pastor Nathan Howell was participating in coaching and realized that he really wanted people in the congregation to get the same kind of "aha's" that he was getting in his coaching sessions. So he started learning how to incorporate a coach approach in his sermon preparation and delivery.

Here's the process he decided to use: in his sermons he talked about a passage of Scripture and then asked discovery questions to help congregants discover ways to apply the Scripture in their own lives and to take appropriate action. He carefully constructed open-ended questions to promote these new insights. He closed the service by asking what new actions people would take based on their new insights. As people left they would often tell him about their insights and what actions they planned to take.

These coaching questions can promote better communication within the church:

◆ What is the main purpose of our church/ministry?

◆ How can you best convey that purpose to the members/ participants?

- What form of communication is most effective for ministry?

- How often do communications need to happen?".

Here are some coaching questions that can be asked about better communication outside the church: "What is the key message you want people outside the church to know about you?, When/where/how does that need to be communicated?, Who is your target audience?"

Faith-Based Culture Considerations

Some faith-based cultures are engrained in having leaders do the thinking and then telling everyone else the answers. If this is the case, you might make the assumption that coaching will not work in that culture, but you might be surprised to find that coaching can be the tool that will start to bring out the best thinking from everyone, not just the leaders.

Often parishioners think of the church staff as the ones who do the ministry. After all, that's what they're paid to do. This can cause the ministry staff to take on the burden of doing all the work of the church. This aspect of church culture can prompt the staff to avoid coaching because they think that if they ask questions instead of providing answers, they will be perceived as not doing the job they are being paid to do. With this perspective, it doesn't take long before the staff is overwhelmed and wondering why the parishioners are not participating in ministry.

When this happens the staff needs to shift their thinking about the purpose of their jobs. Ephesians 4:11–13 talks about ministers as "equipping the saints for ministry." What if you define *equipping* as drawing out the full potential of everyone in the church? What if *equipping* meant getting the whole church to the point of taking personal responsibility to act. What if it included training the laity to evaluate their own results against the standards of Scripture? That could be a refreshing way to have the staff contribute value worth paying for and still get the whole church involved in ministry according to their giftedness.

Faith is such a personal experience that the existence of someone's faith is hard to see or measure. That can cause people to avoid asking questions that are too probing or could be perceived as nosey. Coaching honors the differences in people, in their ways of thinking and in their choice of next steps. It can be the tool that allows people to be at different levels of their faith journey and still help them make progress along the way. If you get pushy or have preconceived notions of what the PBC should be thinking or doing, the PBC will sense that and may be inhibited from coming up with new discoveries and actions. Trust the coaching process, honor the differences in each person—even the different levels of faith development—and trust that God is at work in each person to provide help with insights and motivation for action that is needed.

Faith and Business

As much as people like to think of the spiritual side of churches and faith-based ministries, each of those institutions is also a business, and those who are employed in such endeavors must also deal with business practicalities. For most ministry leaders business skills are outside their core strengths.

Fortunately, coaching can help ministry leaders develop time and money management skills so that they are good stewards of the church's resources. Here are a few issues that are particular to churches and other faith-based organizations.

Tips & Tools

Ministers and leaders of faith based organizations who are not natural business managers can coach other staffers who are more adept in this area to take on greater leadership roles. Ask a volunteer "What are the top three ways you would like to contribute?" and you may be surprised at the answer. You may be missing hidden potential.

Managing Fluctuating Funds

Use a coach approach to help church staff deal with fluctuating funds. In this case, you might be a board member, an elder, or a regional leader for a denomination. You could ask the chair of the finance committee: "What kind of reserves do we need?" or, "What processes need to be in place so we aren't constantly asking for money or talking about money?"

Another way to deal with financial issues is for church ministry leaders to use coaching skills with parishioners. As parishioners are coached, they will learn that the outcome of coaching is personal responsibility, and they will have a deeper appreciation for steady funding.

With a coaching culture members may become more involved with giving. In most churches, 80 percent of the giving is done by 20 percent of the members. With a coaching culture more members may give and become involved in volunteer work, thus reducing some of the church's current expenditures. Sermons about stewardship can move from being thinly veiled guilt trips to a process of creating clarity about what really matters most to parishioners. Picture small groups with one member in each group with some basic coach training.

Here are some questions that might promote clarity and focus about members' priorities:

◆ What are the most important things this church provides that can't be found anywhere else?

◆ What would the ideal budget for this church look like to you?

◆ What can we do this year to work toward those goals?"

Maintaining Membership

When a coaching culture prevails in a church, members have greater ownership and feel more empowered. When they feel empowered, they are more likely to remain members. Church leaders can create a coaching culture by training the pastor(s) and staff to use coaching with members.

Be intentional about creating a coaching culture. Several churches now have coaching services to help members move forward in their lives and faith. Incorporate coaching in women's ministry, men's ministry, and youth ministry.

Another Perspective

People who are further along in faith maturity are most dissatisfied with the organized church, as documented in REVEAL, a Willow Creek Community Church study published in 2007. They speculate that both being coached and coaching others will be a solution for those most dissatisfied.

Generating Growth and Furthering Your Mission

A church with a coaching culture is more likely to stay focused on its mission and calling, thus making more progress in meeting ministry goals. A church that's focused on realizing its full potential is attractive to potential members. It might be a way of getting people interested in the life of your church and ministries.

Benefits of Coaching in Christian Organizations

Everyone benefits from coaching in organizations, and Christian organizations are no exception. The PBCs benefit because they develop new insights and their own plan of action. The ministry leader benefits because they are able to equip others (from Ephesians 4:11–13) and multiply the impact of the ministry. The Christian organization benefits because more ministry is taking place and all constituents, including financial sponsors, can see the progress that is being made.

Aligning Everyone with Giftedness

People in the church experience ministry fatigue or burnout. It can be even more frustrating in church than in business because of the strength of people's religious convictions. Ministry leaders know what the Christian Bible says about giftedness and working out of their giftedness, but many people take on responsibilities that they are able to do but which deplete them. When they realize that this is the case, they have several options. They can learn to do the same task by approaching it through their own gifts or strengths, or they can partner with others to see that the job is done without exhausting the ministry leadership.

The minister who aligns skills with strengths increases his own energy level, experiences a renewed passion for his work, and is able to help volunteers find ministry roles based on their strengths and gifts as well. Too often in the church people are asked to take a job because a hole needs to be filled. Those enlisting workers often know little about the person they are pressing into service. Leaders who understand the Strengths (and gifts) vs. Skills model can coach volunteers to ensure that they are maximizing their effectiveness by working in a role that fits them well.

Clarifying the Mission

Many churches today have a mission statement. Some have it posted on a wall somewhere, and some actually orient their limited resources around that mission. Coaching ministry leaders who in turn use coaching skills with their members not only helps everyone stay more focused on the ministry, it also makes more progress in fulfilling that ministry. The more people who are coached, the greater benefits will accrue because as members focus on the mission they will discover ways they can make a difference. They will take responsibility and take action to move the church forward in its mission.

Preventing Burnout in Ministry Leaders

Ministry leader burnout is a big issue. Part of this comes from leaders feeling the need to do everything instead of leading others to do it. Here's an inspirational story of how coaching can help turn burnout into vital ministry. It points out how the church can help ministers by making coaches available to them.

Frank had been a pastor for more than 25 years. What started out as a desire to preach and take care of people had turned into unending weeks of settling disputes in committee meetings and too much time away from family. Disputes were so petty that he began to wonder if he was having any impact at all in his church. He'd even been wondering if he should leave the pastorate. He talked to his regional leader who had been coaching him for several months. If he was going to leave what he had done for so long, he needed help with the transition.

While talking with his coach, he remembered why he got into ministry in the first place. Answering questions the coach asked, he realized that changing jobs might not solve his problem. His coach suggested that they look at root problems to ensure that he would not take those into a new job. His coach asked, "How will you approach a new position in a different way to avoid these same challenges?" This question led to the "aha" of Frank's asking himself, *What could I do now in this job so things turn out differently and I won't have to leave?*

> **Coaching Cautions**
>
> Senior pastors should have a coach from outside the congregation so they will feel free to answer questions openly. One way to accomplish this is to exchange coaching with other senior pastors or ministry leaders you trust.

He listed things that, if he decided to stay, would have to change to make him feel more productive. He discovered that the church had grown so much that it needed an administrative pastor, and he was not gifted in administration. The church, together with the staff, figured out how to bring on an administrative pastor over the course of the next three years.

Another key discovery was that he had spent 25 years trying to make an impact on the community. That included joining the Rotary Club, becoming friends with the major, and doing many other things that were not in his job description and that kept him away from time with his family. He realized that if he left the church he would want to be more involved with community activities, like being on the city council.

His coach asked: "How can you be involved in your community and still be a pastor?" Frank decided to take this point up with the personnel committee during his next review. When he expressed his desire to be even more involved in the community, they asked, "How will a change in what you do benefit our church and its mission?" He pointed out that when he and other church members were involved in community activities they worked with many people who had no connection with church. That meant their church was reaching more people in the community.

The church started creating new ministries to minister in their own community. The first new ministry was a literacy program for kids who needed help. That literacy project would not have happened if the pastor had not said, "I've always wanted to be involved with community."

Coaching kept Frank in ministry and helped him find his focus again. Many more benefits came from his involvement in community that no one could have envisioned. And it all happened because he had the courage to express his personal desires and his vision for the church and community.

Reenergizing the Laity

With coaching, you can expect new and different ideas to come from the people in the pews. And the ideas they generate are likely to succeed because they are more motivated to participate in making their own ideas become reality.

Tips & Tools _____

Think of the biblical verse John 13: 1–17, in which Jesus washes the feet of his disciples, as a model for the role the leader will take as a coach. The leader-coach takes on the role of a servant to enable volunteers to move forward in their journey but not to do the walking for them. You can think of the dirt that is being washed off of feet as all the obstacles that need to be overcome in order to achieve progress.

A common question in coaching conversations, though not always in church settings, is, "What activities do you need to keep doing, start doing, or stop doing in order to achieve your goals?" It's the "What do you need to stop?" question that is not asked enough in church settings. You may need to cease current activities if they are draining the congregation of its energy. Ministry leaders can promote discovery with questions like: "If this church had no activities at all which ones would you start first?" or "What ministries are you involved with that energize you most?" or "What criteria should we use to determine whether to pursue a new ministry?"

Experiencing God Through Larger-Than-Life Goals

If coaching continues in ministry settings over a long period of time, topics tend to progress through three different phases.

In the first phase, coaching conversations start out addressing day-to-day challenges like staffing issues, project snags, and personality clashes. For example a pastor may need to coach a staff member who is struggling with arrangements needed for an upcoming two-day conference at the church. Questions like: "What are the highest priority tasks for you tomorrow?" and "Who else may be able to help you with this?" may be common.

As trust is built and familiarity with the coaching process increases, conversations start touching on deeper issues. The topics can turn toward life-work balance, purpose for one's life, and changing direction. Questions may include: "How you can have greater impact in helping others?" and "What are the next steps you need to take for your own faith development?"

The third phase involves larger-than-life goals. A parishioner may sense God is leading her toward a goal that is so large she can't see how it could possibly be accomplished. She knows she has strengths in this area but recognizes she can't accomplish them alone. A minister may coach her toward discovering the scope of the goal, establishing an action plan, and understanding how God's guidance and participation will be essential to achieve the goal.

Coaching Cautions

Using coaching as a tool in a faith-based organization doesn't mean you should abandon other tools. Coaching can become a tool to use in addition to mentoring, spiritual development, and pastoral counseling.

The Least You Need to Know

◆ When ministry leaders use coaching, they don't have to have all the answers.

◆ Coaching can lead more people in churches to take action and ownership.

◆ Coaching can be an attractive characteristic of a church, attracting new members and stimulating growth.

◆ Coaching can reduce burnout among both vocational and volunteer ministry leaders.

Coaching as Catalyst

Over several years Tony saw the great impact coaching had on his business as well as other areas of his life. It really was a catalyst for change. He learned that coaching is just one tool—a great tool—that meshes well with other resources for making a difference, especially in the workplace. Even though he'd heard some stories about the pains the company went through to set up a coaching culture, clearly it had paid off. He always volunteered now to help bring the new hires up to speed in his company's culture of coaching.

In Part 5 you'll learn how coaching can be woven throughout the processes of a company and how the coaching culture impacts the company's bottom line. You'll also find out how coaching can be sustained for the long haul.

Chapter 19

Coaching as a Part of a Process

In This Chapter

- ◆ Applying a coach approach to written processes
- ◆ Analyzing processes for a coach approach using the hourglass test
- ◆ Using a coach approach with Lean Six Sigma and other quality management processes
- ◆ Engaging younger generations of adults using a coach approach to processes

Throughout this book, the term coaching has been used to refer to a conversation between two or more people. But people don't operate in a vacuum; instead, they follow company-approved processes, including everything guidelines for submitting travel expense reimbursement forms to personnel procedures to quality assurance certification steps. To really infiltrate a culture with coaching, those processes must be designed to support coaching.

This is a key step to developing a coaching culture. More coaching happens when the processes are supportive of a coach approach; and therefore, more of the benefits of coaching can be realized.

Coaching in a Process Instead of a Conversation

Organizations get their work done by having people follow processes. Some are formal and written down; others are informal and passed down as general knowledge about how work gets done. Some employees work with processes all the time, and some people work with them from time to time. Examples of types of processes also include financial accounting and auditing policies, the steps for developing a new product or business, and the standards from performing management responsibilities.

With a good process in place, everyone can anticipate what will happen and how it will happen, and they have a standard way of communicating about their work. In a large company processes are essential for employees throughout the business to communicate clearly with one another.

Some written processes—the process for handling purchases requiring large sums of money, for instance—have little wiggle room. In those cases the process is so restrictive it doesn't allow for a coach approach to work through the process without a change in the written process document. To try to incorporate a coach approach into such a process will be viewed by management as incorrectly following the process.

Tips & Tools

A common mind-set about processes is they are inhibiting or restrictive. To develop a coaching mind-set about processes, ask "How can a coach approach be used with this process to produce better than expected results?"

Other processes have a lot of leeway; they are more like guidelines than rulebooks. An example of this might be the process for how leaders select and develop their successors. The loose structure of these processes allow for a lot of variation in implementation. In the latter case, two people following the same process may do things very differently and still do the process correctly in the eyes of management. In that leeway is where you can use a coach approach without having to change the written process.

Evaluating Processes

The purpose of this section is to show you how you can evaluate a process to see if it lends itself to a coach approach. By looking at a process through the lens of a coach approach, you can determine if coaching will partner well with the process.

Here's an example of a process that most companies have: the employee evaluation process. It's one of several HR functions that are process-oriented. You can evaluate other processes in the same way.

Although details differ from company to company, the evaluation process at most companies goes something like this:

1. Figure out what you want the employee to do during the year.

2. Have a conversation with the employee about the goals.

3. Give informal feedback during the year.

4. Write an annual evaluation of the employee's performance.

5. Have a conversation with the employee to provide feedback.

6. Give the performance documents to HR to keep on file.

Before you can evaluate a process, you have to determine who is the coach and who is the person being coached (PBC). For the employee evaluation process example, the coach is the boss and the PBC is the employee. That may seem obvious here, but a complex process may have multiple coaches and multiple PBCs.

Let's evaluate how this process fares when matched up with the five phases of the coach approach.

Connect. The process already has a design that includes opportunities for the coach (boss) and the PBC (employee) to talk and connect during the process. You can strengthen this step by being intentional about using a coach approach in each conversation throughout the year.

Focus. This process is already pretty strong on focus. You can strengthen it further by using coaching as a tool for getting focus on midpoint deliverables. The goal of this process is already to focus employees on objectives for the year.

Discover. Nothing in the written process talks about promoting discovery in the employee, related to determining his or her objectives or what can be done to perform well. The evaluating manager can use the conversations outlined in steps 2, 3, and 5 of the process to ask discovery questions even though the process doesn't spell that out. It will require extra intention to promote discovery in this process.

Act. The process assumes the employee will take action and meet all the objectives listed, but it does not specify any explicit conversation with the employee regarding his or her actions. During the discussions through the year, the boss can help the employee determine next actions steps and the intermediate checkpoints that will be used along the way to achieve goals.

Evaluate. Given the nature of this process (employee evaluation) it fares surprisingly poorly in the evaluation phase of the coach approach. This process differs in a major way from a coach approach because the evaluation phase of is done by the PBC not the coach. To strengthen this phase in this process, you would have to add a way for the PBC to self-evaluate, perhaps periodically throughout the year or maybe providing a self-evaluation to the boss as input to the write-up that goes on the evaluation form. The boss can also make sure that self-evaluation becomes a part of the interim discussions throughout the year.

Making Processes Stronger with a Coach Approach

Analyzing the example of the employee evaluation process through the lens of the coach approach allows you to see how a process fosters coaching. It can also show how you can make the process stronger with a coach approach. Here's what you are looking for in each phase of a coach approach.

Connect. The connection phase is all about establishing a relationship, making people want to engage with you and establish trust. The process would get high marks in the connect phase if it gets you to talk to people and build a relationship. If the process spells out whom you interact with and how you interact, it gets high marks. The process scores low if it has nothing about who interacts with whom.

Any written process is already weak in the connect phase simply because it's written. A written process offers nothing for building relationships until it is put into practice.

Coaching Cautions

Don't feel like you must force a coach approach into the written process, especially if it takes approval from the "Grand Poobah of Processes" to change anything. It may be that the best plan is to apply a coach approach in practice.

To improve a process that's not high on connection talk with employees about the way you do the process, why you do the process, how it will benefit them and others, and how all the steps of the process work. Connecting is difficult if you don't understand the purpose of the process, how it will benefit you, or how it will be used. In the employee evaluation process example, the entire process can be scary to the employee. You can strengthen the connect phase through regular meetings, discussion, and coaching conversations.

Focus. The focus phase narrows the scope so action can actually be taken. A process will get high marks on focus if it helps you narrow the scope and clarify which actions need to be taken. A process gets low marks if it is onerous and requires people to take exhaustive steps and includes lists to cover every eventuality. Such a process is too global.

Some processes are focus neutral; you can't tell if they enable focusing or not. But you can strengthen a process in terms of focus. Begin by determining which parts of the process will be done in what order. Create your own focus. For instance, if the process has a hundred steps, you might determine that the most important steps for you to do are steps 1 through 10. You do those first, then come back and look at the next set of other steps—adding focus where it didn't exist before.

As you interact with your colleagues, interpret the essence of the process, and prioritize the elements of the process. That can give the group (and the process) the focus it needs.

Discover. The purpose of the discover phase is to bring out new insights and to tap into potential that hasn't been used. This phase is about generating new ideas.

A process that assumes there is only one right way to do things gets low marks in the discover phase. A process gets high marks if it fosters developing new ideas and new insights.

Most processes are discover-phase neutral, meaning they are neither good nor bad at moving people toward discovery. Typically you will be adding the discover phase to the process in practice. You can improve the discover phase by asking powerful, well-placed questions to get people's brains engaged.

Act. The essence of the act phase in a coach approach is to act on new discoveries and on the content of the focus phase. It goes hand in hand with the discover phase.

Most processes are about action, what to do, and the order in which to do it. But just because it's about what to do, it doesn't automatically fit with the action phase of a coach approach if the action is not directly associated with the focus and discovery phases.

A process gets high marks for action if it acknowledges actions that are a direct result of focus and discovery. A process gets low marks if it just lists steps to be taken that are the same no matter what the surrounding circumstances are.

You can strengthen the action phase by asking:

- Which actions are missing?
- What other actions need to be taken?
- How does this process need to be updated to reflect the changing climate?

Actions need to be specific and clearly identify who will take the action and by when.

Evaluate. The purpose of the evaluate phase is to foster self-evaluation of the person who is being coached. The idea is they are taking full ownership and responsibility for ideas and actions. The PBC is looking at whether his or her actions were successful and what adjustments need to be made. A process receives low marks if it includes no self-evaluation and high marks if self-evaluation is built into the process.

You improve the evaluate phase in practice. In your interactions with colleagues who are performing this process with you, ask one another:

◆ How are we doing?

◆ How will we know when we get there?

◆ What are the criteria for success?

◆ What midcourse corrections are needed?

Evaluating Other Business Processes for Coachability

Some of the key processes businesses use are in the areas of business development, human resources, project management, and quality assurance. A couple examples of these types of processes and an evaluation of how compatible they are with the coach approach provide models for you to use in process analysis.

Business Development Processes

You can define *business development* as the whole process of getting new clients from networking to marketing to sales. For large companies it's a huge, long, and involved process.

Here's a simplified hypothetical business development process:

1. Look at regional demographic trends to identify new potential customers.

2. Develop a strategy for networking with customers.

3. Identify decision makers in customer organizations.

4. Engage customers in discussions to generate interest about your products.

5. Present product or services.

6. Work with customers to budget for purchase of your products.

7. Complete the sale.

8. Work with customer to install and incorporate your product into customer operations.

9. Schedule routine customer follow-up.

10. Engage customer to offer other products or repeat sales.

In this example the lead coach is anyone who works for the company developing business. The main PBC is anyone who works for the customer company.

Connect. This written process has spelled out several places in which the providing company and client company interact. It can be strengthened specifying that the sales rep makes clear to the customer that a coach approach will be used at times. This will serve to gain their agreement and full participation in the rest of the phases of a coach approach.

Focus and Discover. No defined focus or discovery has been written into this process. What's not listed in this simplified process is what you do to bring out the best ideas and to engage client company brains. In practice the coach should help the client focus on his or her goals and promote discovery concerning how the provider company's product and services can benefit the client.

Act. The written process points out the need for the client to budget for the product, install it, and integrate its use in the client company workflow. In practice you can strengthen the process by helping the client identify actions that are the natural result of the focus and discovery phases.

Evaluate. The written process includes customer follow-up, but it doesn't specify whether the client is self-evaluating and making adjustments. You can use a coach approach in practice to foster self-evaluation. It will be better to do this early in the process also, not just in the follow-up step.

Your business development process probably looks different, but the concepts of evaluating a process using the phases of a coach approach will be similar. Look at the steps in your business development process and determine if the phases of a coach approach are represented in the steps. Identify key steps where a coach approach could be integrated. Some companies have such onerous and complex business development processes that people get bogged down. This test may be just the thing to help your business thrive.

Six Sigma and Other Quality Management Processes

Many companies use a process for making sure their company is run in a quality fashion. Six Sigma is one of the most well-known and widely used quality management processes. It encompasses several sets of processes designed to improve quality. A version of Six Sigma called Lean Six Sigma is designed to focus on what really matters to customers rather than providing quality for quality's sake.

Here's a quick overview of Six Sigma process and the key principles of Lean Six Sigma:

Six Sigma Phases

This list of phases is often referred to in Six Sigma process documents by the starting initials DMAIC:

1. Define: Define the project.

2. Measure: Document the baseline of the "as is" process.

3. Analyze: Identify significant potential process causes.

4. Improve: Validate your solutions.

5. Control: Sustain improvement.

Lean Principles

- Value: Act on what's important to the customer of the process.

- Value Stream: Understand which steps in the process add value and which don't.

- Flow: Keep the work moving at all times and eliminate waste that creates delay.

◆ Pull: Avoid making more or ordering more inputs for customer demand you don't have.

◆ Strive for Perfection: There is no optimum level of performance; just continually pursue improvement.

In Six Sigma quality process documentation, roles and responsibilities are spelled out in great detail. The roles of Master Black Belts (MBB), Black Belts (BB), Green Belts (GB), Yellow Belts (YB) and Facilitators (FC) focus on "knowledge transfer" of the Lean Six Sigma process. They are the best candidates for incorporating coaching into the Lean Six Sigma process. The roles of Process Owners, internal customers, and suppliers are the best candidates to be coached.

> **Another Perspective**
>
> In their book *The Complete Idiot's Guide to Lean Six Sigma*, Breakthrough Management Group and Neil DeCarlo present the steps of the Six Sigma process and list the principles of Lean Six Sigma.

Using the standard Six Sigma DMAIC steps outlined in the previous section and the principles of Lean Six Sigma as a process, take a look at how Lean Six Sigma fares in each phase of the coach approach.

Connect. A lot of emphasis is placed on relating to the Process Owners and all the people involved—getting to know the people involved and understanding what they need. The first Lean principle says a company should only do things valued by customers, a connect attitude. You can strengthen this part of the process by continuing this for the purpose of drawing out new ideas.

Focus. The whole purpose of Lean Six Sigma is to get people to focus on what really matters. A coach can strengthen this in practice by helping PBCs prioritize which step of the Lean Six Sigma process is most important. This will flow naturally from the way Lean Six Sigma is designed.

Discover. The Lean Six Sigma process doesn't spell out how to promote discovery, but the coach can promote discovery at various times throughout the process and in so doing improve Lean Six Sigma results.

Act. Lean Six Sigma has elaborate processes for tracking actions and making sure they happen. The process can be strengthened to ensure action by also identifying actions that arise from the process of focus and discovery.

Evaluate. Lean Six Sigma gets high marks for the evaluate phase because it includes steps throughout that prompt self-evaluation and taking new actions that lead to improvement. A minor suggestion for strengthening is to customize the evaluation to individual situations.

Some companies have seen the synergy that can happen with the combination of Lean Six Sigma and a coach approach and have gotten coach training for all the principals involved.

Benefits of Coaching-Enabled Processes

What are the benefits of incorporating a coach approach into your processes?

When you apply a coach approach to a company's written processes, you can expect to find congruence with the company's verbal coach approach. As a result, you build momentum toward a total coaching culture. Using a coach approach with processes may even lead a company to incorporate coaching when it writes or rewrites its policies.

Using a coach approach with processes could eliminate wasted energy and help improve the company's bottom line. Sometimes people blindly follow a process simply because they've been told to do so. A coach approach–enabled process involves the employee in the process, allowing them to make more efficient decisions about the next steps to take. What's more, using coaching with processes can make people less process averse.

If you embark on creating a coaching culture, that in itself is a process. The process of creating a coaching culture involves multiple steps, many of which will be common to

Another Perspective

"The important thing is to start, to lay a plan and then follow it step-by-step, no matter how small or large each step by itself may seem."

—Robert Louis Stevenson, author

all intra-company coaching initiatives. These have been discussed in earlier chapters and include introducing coaching, getting executive buy-in, running pilot programs, tweaking how it works, training more people in basic coaching skills, and rolling out to larger groups. As you design your process, make sure it incorporates each phase of the coach approach model.

The Least You Need to Know

◆ Restrictive processes allow little room for a coach approach.

◆ Breaking down complex processes with many steps into small groups of steps can provide much-needed focus.

◆ Written processes tend to be weak in the connect phase of the coach approach.

◆ The evaluation phase of any process fits a coach approach only when it includes self-evaluation for the PBC.

Chapter 20

The Business Impact of Coaching

In This Chapter

- ◆ Moving through chaos to achieve success
- ◆ Rowing in the same direction with a coach approach
- ◆ Coaching a cross-functional team
- ◆ Measuring coaching's impact
- ◆ Documenting the improved business results

Coaching is one of those processes that people think offers only an intangible impact. Its nature seems a little amorphous and not something you would count on to make progress in business. Yet, time after time companies that have implemented a coach approach have seen an improvement in their bottom line. Organizations that stick with coaching reap benefits in the end.

It Gets Worse Before It Gets Better

Lindsey was a vice president of marketing in a medium-sized pharmaceutical company, and she was stuck. Her division was responsible for the rollout of new drugs. When there was a rollout on the horizon, all of her staff worked long days and every weekend. After the rollout was complete, they had routine work but not always enough to keep everyone busy. She needed to find ways to even out the work load. Not only was the current scenario exhausting her employees, and even causing some of the bright young crew to leave, but it was costing the company money because some of the employees were paid overtime when the long hours of the rollout ensued.

Lindsey's peer, Paul, and his team had really embraced coaching, and others in the company started noticing the positive impact of the coaching culture. Paul's success got Lindsey's attention.

She could see how it might help someone's personal life, but she was a bit skeptical about whether it could have any impact on her department. She decided to ask Paul to coach her.

In the first coaching conversation, Lindsey brought up her frustration about the highs and lows of demands on employees. As a result of the conversation, she began to think of shortcuts for the rollout paperwork that could be done in advance.

When it came time for the action phase of the coaching conversation, her action was to give new direction to her executive direct reports. She was excited and pleased about her new insight and the potential benefit to the business as a result.

Dealing With Resistance to Change

At the next staff meeting she shared the idea for changing the paperwork and other ideas for new rollout procedures with all her direct reports and instructed them to look for ways to even out the workflow as well.

After the staff meeting was over, several of her direct reports met together and said, "What was that about?" What she had just said was so counter to everything she had said before that they decided she was just having a bad day and ignored her statements, hoping that was the last they would hear about changing their rollout procedures. In their experience all pharmaceutical companies dealt with the crazy work hours. It was just the nature of the industry. They were used to a boss who played by the book, held information tightly but shot straight with them, and rarely changed. What was it with the idea of coaching? It seemed a little too relational and touchy feely for Lindsey and for them as well. They all agreed that just ignoring her directives was their best plan.

Then Lindsey started having individual meetings with the executives. When she asked about the new directives, they stalled and said they hadn't gotten around to the actions. She first thought she had done something wrong and was looking forward to talking to Paul again to discuss this.

During Lindsey's next coaching conversation, she told Paul about the challenge she was facing with her employees. She had tried to take the actions she and Paul discussed but she was getting nowhere with her executive staff. She decided to present her ideas differently at the next staff meeting.

During the meeting, Lindsey presented the workflow challenge as very serious. She told them that she expected their action plans to be on her desk in a week.

When she said this, all eyes cut sideways to one another. "She's serious. Are we really going to have to do this?" This gave rise to a heated discussion about whether this was a good idea. A new rollout plan that didn't work as planned could be a nightmare.

The staff meeting went long. They discussed the pros and cons of the new direction. There was no consensus at end of the meeting. Lindsey was so convinced that they needed to take new action that at the end she said, "This is not a consensus organization. I'm the leader, and I want to see your plans for a new rollout process in a week."

She didn't feel good about the staff meeting; but after thinking it through during two coaching sessions, she felt confident that progress was being made.

Over the next week the executives delivered their action plans. But when she read them, she found variances from her directives and lots of reasons each person didn't think change was a good idea. This was becoming complicated. All the one-on-one meetings were as tough as the staff meeting.

She began to second-guess her own ideas and the method that got her to that idea, which was a coach approach. But eventually everyone got with the program. Now these executives who reported to Lindsey had to do the same thing with their direct reports. The executives got similar no-change feedback.

> ### Another Perspective
>
> "... all things, even life itself, are a seamless blending of chaos and order."
>
> —Dee Hock, *Birth of the Chaordic Age* (Berrett-Koehler Publishers, Inc., 1999)

Within a month of the first meeting, chaos reigned within the organization about new approaches to rollout and about Lindsey's new ways of working.

When she started seeing the chaos at the lower levels, she really started to get concerned. She frequently checked in with Paul, and he kept reassuring her that organizational change was painful but worth it.

Lindsey persisted. Gradually, people began to come up with new ideas that they tried in the next rollout. Some of them helped even out the workflow, but more changes were needed. She was feeling a little bit better about the procedures and a little more confident that coaching was helping her get to where she wanted her team to be.

The executives and their employees were slowly beginning to see the positive results of changing their rollout process. Eventually enough positive results accrued that the organization began to see this was the right direction. Lindsey breathed a big sigh of relief.

The period of time between the first coaching conversation "aha" until the sigh of relief was months. That first major shift Lindsey went through with the organization was the most painful, because not only was she pushing her team to change, the whole team had to come to grips with the idea of change. Future shifts were not as bad.

Lindsey's experience is typical of how organizations change course. It's painful and requires good communication with one another during the change. A coach approach is a process that fosters change. If you go into it knowing things can get worse before they get better you can more easily roll with the growing pains that accompany change. When you don't anticipate the challenges, if you think a coach approach will solve all your problems and make everyone happy, that's when you tend to loose faith in the process. It's actually very organic.

Weathering the Chaos

At the beginning of implementing a coach approach, you'll likely find yourself dealing with a lot of chaos. Any significant change requires chaos to get to order.

Here are some tips you can use to deal with the chaos.

◆ Know that it's coming.

◆ Celebrate it when you see it.

◆ Use the period of chaos to refine your decisions, plans, and strategies. Make sure you haven't left out anything.

◆ Notice how your organization responds to change and learns how to change. Celebrate an individual's new ability to change. You want to build momentum for how quickly your organization can adapt to change.

 Coaching Cautions

Don't be blindsided by the chaos, or you are likely to think the coaching process is flawed. If you are expecting it, you celebrate it and think, *Wow, it's starting to work; we're getting very different views.*

The Organization Starts Rowing in the Same Direction

A rowing team must do several things well in order to succeed: everyone must focus, communicate, develop a rhythm, and use their strength to its full potential. When you create a coaching culture in an organization, you're training people to row the organization's boat. When a work team is "rowing in the same direction," they all want to achieve the same goals; they have the same vision, and they have all participated in creating that vision.

Tips & Tools

The test of a compelling vision is if it ignites passion that fuels action. Coach the team to keep that vision in sight constantly as they "row."

"Rowing in the same direction" does not mean everyone thinks the same and always agrees with one another. Rather, it means everyone respects varying worldviews so they can work together on projects while still having differences of opinion. The members of a rowing team may not be friends off the clock, but that doesn't matter as long as they put their differences aside while rowing.

Harry is an HR professional who learned about coaching and used it whenever he could even though his company was not totally immersed in a coaching culture. He'd let it be known that he is available to coach individuals and teams.

When a sales team invited Harry to coach them, he learned in their first conversation that they were very intertwined in a cross-functional team. He thought it would be good to coach representatives from each function—sales, marketing, customer service and development—as a team. Harry hadn't done this before, but he was excited to try it.

While coaching the cross-functional team, if something was specific to one area, people from other areas could give different points of view. The resulting actions yielded dramatically better business results because they reflected input from all areas.

The result was their biggest sales to date. The insights that lead to their improved bottom line were generated because all areas were represented—in other words, everyone was rowing in same direction. The team was originally put together to solve one problem but ended up staying together about 18 months because they realized it was a great way to get work done.

Small companies automatically are cross-functional, but in large companies teams tend to be organized along lines of specialization. Cross-functional teams are a way to regain some of the synergy found in smaller companies. Teams like this are difficult to keep intact, but with a coach approach the results that come out of the meetings are usually of enough value to keep them together.

Improves Business Results

The main point of this book has been that you can do your job better by coaching others. It's a matter of finding those coachable moments and knowing what to do when they occur. You are harnessing the brain power of others to help you make progress in a very focused way. You are adding their actions to your actions to increase productivity. And you are encouraging them to join you in constantly striving to improve results.

So what is the real business impact of such an approach?

Some would say that it is impossible to measure. In the June 5, 2007, issue of *Personnel Today*, Helen McCormick writes in an article entitled "Made to Measure?" that they surveyed 500 readers and found that "67 percent of respondents say ROI in relation to coaching is not formally measured within their organization." Part of the difficulty is in knowing what to measure and knowing if it is valid to give credit to coaching for the improved business results.

Others, like Booz Allen, who have measured the business impact of executive coaching, say that coaching can conservatively give a 600 percent ROI.

The International Coach Federation's Prism Award recognizes organizations that have enhanced excellence and business achievement through their commitment to coaching as a leadership strategy. Here's what some of them have experienced.

Oracle Corporation, Public Sector. Ed Allen from Oracle received the 2004 Prism Award from the ICF North Texas chapter. Ed says, "Oracle's primary goal of coaching was to strengthen Sales performance, both from individual Sales Representatives and geographically based Sales Teams. In addition to increases in revenue and margins, there was an increase in the number of deals and shortened sales cycles. In one case, a Sales Team increased their performance from 70 percent to 130 percent of plan as well as a 43 percent increase in the next year's pipeline. According to the Sales professionals, 'coaching made the difference.'"

Verizon Business. A 2006 press release from the ICF, quotes 2006 Prism Award winner Renee Robertson from Verizon Business who said, "The coaching initiative is considered fundamental to the organization's strategy for leadership development, and has been in increasing demand across broader segments of the organization over time." The press release went on to say, "the coaching initiative has delivered a consistently high return on investment (14:1 in the most recent analysis), as measured by an annual impact study. Clients cite the following as having been directly and positively impacted by participation in the coaching program: improved bottom line results, improved overall effectiveness, alignments of business priorities, employee engagement, management team awareness, improved goal setting and strategic thinking, and leader retention."

Deloitte U.S. Firms. As one of the 2007 recipients of the ICF Prism Award, Tracy Sullivan shared that, "The Deloitte U.S. Firms have measured their internal coaching service's success in a few ways. First, by interviewing employees, they have identified over 750 employees who stayed with Deloitte and cited their interaction with coaching as an influencing factor. Thus, they conservatively estimate the total service benefits since inception in 2002 at over $115 million. An anonymous survey of employees in July 2007 also shows that coaching is having a strong positive impact on business success as well as the employee's success, connection, and perception. Ninety-four percent of respondents said they were 'better at my current role or better prepared for my next role', 88 percent said there was a 'positive effect on my view of the Deloitte brand', 57 percent said there was 'positive impact on my business output', and 66 percent said there was 'positive impact on business quality'."

Focus on Measurable Results

Coaching makes a more credible impression if you actually measure the results and have numbers to back it up. The business improvements you might measure include retention of key talent, recruiting, attracting top-notch people through coaching, increased revenue, keeping customers, and adding customers.

Some organizations even include intangibles such as improved business climate, good will, and morale. In *Coaching That Counts* (Elsevier Butterworth-Heinemann, 2005), Dianna Anderson and Merrill Anderson provide readers with a number of useful tools for measuring the business impact of coaching initiatives.

> **Tips & Tools**
>
> In *Coaching That Counts* by Dianna Anderson and Merrill Anderson, there are several detailed forms and step-by-step instructions for helping you calculate the return on investment (ROI) of coaching.

Coaching That Counts offers five levels at which you might choose to measure coaching's impact. Here's an overview of the five levels for gauging coaching's success:

- ◆ **Level 1: Reaction**   Measure the initial reactions of participants.

- ◆ **Level 2: Learning**   Measure all that is learned by participants.

- ◆ **Level 3: Application**   Measure how participants have applied what they learned.

- ◆ **Level 4: Business Impact**   Measure the impact on business goals, efficiency, and productivity.

- ◆ **Level 5: ROI**   Calculates the ratio of monetary gain to monetary investment.

If you are interested in documenting the improved business results for your coaching initiative, *Coaching That Counts* is the handbook you need.

Self-Sustaining Momentum—A Personal Story

When IBM Coaches Network was started in the late 1990s, coaching was emerging as a new business tool. People were beginning to talk about it at conferences and read about it in trade journals, but at the time there was no formal, company-wide coaching initiative within IBM. Few in the corporation knew what it was or how to do it. I had been coaching for about a year and had experimented with coaching in the organization. After hearing me speak at a couple of conferences, some of my colleagues at IBM asked me to work with them. I agreed to coach them to implement a coach approach in their respective areas of work.

> **Another Perspective**
>
> "The leader of the past knew how to tell—the leader of the future will know how to ask."
>
> —Peter Drucker (1909–2005), business management authority

We met via conference call twice a month. I and three other coaches started by asking about the challenges of using coaching in their current jobs. We brainstormed about how to be better at noticing coachable moments. We talked about what to say, what made questions powerful, and what challenges they could use to get people to self-evaluate. Basically, we discussed all the challenges people would face when using a coach approach.

The group started to grow. IBM did not incur a large expense because the group only met by conference call once or twice a month. Soon, however, each of the people participating in the network began adding value to the organization through coaching.

Other divisions noticed, and the network grew from the three initial coaches sharing ideas with one another to 40 people. As it grew, some decided to write down what it was like to use a coach approach and put it in a database. Because they used the networking function of a database, they soon became known as the IBM Coaches Network. They stored PowerPoint files, coaching guidelines, and tips for other coaches in that database.

After a few years so many people were participating in the conference calls it was difficult to discuss everyone's challenges on the calls. To accommodate the numbers, the format changed to having a guest speaker for 20 minutes followed by questions and answers.

I left the company, but the process continued for about six or seven years, eventually developing into a formal Community of Practice (CoP). The network now has more than 500 members in 26 countries.

What makes a coaching initiative self-sustaining? Often coaching begins in a company as a grassroots movement by a small group of passionate people. They directly experience the positive results, and it makes them want to keep using it.

To sustain this momentum people need to feel they are valued contributors when they use a coach approach. One way to achieve this is to form coaching communities such as the one just described. These groups thrive when there is some type of recognition for those who use coaching. People want to matter.

A key to passing the torch is setting up systems to identify people who have the strengths for coaching, give them opportunities for continued training, and challenge them to hone their coaching skills continually by using them in different ways and in different situations.

The Least You Need to Know

- Organizations that stick with coaching through the chaos reap benefits in the end.

- If you are blindsided by the chaos, you'll think that coaching doesn't work.

- Trying to get everyone to think the same way is unrealistic; it's distracting and doesn't help everyone get to the goal together.

- Cross–functional teams are a way to regain some of the synergy found in smaller companies.

Appendix A

Glossary

coach approach   Specific attitudes, skills, and conversation models used to help other people at work discover new insights and take new action to achieve the organization's goals. It could consist of only one question that promotes discovery.

coachability   A combination of willingness, readiness, and respect for the coaching process. People go in and out of coach-ability based on their personality and circumstances. Always determine a person's coachability before attempting to coach him or her.

coachable moment   A moment in which someone is ready to benefit from learning something new related to a specific focus area and is willing to take action on it.

coaching   According to the International Coach Federation (ICF), coaching is partnering with clients in a thought-provoking and creative process that inspires them to maximize their personal and professional potential.

coaching culture   An organizational environment that is created when connection, focus, discovery, action, and evaluation are routinely fostered through conversations and processes.

Communities of Practice (CoPs)   Groups of people who have an interest in sharing their knowledge and learning together.

distinction   Coaching jargon for a process of exploring the nuances behind a PBC's choice of words and using the underlying meanings to promote discovery. It goes well beyond just noticing that different words are used.

equity of exchange   The knowledge management concept at play when a PBC believes he or she will receive something of equal or greater value from the coach than he or she is expected to offer in the conversation.

hijacking   Coaching jargon for turning the agenda from focusing on the PBC to focusing on the coach as the expert. Once the conversation is hijacked, it is very hard to turn the focus back to the PBC and generate an "aha" moment.

internal coach   An employee of a company whose focus is primarily coaching. Coaching is written into his/her job description and involves formal, regularly scheduled coaching sessions.

intra-prenuership   Operating as an entrepreneur inside a large organization; the practice of approaching your role with the same drive, attitude, and behaviors that you would if you owned the business.

Level 1 coaching   Direct coaching with an employee.

Level 2 coaching   A coaching conversation to help someone improve coaching skills in any of the coach-approach phases. Coaching on this second level often applies to HR personnel but could apply to others as well.

meaning   The speaker's intent, as compared to "understanding," which refers to how well the listener grasps the intent.

nonanxious presence   The state of being focused on what is being said to you as the coach without constantly reacting, evaluating the content, and comparing it to what you would have said.

onboarding   The process of assisting an employee in dealing with being a new hire or being newly promoted or redeployed.

pace   Refers to how much "slow motion" (every thought is voiced) or "fast forwarding" (some thoughts are skipped because they seem obvious) goes on between the coach and PBC(s).

PBC   Shorthand for "person being coached." Preferred over "client" when coaching others at work.

PBC's agenda   More than just a plan for a coaching conversation, this concept conveys the fact that everything associated with coaching—the topic, the pace, the "aha," the action, the evaluation—is centered around the PBC.

shift   Term used to refer to the change that happens when a PBC has had such a huge new insight that his or her perspective is immediately changed to see the situation from the new perspective.

stacked questions   Asking two or more questions one right after another, before the PBC has a chance to answer the first. Asking stacked questions often results in confusion.

systems resources   A variety of tools designed to help replicate results by facilitating a common or standard way operating in a given situation. Examples are: a process, database, software tool, website, or maybe just a standard way of doing things.

toleration   Coaching jargon for enduring something objectionable that blocks progress. Once "tolerations" are removed the PBC often has "aha's," creative ideas, and makes new action plans. Examples are: a cluttered work space, a faulty computer, or an unnecessary committee meeting.

understanding   How well the listener grasps the intent of the speaker. Compare this to "meaning," which refers to the speaker's intent.

Appendix B

Resources for Coaching

Coaching

Anderson, Dianna, and Merrill Anderson. *Coaching That Counts.* Burlington: Elsevier Butterworth-Heinemann, 2005.

Bacon, Terry R., and Karen L. Spear. *Adaptive Coaching: The Art and Practice of a Client-Centered Approach to Performance Improvement.* Palo Alto: Davies Black Publishing, 2003.

Blanchard, Scott, and Madeleine Homan. *Leverage Your Best and Ditch the Rest.* New York: HarperCollins, 2004.

Crane, Thomas G. *The Heart of Coaching, Second Edition.* San Diego: FTA Press, 2002.

Dotlich, David, and Peter Cairo. *Action Coaching.* San Francisco: Jossey-Bass Pfeiffer, 1999.

Hargrove, Robert. *Masterful Coaching.* San Francisco: Jossey-Bass Pfeiffer, 2003.

Homan, Madeleine, and Linda J. Miller. *Coaching in Organizations: Best Coaching Practices from The Ken Blanchard Companies.* Hoboken: John Wiley & Sons, 2008.

O'Neil, Mary Beth. *Executive Coaching*. San Francisco: Jossey-Bass Pfeiffer, 2000.

Rosinski, Philippe. *Coaching Across Cultures*. London: Nicholas Brealey Publishing, 2003.

Whitmore, John. *Coaching for Performance*. London: Nicholas Brealey Publishing, 1992.

Whitworth, Laura, Henry Kimsey-House, and Phil Sandahl. *Co-Active Coaching*. Palo Alto: Davies Black Publishing, 1998.

Christian Coaching

Creswell, Jane. *Christ-Centered Coaching: 7 Benefits for Ministry Leaders*. St Louis: Chalice Press, 2006.

Larsen, Kate. *Progress Not Perfection*. Andover: Expert Publishing, Inc., 2006.

Miller, Linda J., and Chad W. Hall. *Coaching for Christian Leaders: A Practical Guide*. St Louis: Chalice Press, 2007.

Stoltzfus, Tony. *Leadership Coaching*. Virginia Beach: Stoltzfus, 2005.

Whitcomb, Susan Britton. *The Christian's Career Journey*. Indianapolis: JIST Publishing, 2008.

Teams

Lencioni, Patrick. *Five Dysfunctions of a Team*. San Francisco: Jossey-Bass Pfeiffer, 2002.

Payne, Vivette. *The Team-Building Workshop: A Trainer's Guide*. New York: AMACOM, 2001.

Pell, Arthur R., Ph.D. *The Complete Idiot's Guide to Team Building*. Indianapolis: Alpha Books, 1999.

Tapping Potential

Buckingham, Marcus, and Donald O. Clifton. *Now, Discover Your Strengths*. New York: The Free Press, 2001.

Fletcher, Jerry L. *Patterns of High Performance*. San Francisco: Berrett-Koehler Publishers, Inc., 1993.

Other Related Topics

Allen, David. *Getting Things Done*. New York: Penguin, 2001.

Eblin, Scott. *The Next Level: What Insiders Know About Executive Success*. Palo Alto: Davies Black Publishing, 2006.

Friedman, Thomas L. *The World Is Flat*. New York: Farrar, Straus and Giroux, 2005.

Heath, Chip, and Dan Heath. *Made to Stick*. New York: Random House, 2007.

Hock, Dee. *Birth of the Chaordic Age*. San Francisco: Berrett-Koehler Publishers, Inc., 1999.

Horan, Jim. *The One Page Business Plan*. El Sobrante: Business Plan Company, 1998.

Jones, Laurie Beth. *The Path*. New York: Hyperion, 1996.

Morrison, Terri, Wayne A. Conaway, and George A. Borden. *Kiss, Bow, or Shake Hands: How to Do Business in Sixty Countries*. Avon: Adams Media, 2006.

Pink, Daniel H. *A Whole New Mind*. New York: Penguin, 2005.

Pomerantz, Suzi. *Seal the Deal*. Amherst: HRD Press, Inc., 2007.

Ratey, John J. *A User's Guide to the Brain*. New York: Vintage Books, 2001.

Schein, Edgar. *The Corporate Culture Survival Guide*. San Francisco: Jossey-Bass Pfeiffer, 1999.

———. *Organizational Culture and Leadership*. San Francisco: Jossey-Bass Pfeiffer, 1992.

Websites

www.coach22.com   A great source for Christian coaching resources, developed by Tony Stoltzfus.

www.coachfederation.org   The official site of the International Coach Federation, where you can find coaches, coach training schools, information on certification requirements, and research symposium findings.

www.coachingconsortium.org   Supported by the not-for-profit International Consortium For Coaching in Organizations (ICCO). The site provides resources for those interested in coaching within organizations.

www.internal-impact.com   This site is maintained by the author and provides more information on how she helps organizations create a coaching culture.

www.CA-Ministries.org   Coach Approach Ministries provides a variety of coaching resources for Christian ministries including individual and team coaching, coach training, leadership development, and tools for creating a coaching culture. The author is one of the partners along with Linda Miller, MCC, Chad Hall, PCC and Bill Copper, ACC.

Questions for All Occasions

One of the most important aspects of adopting a coach approach is asking powerful questions. Here are some examples to help you get started. These questions were suggested in various chapters of this book and are compiled here for quick reference.

General Questions

These can be used with just about anyone on a large variety of topics.

Connect

How can I be of service to you?

What do you want me to know about you that will help us connect?

Focus

Where do you want to focus (or start)?

Where are you now and where do you want to be?

What is the most important thing you need to deal with today?

How can you narrow your focus for greatest impact?

What topic would give the biggest return for this investment of time?

Discover

What initial thoughts do you have about this challenge?

What are all the options for dealing with this situation?

What is another perspective on your situation?

What is at the very root of this challenge?

How will you determine between good and best options?

What are the three to-do's on your list that will have the greatest impact when completed? For the company? For yourself?

What were your underlying assumptions? Which of those assumptions need challenging?

Act

What next steps need to be taken?

What is stopping you from taking that action?

What can you do to move forward on this?

Which of these ideas would be the most feasible and effective given the time and resources available?

What action do you plan to take by when?

What can you do to mitigate the risks involved with this action?

What milestones do you envision along the way?

Evaluate

How will you know if the options you choose will be good?

What would be the consequences, both positive and negative, of taking that action?

What would be the consequences of no action?

How will you evaluate the results of this action?

What systems do you need to put into place to measure progress?

Questions for PBCs in Specific Roles

These questions were formed with the unique role of the person being coached (PBC) in mind.

Teams

What are your top challenges as a team?

What perspective do you need to take as a team to be able to collaborate?

How would each of you define success?

How can you convey the new idea in a way that everyone on the team can see it?

What is the team process for addressing lack of necessary progress ASAP?

What else needs to be explored so everyone on the team participates in the action based on today's discoveries?

Regarding team dysfunctions:

How often do you admit mistakes to each other?

What would have to happen for you to feel safe admitting mistakes with your team?

What are the benefits of conflict?

How will you handle disagreements?

What are the most important goals for your team?

What is the process for communicating goals or changing them?

What are the performance standards for your team?

How will you communicate to each other when performance standards are not being honored?

What are the current inhibitors to putting the goals of the team above individual goals?

How and when will you eliminate those barriers?

Regarding multicultural teams:

What has worked well to establish trust on multicultural teams before?

What do you need to learn about these specific people in your meeting?

How can your teammates' diverse backgrounds be used for the good of your organization?

Managers Coaching Employees

What department functions/processes distract you from focus?

What actions can be taken to eliminate those distractions?

What system do you need to put in place to stay focused on your annual/quarter objectives?

What resources may exist but are underutilized?

What impact would taking this action have on the rest of the team?

How will we as a team know you have been successful in your actions?

What systems will you put in place to alert the team at the first sign of trouble?

What problem-solving strategies will you use to course-correct midway?

How will you celebrate your success?

Regarding progress:

What client contacts will you need to make to have significant progress in your goals this month?

What new approach can you use to gain client commitment?

What obstacles can you anticipate and avoid?

What milestones need to be put in place to measure your progress?

How much progress is enough, by when?

How can you make progress with less effort (or less expense, or a smaller team)?

What will be the trigger to know you should choose a different strategy?

Regarding setting priorities:

How would you recommend the priorities be set for this project?

How will you measure whether the effort you are spending is worth it?

What are all the factors that go into the investment?

What are your expectations about the return—financial and intangible?

What is the return you will get for this investment?

How will you reset the priorities if the return on investment (ROI) doesn't happen as anticipated?

Regarding a challenge with another co-worker:

What are the benefits of your co-worker's perspective?

What strategy can you use to show your perspective in a better light?

How have you solved this type of problem before?

What would successful resolution look like?

Based on your Meyers-Briggs Type Indicator (MBTI) results, who would you guess is going to have conflict with each other?

What can be done to communicate well with each personality type defined in the MBTI?

Who on our team will give a certain perspective on (a variety) of challenges based on his or her MBTI?

Regarding fostering intra-prenuership:

If you were the owner, how would you decide?

If you changed your perspective and made decisions as if you are the owner, how would that change your behaviors?

What do owner's care most about?

Sales Team

What is most pressing from the customer's perspective?

What is our biggest inhibitor to closing this sale?

What are all the ways we could eliminate those inhibitors?

Marketing Team

Regarding trade shows:

What do you think would be an ideal outcome?

What would have to happen at the trade show to allow you to feel like you've made progress instead of lost time?

What would be the absolute best outcome of someone coming to your booth?

What do you need to do to make that happen?

Regarding improved communications:

What are you intending to communicate?

What's the key message you want to convey?

What details would aid understanding?

How could you simplify what you just said?

How would you explain this to someone sitting next to you on a plane?

Customers

Regarding closing a sale:

What next steps do you need to take to purchase our product?

What approvals do you need to make this sale complete?

What obstacles might prevent you from purchasing our product?

What strategies could you use to overcome those obstacles?

When can you take delivery of the product?

Regarding trade show conversations:

What does the decision maker think are the most important criteria for selecting a product?

What objections have you already heard voiced?

What information do you need to address these objections? How can you convey this information with the decision maker's perspective in mind?

Regarding focus group participation:

What would you like to get out of the time you invest today?

What new insights did you gain and how can you apply them to your own work?

What will you do with what you've learned today?

What actions can you take as a result?

How will you know today was worthwhile?

Regarding services provided:

How will my services best help you achieve your objectives?

If you don't know what you want specifically, what is the essence of the service you desire?

What responses would you like to receive once others see what I've provided for you?

Small Business Owners

What signs do you see before revenue is about to drop?

What strategies have helped you manage revenue in the past?

How have you tried to trim costs in the past?

Of those areas, where have you found the most potential savings?

What might be the negative consequences of growth? And, how can you anticipate those consequences and mitigate them within your current plans?

What should our business look like in 10 years?

What are the key things you should be doing now to make that happen?

What obstacles are you likely to encounter?

What would you have wanted to know before you started the company?

How can you communicate those insights to a new owner?

Nonprofit/Government Leaders

Regarding planning:

What are your goals for the next 6 to 12 months?

How will you know you're successful?

Where do you see yourself in two to three years?

What types of financial needs will you experience during that time frame?

What will your staffing, space, and equipment needs be?

What are some potential sources for providing for those needs?

Who can help you obtain those resources?

What data do you need to make informed decisions about the future?

Regarding budget management:

What are the major budget hurdles you can expect this quarter?

What patterns of cash flow have you noticed?

What patterns have you seen in donations from small donors? Large donors?

What adjustments to expenses are possible during slack times?

What can we do to smooth out the effects of fluctuation in funding and expenses?

Regarding grants:

What criteria will you use for selecting grants to pursue?

What will you need to change in your operations to meet the requirements of the grant?

How different are your needs now than when you wrote the grant proposal?

What are your options for dealing with the change?

Who can help you clarify the options acceptable by the granting agency?

What can you learn from this experience to help plan for future contingencies?

How well did you do in managing the grant?

What will your report back to the granting agency contain?

What criteria will you use in selecting future grants?

Ministry Leaders

What activities do you need to keep doing, start doing, or stop doing in order to achieve your goals?

What ministries are you involved with that energize you most?

What criteria could you use to determine whether to pursue a new ministry?

How you can have greater impact in helping others?

What are the next steps you need to take for your own faith development?

What new insight could come from looking at this situation from God's perspective?

What resources do you already have at your disposal?

What is the ultimate destination for this ministry?

What are all the routes you could take to get there?

What strategies can you use to avoid roadblocks along the way?

Questions for Specific Topics

These questions are oriented toward specific topics that might be identified by PBCs at work.

PBC is new to coaching:

May I ask you a few questions to help get at answers you might have?

I've been practicing coaching skills recently. It sounds like coaching might be helpful in your situation. May I use this approach while we talk to see if it can help you get unstuck?

What do you need to think about in advance to make your first coaching conversation productive?

PBC is stuck:

What was the point at which you got stuck?

Whom can you get advice from to get unstuck?

What new perspective have you not explored to address your situation?

What personal system will you put in place to minimize lost time the next time you are stuck?

What successes have you had in the past when facing similar challenges?

PBC is overwhelmed:

Who do you need to say no to in order to make this a more reasonable work load?

Who will it impact?

What can you do in the first hour today to get the momentum going?

What will you need to do to protect that time?

Who can you collaborate with that might help you get unstuck?

PBC is dealing with conflict/difficult situation:

What process will you use for settling differences of opinion?

What issues are beneath the surface?

What are the sources of friction here?

How much agreement do we need to be effective? What would it take to get to that point?

PBC is drained and wants to be creative:

What are most critical issues you need to focus on today?

What can you change about your routine to allow more space for looking for new ideas?

Who can you connect with to create synergy?

PBC fears taking a risk:

What new things would you like to do that you have been afraid to attempt?

What would you need to put in place to make this a successful trial?

What would you do if you knew it would be successful?

PBC realizes he or she has made a mistake:

What do you need to do to fix this?

Who has been negatively impacted that needs to be informed?

What strategy will you put in place to avoid this in the future?

How can the organization leverage what you've learned in this experience?

PBC's words and actions don't match:

Which one, words or actions, needs adjusting?

What is getting in the way of aligning your words and actions?

What system can you put in place for yourself to notice when your words and actions get out of sync?

PBC is ready to be challenged:

What would it take to accomplish that in half the time or with half the resources?

What would you need to do to significantly broaden the impact?

What would you do if you knew you could not fail?

PBC wants to focus on self-care:

When you are at your peak level of self-care, what are the daily habits that contribute to that?

On a scale of 1 to 10, where are you on self-care today?

What action could you take to move that number up two notches?

PBC has financial decisions to make:

What do you hope to do with proceeds from your financial investments?

What are you willing to do now for future results?

What challenges can you anticipate when it comes to the way you deal with money?

Who else needs to be consulted in your money matters?

PBC is asked to plan a large event:

What's the overall objective for the event?

How would you describe a successful event?

What are some unique aspects of this event?

What elements do you need to consider?

What are the time constraints with each element?

What resources will you need?

What can you delegate, and what do you have to do personally?

What problems can you anticipate?

PBC wants to focus on time management:

What have you done in the past that has worked well?

What tends to get in the way?

Are there better times of the day for certain types of tasks?

What systems do you need to put into place to help?

What are the consistent sources of interruptions and what strategies can you use to deal with them?

PBC wants to focus on managing details:

What will help you capture all the details?

What kinds of details are likely to slip through the cracks?

What organizational methods can you put into place to make sure you track all the details?

What standard set of questions can you ask when you receive a request to make sure you get enough information to cover all the details?

If you are not a detail-oriented person, what can you do and whom would you contact to learn from or get advice?

PBC wants to focus on follow-up:

What types of projects need follow-up and when?

How will you know you're doing a good job of following up?

What system do you need to put into place to make sure follow-up happens and is thorough?

PBC wants a promotion:

What are your goals?

What can you do in your current job to make progress toward those goals?

How can you tweak what you're currently doing to help with career goals?

What do you know about being a manager that would indicate management is a good fit for you?

Who knows you well that you could ask whether you would be satisfied in management?

PBC is considering leaving the organization:

What part of your job now would you miss most if you took a new position?

What will you be glad to move away from?

How many of those conditions will your potential new position contain?

What elements have to be present in a job for you to perform at your peak?

How many of those elements are present in the new job?

What are some other things you need to consider in addition to the pay, work environment, and culture?

PBC is considering a career change:

What plans need to be in place to make a smooth transition?

How will peers react, and how can you gain their support?

What are some obstacles?

Whom do you need to be developing to make a smooth transition?

Questions for Yourself as Coach

You can use these to hone your coaching skills. You can also use these while coaching others who are using a coach approach.

Regarding coachable moments:

Is the person ready to look for new insights?

Is this a situation the person can control, decide what to do, and take actions?

Is the person interested, searching for answers but not in deep distress, or worry over the issue?

Do you have a good relationship with the person so your questions are not viewed with suspicion or as a trap?

Regarding your use of a coach approach:

What evidence shows you made a solid connection with the PBC?

Which of your questions prompted focus?

What was the evidence that a clear focus was achieved?

What new insight was created? If none, what could you try next time?

On a scale of 1 to 10, how committed was the PBC to his or her action?

How specific was the action?

Did the PBC establish a target date for completing the action?

How well did the action align with the focus topic?

How did you set the stage for the PBC to evaluate his or her results?

Regarding your coaching skills:

How often did you find yourself telling versus asking, and what can you do when you find yourself doing this?

What criteria will you use to determine when to coach and when to tell?

How much time did you spend talking compared to the PBC?

How often did you formulate another question before the PBC finished answering?

What were the indicators that the PBC felt heard?

Which of your questions could have been improved?

Index

HILLSBORO PUBLIC LIBRARIES
Hillsboro, OR
Member of Washington County
COOPERATIVE LIBRARY SERVICES